DAVID BALL

ON

DAMAGES

THE ESSENTIAL UPDATE

This book is for plaintiff's attorneys. Defense attorneys will be wise to eavesdrop.

—David Ball, Ph.D., 2005

Note To Readers

Dr. Ball's opinions in this book, especially those in Chapter Eleven, do not necessarily reflect the opinions of the National Institute for Trial Advocacy—or its membership.

DAVID BALL

ON

DAMAGES

THE ESSENTIAL UPDATE

A Plaintiff's Attorney's Guide
for Personal Injury and
Wrongful Death Cases

SECOND EDITION

Revised and Expanded

DAVID BALL, PH.D.

NATIONAL INSTITUTE FOR TRIAL ADVOCACY

Reproduction Permission
National Institute for Trial Advocacy
361 Centennial Parkway, Suite 220
Louisville, CO 80027
(800) 225-6482 Fax (720) 890-7069

Ball, David, *David Ball on Damages—The Essential Update, A Plaintiff's Attorney's Guide for Personal Injury and Wrongful Death Cases, Second Edition, Revised and Expanded* (NITA, 2005).
6/05
ISBN 1-55681-940-4

Library of Congress Cataloging-in-Publication Data

Ball, David (David A.), 1942-
David Ball on damages : a plaintiff's attorney's guide to personal injury and wrongful death cases / David Ball.--2nd ed.
p. cm.
Includes index.
ISBN 1-55681-940-4 (alk. paper)
1. Damages--United States. 2. Wrongful death--United States. 3. Personal injuries--United States. 4. Trial practice--United States. I. Title.

KF1250.B355 2005
346.7303'23--dc22 2005047929

This second edition is dedicated to

Bruce Rasmussen.

His trials are ended.

His teachings and inspiration continue.

CONTENTS

Dedication to the First Edition

As a trial consultant, I have worked on many hundreds of cases for a wide variety of trial attorneys on both sides of the aisle. The strategies in this book have as their source many of the good ideas from these attorneys, along with principles generated from years of research, focus groups, mock trials, and post-trial interviews with jurors, and the advice and strategies gleaned from trial consultants and teaching attorneys with whom I have worked and taught CLE seminars across the country.

This book is dedicated to all those who will spot their ideas and strategies as the inspirations for these pages—especially Atlanta's Don C. Keenan, from whom I have borrowed the most. It is also dedicated to the National Jury Project's Susan Macpherson, who for years has provided me with enough wise guidance to deserve more gratitude than I can express; and to Raleigh attorney Donald H. Beskind, whose years of advice and friendship have shaped more things in my life than just this book.

I also dedicate this book to the insurance companies, chambers of commerce, and politicians whose methods of doing business inversely inspired this book.

David Ball, Ph.D.

Acknowledgments for the First Edition

It is easy to go astray while sitting alone writing on a North Carolina porch. Among the patient guides who read what I wrote for the first edition and tried their best to keep me from straying too far were two remarkable trial consultants: Susan Macpherson (Minneapolis) and Eric Oliver (Canton, Michigan), and four exceptional trial attorneys: E. D. Gaskins, Jr. (Raleigh); Thomas A. McNeely (Charlotte); the late Bruce D. Rasmussen (Charlottesville, Virginia); and Donald H. Beskind (Raleigh).

Katharine M. Wilson, one of the country's best professional technical writers, has read my writing with the patience of a saint and the acuity of a schoolmarm to tell me what needed to be better and how to make it so.

Susan Chapek took many long hours from her own writing to ensure that mine was better than I could do on my own, and almost as good as hers.

Acknowledgments for the Second Edition

Donald H. Beskind, Susan Chapek, Susan Macpherson, and Kate M. Wilson, all of whom have more than enough of their own work to do, have once again selflessly martyred many of their own hours in the cause of advising and correcting me on this edition. As with the first edition, they have made this a far better and more readable book. I thank them deeply. So should every reader who otherwise would have had to read my unvetted work, not always a pretty sight.

Jude Phillips, NITA's cover artist, has done it again: a perfect cover. You *can* tell a book by its cover when it's Jude's cover.

I also want to acknowledge the enormous contribution to our cause (and to my work) made by two of the best advocacy guides and teachers we have: Phoenix's David Wenner and Alabama's Greg Cusimano. Both are trial consultants as well as first-rate plaintiff's attorneys. Their coast-to-coast research into the real behavior of jurors has not only helped show many of the most important paths to traverse, but has also led to the widespread teaching of how to traverse them.

Debra Miller, who has been working with me on case after case since this book's first edition four years ago, has shown me the value of having a brilliant partner at JuryWatch. And our erstwhile intern, Artemis Malekpour, is now our formidable colleague Artemis Malekpour, Esq.—an extraordinary addition to what we do at JuryWatch. These valued and cherished colleagues have been wellsprings of much of this edition's most important new material.

FOREWORD

by Don C. Keenan

I am fortunate to have been associated with many large verdicts, and that is the light in which most people know me. But like every attorney, I have also tried my share of small cases. So I can report that *David Ball on Damages* will be useful to you whether you are trying to win a few thousand dollars for a client with only minor injuries, tens of millions of dollars for cases as large as those of the catastrophically injured children I now represent, or any figure in between. David explains why jurors give, why they do not, and how to motivate them to do the former instead of the latter. His book is one of the most useful trial advocacy books I know. It is certainly the best thing I have read on damages.

I wish I had had his book years ago when I started. I am grateful for it now. As I am sure you know, until now there have been few if any helpful articles or books about damages, even though that is what we mainly need help with. Most of what I know I had to make up myself, and I am flattered David saw fit to include some of it. But there is far more in his book than what I already knew, and it is indispensable. David walks you in detail through voir dire, opening, testimony, and closing, providing step-by-step practical, effective, and innovative methods for pursuing damages.

David points us squarely at the goal we often lose sight of in the rush and blur of trial: that we are in trial solely to get money for our clients. Then he explains how to do it. He shows you how jurors view damages. Then he explains how to shape what they see.

David marries the practical to the theoretical. He avoids the kind of generalized advice we get so much of that sounds good but does not really advise. He tells you what to do, why to do it, and exactly how.

Among his many innovations, David has even invented a way for you to teach jurors how to calculate intangible damages, an easy method that will surely become the standard approach and help you argue for intangibles as effectively as tangibles. His many such innovations are accompanied by necessary reminders of things we already know but easily forget or let slide.

Those of us who have been athletes will appreciate the fact that David is like a great coach. He makes you the best player you can be. He will not let you settle for less out of yourself than you can achieve. He has told me that he assumes there is greatness in almost every one of us who works in front of juries, and he shows us how to tap into whatever greatness we are each blessed with. On every page he teaches something new about pursuing damages. And by the end of the book you will have learned a whole lot new about yourself.

I have worked with David in trial so I have had the direct benefit of his insights. Now his book puts him at my elbow whenever I need him, whether he is here or not. Given the many reasons today's jurors have for not fairly compensating our clients, we all need David at our elbows with every case. Keep his book in easy reach. A cover-to-cover re-reading before each and every case will be your most valuable preparation time.

Introduction to the Second Edition, 2005

If you leave the jurors alone on the topic of harm and damages, they will return the favor.

—David Ball

Since 2001 a revolution has taken place in the way good plaintiff's attorneys have been seeking damages. I'm proud to say this book's first edition flagshipped those changes.

But the times are still changing. Opposition tactics grow more sophisticated, and the public mood along with laws and rules grow more hostile. And tort "reform" grows like kudzu with an attitude. Staying a step ahead requires some leaps.

Those who thumbed ragged their copies of the first edition will see in this edition that we must begin in the same place: Continuous awareness that the goal of going to trial is to *get money for your client.* Throughout the havoc of case preparation, harm and damages must remain uppermost in your mind and work—and stay there throughout trial.

Cut out and frame (5 x 7-inch frame) the next page. Hang it on your office wall with nothing near it. Read aloud daily. And let it underlie all your trial preparation and execution.

The *only* goal of trial is to get money for your client.

—David A. Ball, Ph.D.

Preface

Over the past few years at my damages seminars, I have asked thousands of personal injury attorneys, "How many of you tell jurors that preponderance applies not only to liability but also to verdict size?" Fewer than 2% raise their hands. Traditionally, plaintiff's attorneys have thought so little about damages that they have not mentioned the burden for decision making about money.

As a result, a common juror comment in deliberations is, "Well, I'm just not completely convinced that the verdict should be $__________. They didn't absolutely prove it." Not even the most favorable plaintiff's jurors argue with that, because they don't know they should and they don't know how.

This failure is a perfect example of how attorneys ignore damages. Until this book's first edition in 2001, books, articles, CLE seminars, and law schools had little to say about damages persuasion—despite the fact that a plaintiff's injury attorney has no other purpose. Damages was treated like pornography: something to be ashamed of. Bogus theories sprang up: "Don't talk about damages until after you convince the jury of liability." "Don't mention a specific figure; leave it to the jurors." "Do liability witnesses first, then damages witnesses."

Every one, gifts to the defense. If you have not yet joined our damages revolution, I hope this book will enlist you now.

Caveat Number 1: This is no cookbook. It's not a compendium of tricks. You need to understand the principles that underlie the methods. This will prepare you to best use the methods and develop more of your own.

Caveat Number 2: Michigan trial consultant Eric Oliver points out that "It's not what you say, it's how you say it." When using the techniques in the chapters below, keep in mind that the way things are worded is important. It is not enough to learn just the concepts. The way you say them is crucial. The more closely you use the words I suggest, the more effective the techniques will be.

CHAPTER ONE

THE BASICS

Impure Thoughts

Especially in today's climate, jurors usually incorporate immaterial factors into their decision making about money: "The money won't do any good," or "A big verdict will drive up insurance prices," or "Her health insurance probably paid for it," or "No one deserves a windfall just because they got hurt." Deal with this ever-worsening problem head-on in every element of trial. This book will show you how.

The Other Ten Basics

Ten other basics shape juror decision making about money.

1. Degree of harm and loss
2. Worthwhileness of the money you seek
3. Jurors' job: to fix, help, and make up for
4. Proportion of time spent on harms, losses, and money
5. Defendant conduct
6. Who gets the money?
7. Who *really* gets the money?
8. Client's point of view
9. Handling why jurors give less
10. You

1.1

Basic Principle One: Degree of Harm and Loss

Degree of harm and loss is rarely the most important decision-making factor, though it carries significant weight. Yet few attorneys do enough to find out what all the harms and losses were or will be, and few present those harms and losses as effectively as possible. You must seek out and present information about your client's harms and losses as vigorously and thoroughly as you pursue and present liability matters.

I once asked an attorney for a list of the harms and losses in his wrongful death case. He gave me the following:

1. Death
2. Loss of a husband
3. Loss of a father

A guy dies and the whole loss takes only nine words? To anyone who cares about him it should be more like nine volumes. And you want the jury to care about him.

Learn the full range and depth of your client's harms and losses. "Harms and losses" means all the bad things that happened because of the defendant's negligence. It is never only nine, 90, or even 900 words. The best sources include the client, the people who know or knew him, the people who worked with him, helped him, observed him, and experts—such as social workers and other counselors—who work with people with similar harms and losses. The more you listen to those sources, the more you will learn about the harms and losses to your client.

1.2

Basic Principle Two: Worthwhileness of the Money You Seek

For years, the National Jury Project has been telling us that jurors provide money mainly when they think money will serve some worthwhile purpose. The fact that your client "deserves" money has little persuasive power. Jurors are more likely to provide money for worthwhile purposes such as medical bills or providing for surviving children. Like shoppers, jurors want something for the money. They want to know it will serve some purpose: *What makes it worthwhile*?

When a juror says, "Money can't bring back the dead" or "Money won't make the pain go away"—common sentiments in deliberations—she is arguing for a small verdict on the grounds that money serves no purpose. This is why death cases usually get less than serious injury cases, where money serves the purpose of care.

When it comes to non-economic damages, you must seek out and show worthwhile purposes. Jurors often don't see purposes unless you show purposes.[1] There are ways to do this, as you will see.

In long-term cases, jurors tend to provide less when you paint a picture of hopelessness and despair. If there's no hope, what purpose can money serve? So as soon as you get involved in a case, keep your antennae tuned to anything that can be positioned as hope—especially hope that can be fulfilled or encouraged by means of a fair damages verdict. Can money provide training that will put your client back to work? Can money help make a defendant meet his responsibility?

In cases where the harms and losses are already over, it can be even harder for jurors to understand what good money will do. Money for last year's pain does not seem compellingly worthwhile. This book will offer some ways to make it so.

1.3

Basic Principle Three: Jurors' Job: To Fix, To Help, To Make Up For

The purpose of a jury is to fix, help, and make up for. Atlanta's Don Keenan wisely teaches not to make your jurors think their job is to *judge* or to *decide*—as when you say: "Your job will be to decide whether the defendant was negligent." "Deciders" and "judgers" tend not to incorporate caring into their decisions. Helpers and fixers do.

So, for example, instead of telling jurors they will *decide* who is right or *decide* how much the verdict should be, explain early that

1. Never say "non-economic damages" to jurors. Even when explained, it sounds like "requiring no money." Every legal term you use hinders your effectiveness. The defense loves it when you talk that way.

you expect that they are here to *figure out how much it will take to make up for the harms and losses.*

Explain their three jobs:

1. **To *fix* what can be fixed**—such as by repaying lost income and medical bills.
2. **To *help* what can be helped**—such as by paying for therapy that will help but not cure.
3. **To *make up for* (balance) what cannot be fixed or helped**—such as past pain, or injuries that cannot be treated in the future.

"Fix, help, and make up for" is a primary theme[2] of every case. Use it to shape your trial preparation and every element of trial. So don't dress jurors in judicial robes. Dress them as caretakers: *healers, fixers, balancers.*

1.4

Basic Principle Four: Proportion of Time Spent on Harms, Losses, and Money

A book, a play, a trial, a sermon, a TV show, a movie: Each is about *whatever it spends its time being about.* It cannot be about what it spends a small proportion of its time on.

A sprinkling of testimony about damages followed by a quick mention of damages in closing will not make jurors think the trial's purpose is money. So they won't fight hard to provide it.

Some literary scholars think that a two-minute piece of *Hamlet*—in what is called the "closet scene"—means the play is about an Oedipus complex, though the play's other 138 minutes have nothing to do with mother-coupling. Every audience—always miles ahead of literary scholars—knows *Hamlet* is about revenge. How? Because *Hamlet* spends most of its time being about revenge. A play is about mother-coupling only if it spends a large proportion of its time being about mother-coupling, such as *Oedipus Tyrannos* does.

2. A theme is not merely a phrase, such as "Didn't have to happen." The phrase is just the theme's label so the jurors can quickly identify it. The theme itself is a *concept* that you weave into every element of trial.

Jurors are like an audience reacting to a play. They make their decisions based on the information made available to them. So you must control the proportion of time your trial spends on damages. A third to a half should be on harm, losses, and money.

Smart defense attorneys try to force you to spend a lot less. They know that the smaller the proportion of time jurors hear and think about harm, losses, and money, the less the jurors will be moved to do much about them. As Don Keenan points out, *liability is defense turf. Damages is your turf.* Fight on your own turf as much as you can. Whether you have a few minutes or a few weeks for jury selection, spend half on harms, losses, and money. Spend a third of opening and direct testimony, a significant chunk of your cross-examinations, and half your closing on harms, losses, and money. Do this no matter how much attention your liability case needs. And to do this, don't abbreviate your liability case. Expand damages to meet the necessary proportions.

Time is money.

1.5
Basic Principle Five: Defendant Conduct

Kentucky's Gary C. Johnson has the long-term track record to support his observation that juror giving is based heavily and often mainly on the bad stuff the defendant did or is doing.

Jurors look at two things to gauge defendant conduct. First, the defendant's negligence. Jurors don't think badly of a defendant who did something inadvertently. An "accident" such as "the trucker missed seeing the red light," is barely "conduct." Jurors tend to forgive such an easy mistake and thus provide less money for it. But they are less likely to discount the trucker's *choice* not to look where he was going. This distinction between inadvertence and choice often makes the difference between an economic-damages-only verdict and one with some non-economic damages.

Further, most jurors expect a defendant to have acted the way most others in the same position would have acted. The more you show that a defendant violated that expectation, the more the jurors are likely to gauge the defendant's conduct as wrong. Jurors gauge conduct by the norm.

Finally, the more outrageous you show the defendant's choices to be, and the more outrageously distant the defendant's conduct is from the norm, the angrier the jury.

And juror anger is our best antidote to tort "reform."

The second way jurors gauge defendant conduct goes beyond the actionable negligence. What the defendant does right after the negligence can matter to jurors. The worse it is the less they like it, and that can increase your verdict.

For example, show the defendant's initial attitude towards the negligence. Did he sit in his truck talking to his boss by cell phone while Jane was bleeding in the road? Did he go out in the rain to wave traffic away so Jane would not get run over again? No. Did he hold an umbrella over her? No. Did he help in any other way? No. Did he even call 911? Or apologize?

In a med mal case against a hospital, who showed up first in your client's hospital room after the negligence? A social worker to help the family deal with what had happened? Or the hospital's risk manager to put a lid on things? Where was the negligent doctor? What did she say when she realized what happened? Did the hospital tell the family what had happened or hide it? And for how long?

Since the day of the negligence, what machinations has the defense been using to get out of meeting its responsibility? Did the railway company conveniently "lose" the engine's speed records? Did the defense stipulate to liability the day before trial—not out of honesty but as a trial tactic? Is the defense adding insult to injury by attacking your client's good name in saying he is lying, exaggerating his injuries, or malingering? (See 9.23)

By choosing to deny responsibility all this time, did the defendant deprive your client of funds needed for care or safety? Deprive him of the peace of closure? Or force him into the stress and delay of litigation?

A defendant's refusal to accept responsibility (which means full compensation) can add significantly to the plaintiff's suffering. Your client's pain and disability are bad enough. They are harder to bear when the defendant says the equivalent of, "Not our fault." Even worse is when the defense stipulates to fault, because then they are saying "We did it and we don't care." These things are harm piled on harm.

Many jurors are reluctant to make "good" people or "good" corporations pay as much as it will take to balance the harms and losses. But jurors have less trouble making "bad" defendants pay. This can neutralize the entire tort-"reform" movement. Jurors who say they would never give money for pain and suffering suddenly give lots of it—and sometimes even add extra to make up for your fee.

To anger jurors at the defendant, don't show your own anger. And don't tell jurors what to think and feel. Instead, show the facts that got you angry. Angry jurors punish with or without a punitive damages issue.

Be thorough in your search for things to anger the jury. For example, point out that the defendant's company representative at trial has not been anyone who knows about the case and who cannot make decisions in the company about the kind of thing that happened in this case. "They didn't care then; they don't care now."

As Phoenix attorney David Wenner points out, most cases are essentially punitive. So try to show defendant conduct in the light that gets jurors angry.

1.6

Basic Principle Six: Who Gets The Money?

Jurors care how deserving the verdict recipient is. They gauge this by characteristics—*the kind* of person she is—and the extent to which she could have avoided the harms and losses.

Characteristics. Just as jurors will punish a "bad" defendant, so will they withhold money from what they see as a "bad" plaintiff, even if the "badness" has nothing to do with what happened in the case. In this respect, obviously some clients are better than others. Maximize whatever you have to work with. Emphasize the good parts—such as having done good works, having accomplishments, working hard, striving to overcome the injuries, being a dedicated parent, helping others, being honest, etc. To the extent you can, show that your client is a responsible person regardless of his station in life.

Try to bar any characteristics or histories from evidence that may be unpalatable to some jurors. Is your client's DWI eight years ago really relevant to any case issues the jurors will decide? Did your client use drugs 30 years ago? Some jurors will worry that if he gets money now, he'll revert and blow it all on drugs.

Personal manner can play a large part. Work with your client—or bring in a specialist—to minimize off-putting characteristics such as arrogance, defensiveness, or vengefulness. With problem clients and other problem witnesses this is always worth the effort. Even—perhaps especially—if you have been preparing witnesses for years, outside advice can help. It is easy for you to do more harm than good on your own.[3] Do not assume that your failure to make coaching headway is your client's fault. It rarely is; progress is almost always possible.

You cannot make your client seem good just by telling the jury that she's good. Show the facts that allow jurors to make their own judgments that she's a good person. This can make all the difference in verdict size. Show how her children have turned out well despite the family's economic status. Tell stories that illustrate how he was always the one who helped everyone else.

Avoiding the harm. Many jurors look at what your client did or did not do to avoid or minimize the harm. This is the "If-it-had-been-me" response. Jurors do not want to think that this kind of harm could have happened to them, so they make themselves believe they'd have avoided it. This impulse can lead jurors to blame your client even when there's no contributory or comparative negligence claim. "I would not have done it that way," "Dark or not, I'd have seen that boulder in the road," "If it had been my kid he wouldn't have been using that kind of lawn mower," "If I were 60 and my doc told me my prostate was fine, I'd say, 'Okay, Doc, but I want a second opinion.' " Many such thoughts are nonsense, but jurors believe them. This can cost you the case on liability. Even when it does not, it can drive your damages verdict lower, often much lower.

---

3. See *Theater Tips and Strategies for Jury Trials, Third Edition,* Chap. Two, by David Ball (NITA, 2003).

Even when the juror knows he would have done exactly what Jane did, if the juror can find anything even mildly wrong with it he'll often lower the verdict. "We all speed, but we take our chances when we do and we're responsible for it if we get hurt." Sometimes jurors even fault things your client did that neither were wrong nor had anything to do with what happened to her: "If you're going to live in a place like that, you have to expect drivers like that."

1.7

Basic Principle Seven: Who *Really* Gets The Money?

Jurors worry about money getting into the wrong hands. The injured child needs treatment, but dad is a rat who could take the money and run. Or Mom and Dad are great folks but could get run over and bad Uncle Benny would take the money. Don Keenan says every case involving a potentially significant verdict for a child should have a trust account for the child so jurors know the money will go for the *worthwhile* purposes they intend. Keenan also suggests naming the trust holder as a plaintiff: "First National Bank and Bobby Smith versus Acme Trucking." This can allow the trust officer to testify how the money will be controlled for Bobby's benefit.

Not as strong but adequate is to explain or have the judge explain that the court will control the money. But not every judge will allow such an explanation. A legal mind can find it immaterial, but jurors find it extremely material. Even jurors who mistrust the courts would rather have the money there than where Uncle Benny can get his paws on it.

Even with adults, jurors often keep verdicts low because they are worried about who will get their hands on the money. Is the quadriplegic's young wife going to grab it and run? Such thoughts breed smaller verdicts. Be on the lookout for anything that can start such thinking so you can take steps to offset it.

1.8

Basic Principle Eight: Client's Point of View

Jurors cannot gauge the full weight of the harm unless you get them to walk in your client's shoes. If you do not, they measure the harm by how it feels to an observer, not the harmed person. "*Your* broken leg is unfortunate and slightly comic. Can I sign your cast?" But, "*My* broken leg is a tragedy! What are you laughing at?" All non-economic harms and some economic harms are subjective. They can be gauged fairly only from your client's point of view.

Think about a four-year-old child as an emergency room patient. The child's terror—a harm that can be fathomed only through the child's eyes—results in panicky screams as the nurse comes near with a hypodermic. Onlookers who do not view this through the child's eyes are amused at the child making such a big deal out of it, or annoyed at the little brat's racket. That's how jurors can view your client's harms. Only by helping jurors *subjectively* understand your client's harm—as if standing in your client's shoes—can they gauge its full weight.

But be careful. Violating the "Golden Rule" can lead to a no-brainer reversal: "Ladies and gentlemen of the jury, if *you* run a blowtorch up and down your arm . . . " or "How would *you* feel if it were your dad lying there in pain?" Ethical and effective ways to help jurors see the harms from your client's point of view are covered in upcoming chapters.[4]

1.9

Basic Principle Nine: Handling Why Jurors Give Less

You need to identify every reason jurors may find to minimize money in your particular case (see, for example, Chapter Three). Jurors sometimes minimize because they are inhumane, selfish, or uncaring. More often they minimize because they think minimizing is the right thing to do. And many give less because they have bought into tort "reform."

4. Beware the fad of first-person storytelling. ("I am hit from behind by a delivery truck . . . .") While it can help put the jury in your client's shoes, opening statement is too early to use such an openly manipulative technique. Even later, it can blow up in your face by inadvertently making your client seem like a whiner. Never use a first-person story in opening, and before using it in closing, learn and avoid its pitfalls and test it case-by-case in focus groups.

Many reasons are case-specific, and are found by doing focus groups.[5]

Many specific reasons crop up in many cases: "Money won't make the pain go away." "Public assistance programs will take care of this." "He had health insurance, so why should we pay the hospital bill?" "The plaintiff (or the deceased's family) would never have had that much money, so why give it now?" "The President of the United States says not to give much." "You can ruin a person's life by giving too much money." "It's a windfall." Or . . . Well, the list is long. Chapter Two covers many. The more you can identify the more you can head off at the pass, as the later chapters of this book show you.

1.10
Basic Principle Ten: You

Jurors know you get what they see as an unreasonably hefty chunk of the verdict, and many jurors regard that as your primary if not sole motivation. On this basis, the tort-"reform" campaign has convinced the public that you and your kind are a crisis in America. This becomes a factor in the decision making of many jurors, including decent-minded citizens who believe in justice and want to help people who have been harmed. As a result, liability is a steeper mountain to climb and damages—especially since the beginning of 2005—is often a formidable cliff looming over you.

The solution is no longer simply a matter of you being credible and decent. That used to be enough, but today the more credible and decent you are, the more some jurors think it is a result of law school training.

Many of this book's methods have been developed to contend with the way many of today's jurors think about lawyers and their clients. Even some of the best of the old ways can ruin your case—such as saying anything about your client before the jury knows all about what the defendant did. And some new ways that are necessary in

5. A focus group (or "mock trial" or "jury simulation" or "trial simulation") involves telling a group of laypeople about your case and then gathering their reactions. If you don't do focus groups—even for small cases—you need to start. See *How to Do Your Own Focus Groups* by David Ball (NITA, 2001), as well as the video from the same publisher.

today's climate may seem anti-intuitive—which is probably why they work.

1.11
Conclusion: Keep Your Focus

As you prepare for trial, review this chapter's ten basics regularly. During trial, review them daily. Don't let them out of sight. Here they are again:

1. **Harms and losse**s (degree)
2. **Worthwhileness** (of money)
3. **Jurors' job** (to fix, help, and make up for)
4. **Time** (proportion spent on harms, losses, and money)
5. **Defendant conduct**
6. **Who gets the money?**
7. **Who *really* gets the money?**
8. **Client's point of view**
9. **Handling why jurors give less**
10. **You**

CHAPTER TWO
MOTIVATIONS FOR GIVING

This chapter describes juror motivations for giving money. Chapter 3 describes motivations for not giving. Analyze every case in light of both sets. This will help you decide whether to take a case and how to negotiate, prepare for trial, pick a jury, and present the cases you take.

2.1
To Fix

Jurors tend to provide money when they believe it will fix or heal a loss. The costs of care, medical treatment, and lost wages can be entirely fixed with money. Some kinds of physical harm can be fully healed, and jurors will usually pay for that. Most jurors will replace lost income, but a few will find it speculative—past as well as future.

The total of the economic damages can serve as an anchor on which to base a proportionality argument for intangible damages: "John's pain is a far greater harm than just the medical bills, because medical science could do only so much to help him, so. . . . "

2.2
To Help

For harm that cannot be completely fully fixed or healed, jurors tend to provide for assistance that can partly offset it or help the victim deal with it. The paraplegic will never walk again, but an electric wheelchair and a van will get her around. The dead cannot be brought back to life, but money will support the surviving young children.

Because jurors are likely to provide money to fix and help, they will usually fully fund your minimum life-care plan[1] if you present it

1. See 7.7 on "minimum life-care plan."

properly. Even without a formal minimum life-care plan, you can create an effective list of things that fix and help.

Jurors more easily provide money that fixes and helps in ways they find familiar or understandable. Most jurors will provide support for a child because they are familiar with the financial needs of children. Less familiar needs must be explained. For example, some jurors may not easily provide speech therapy unless you teach them what it is, why it is needed, how it will heal or help, and what will happen without it.

2.3
To Balance (To Make Up For)

When harm cannot be healed or helped, all jurors can do is make up for it.

But some jurors see no worthwhile purpose in doing that: "If the pain can't be diminished, why pay her for it?" "How can we put a price on it?" Teach jurors why making up for such harms is the most important part of their job. And teach them how to do it. This teaching starts its trial-long journey in jury voir dire (see Chapter 5), or, without voir dire, in opening.

Without this teaching throughout trial, jurors who want to make up for harms will not know how to argue their positions in deliberations.

The teaching involves four steps:

1. In voir dire, identify and remove prospective jurors who have trouble with intangible damages. (See 5.19)

2. Teach seated jurors that making up for harm is fair and required by law. (See 5.9)

3. In voir dire (or opening, if the judge conducts voir dire), promise that you will explain in closing how to figure out money for harms that cannot be fixed or helped. (See 9.18)

4. In closing, show that time is an easily calculable component of all intangible losses. (See 4.2, and the non-economics arguments in Chapter 9.)

2.4
To Express Anger

As explained in 1.2, jurors who are angry at a defendant tend to provide more money. Greater anger, more money. Jurors can become angry not only at a defendant's wrongdoing but also at her in-court behavior (lies, evasions, refusal to accept responsibility, not taking the situation seriously, etc.). Jurors get angry when a defendant corporation seems not to take the case seriously, as by sending a representative who knows little about the case. (If you can—depending on who's on the defense witness list and whether you have listed "all defense witnesses" on yours—call that uninformed representative to the stand before he has a chance to get comfortable or to learn about the case from the proceedings. You might even call him first, if you are experienced enough to handle him no matter what he says. If his ignorance angers jurors right from the start, they are likely to look at the whole case through those lenses of anger.)

Responsibility. Jurors become angry when they understand that the defendant's refusal to meet his responsibility has caused harm beyond the original wrongdoing. For example, because the defendant refused to meet his responsibility and provide the necessary money, the plaintiff could not afford therapy that would have done more good soon after the injury than it can now.

Motivations. Go beneath the defendant's wrongdoing to show his motivations. Jurors get angry at negligence motivated by greed, dishonesty, hostility, corruption, callousness, or selfishness. Motivation, though rarely a legal element, is always persuasive. When you show the defendant's motivations, jurors are more likely to believe she did what you say she did. And bad motivations tend to maximize verdicts.

Make sure the motivation you suggest is believable. When you say that a manufacturer's choice to put no warning label on a product was driven by the motivation to save a penny per unit, it has little effect. It's hard to believe. Why bother saving a penny on a $600 unit? Sure, you can multiply it out by the number of units, but the amount remains comparatively trivial. So jurors are not quite convinced that the lack of label was due to any nefarious cause. The choice to use no label was driven by a more nefarious motivation: Manufacturers don't want warning labels on their products when there are no warning labels on the competing products from other manufacturers. If the Ajax mower is the only one with a particular warning, customers buy the one without the warning. No manufacturer wants to be first. (This is why manufacturers don't care as much when the government forces everyone to add the warning label.)

Look for and find persuasive motivations. They help you convince jurors that the defendant did what you say he did, and they can help stir juror wrath.

Defense Counsel. Defense counsel can anger jurors. Questionable tactics, too many objections that jurors find pointless, bullying a witness, and other such practices can lead some jurors to express their anger in verdict size. This does not happen automatically; you have to work at it, using such methods as described in this book. (Jurors can get angry at you, too, for the same tactics. That can minimize the verdict. For example, being nasty to a witness may feel good but is almost always a blunder. One of New York's otherwise best plaintiff's attorneys regularly irritates jurors with his unrelenting, biting, often pointless sarcasm and anger on cross: he's overbearingly nasty. This often affects verdict size because jurors who are repeatedly annoyed at counsel are less enthusiastic about making counsel happy. So don't try creating juror anger at the defendant or an opposition witness by displaying your own anger. If your facts and arguments do not anger the jury, neither will your display of anger. Stay slightly less angry than you think the jury already is. And save your outbursts for specific and rare moments.)

2.5
To Get Revenge for the Juror

A juror can use a large verdict to strike a blow against forces in her own life that she perceives have harmed her.

For example, in one affluent community with world-famous medical facilities, many members of an economically disadvantaged racial minority have long felt that they have been locked out of much of the wonderful care due to their inability to pay and their minority status. Older members remember when the world-famous hospital had racial quotas. Members of that minority still hold the lowest-paying and most ill-treated service jobs in these medical facilities.

Thus, that population has reason to resent and be suspicious of the medical establishment. Since medical care is a personal and family issue, the resentment and suspicion are intensely personal. Such jurors readily believe that the hospital, and other medical providers as well, are very capable of wrongdoing. Such jurors are easily angered by such wrongdoing, and take some pleasure in the opportunity to exact some revenge in the form of high verdicts.

When you may have such jurors, emphasize the parallels between the defendant's wrongdoing and the particular factors that those jurors perceive as having hurt them. For example, the minority population that feels shut out of the world-famous medical center can respond sharply when they hear that the plaintiff—minority member or not—had trouble getting access to decent care, even at a different hospital. When the wrongdoing reflects jurors' own experience, they are more likely to believe your side of the story, and can revenge their own situation by generously evaluating your client's harm.

Caveat. Some jurors can be so angry that they have turned too cynical to think that revenge—or much of anything else—can do any good. Such jurors are not motivated to provide anything beyond the minimum basics of economic compensation.

2.6

To Make a Social Statement

When jurors see that the defendant's kind of wrongdoing has consequences beyond the case, or that the wrongdoing represents what they feel to be a wider problem in society, they take their tasks more seriously and may decide on a larger verdict. They feel they can improve the world by compensating well for this kind of case.

This can work against you if jurors feel your claims can do social, political, or economic harm. Some jurors see tobacco, sexual harassment, and many other kinds of cases as harmful. And the tort-"reform" movement has made some jurors see everything you do as harmful. In voir dire, you need to discover which jurors hold such beliefs deeply enough to affect a verdict.

2.7
To Make an Example of the Defendant

Even without punitive or exemplary damages issues, jurors can use full and fair compensation to make an example of the defendant.

To encourage this, argue that it is important for the defendant to be forced to meet his responsibility—that "this is society's only way of making a negligent trucker (or whatever) meet his responsibility." This does not cross into punitive damages, but it helps jurors understand the relationship between justice for your client and the welfare of other people. (See 9.18)

2.8
To Make the Defendant Face Responsibility

Jurors tend to give more money when they see that the defendant's wrongdoing was a failure of responsibility and that the defendant continues to try to evade responsibility in court.

Jurors know it is proper for a defendant to defend himself, and will allow a lot of leeway for how he does it. But if they decide the defendant was wrong, you can lead them to see the liability defense or the attempt to pay less money as an attempt to evade responsibility.

In closing, argue:

> It's fine to defend yourself when you've done nothing wrong. But when you're wrong, you are supposed to stand up and accept responsibility—not sidestep responsibility at the further expense of the person you hurt in the first place. Defendant Smith failed in his responsibility first by not looking where he was driving. Then he refused to accept his responsibility for more than two years, depriving John of the care he needed and forcing us to come to trial. And now you have seen the defendant spend ten days

> trying to evade his responsibility right here in front of you. That's why you have to make Mr. Smith pay to fix what can be fixed, to help what can be helped, and to fully make up for everything that cannot be fixed or helped. Anything less, and Mr. Smith will permanently escape his responsibility.

(You may want to add an aggressive ending: "If you decide on less, then after you've announced your verdict, when you're walking through the parking lot to your car to go home, you'll see that defendant and those lawyers congratulating each other for having permanently escaped responsibility." This is not an attack on opposing counsel; it is an observation of what often happens.)

A defendant's attempt to avoid responsibility often begins right after the wrongdoing. What he does at that point can be revealing. Examine records and other sources to see what the defendant did immediately afterwards, or as soon as he learned what had happened. Contrast that with what your experts say he had the responsibility of doing. Did the doctor report everything properly? Did his report include the harm he did? Did his failure to properly report aggravate or prolong the harm?

Show how the first thing on the defendant's mind after (or during) the wrongdoing was to escape responsibility. This can show that he knew he had done wrong. And it can undermine his integrity.

Bring up responsibility in jury voir dire. Ask what values the jurors most hope to instill in their children, and why those values are important. When a juror gives responsibility as an answer, ask that juror and the others why they think responsibility is important.

Then ask, "What makes it hard for children to own up to responsibility when they've done something wrong?" "Why is owning up important?" "What do your children see in the outside world that you worry can teach them they don't have to accept responsibility for the things they do?"

These questions help distinguish jurors who value responsibility from those who do not. These questions also introduce your themes of responsibility and the defendant's continuing bad behavior.

"Responsibility" is an especially powerful theme when the wrongdoing was inadvertent. Argue that anyone can make a mistake—but that when we make a mistake, it is wrong to try to evade responsibility. (Also see 5.43.)

Lack of remorse. A lack of remorse on the defendant's part can anger jurors. Few defendants know how to be remorseful and defend themselves at the same time. You can usually point out that the doctor energetically tried to escape responsibility throughout trial but never showed remorse for what she had done.

When the defendant or defense counsel does express remorse during trial, show how this remorse was just a trial strategy. If it had been real, it would have been expressed long before trial. For example, instead of sitting in his truck talking to his headquarters by cell phone, the defendant would have climbed down out of his cab, offered to help your injured client, come visit him in the hospital, or call or find some other way to express his concern. Argue in closing that the defendant's late-in-the-day expression of remorse is not remorse but a manipulative tactic.

Attacks on your client. When the defense attacks your client, argue that it is salt on the wound. First the obstetrician's negligence killed the baby, and now to evade responsibility, the doctor blames Mom—knowing she will have to live forever with having been accused on a permanent public record of killing her own infant.

Malingering, exaggeration of symptoms. If the defense claims your client is malingering, point out that publicly branding your client a liar in this way is literally adding insult to injury. (See 9.23.) Jurors do not automatically see the malevolence or the destructiveness of such attacks. Point it out, so that if jurors decide the defendant is liable, they will be more likely to make her pay full measure for the compensable harms.

2.9
To Take Care of Someone Likable

Verdict size is influenced by how jurors feel about the plaintiff or the plaintiff's family. Jurors who like the plaintiff or consider the plaintiff's family "good folks" tend to give more money. Jurors find likable people more deserving than unlikable ones.

The way a juror feels about the parties is partly, often largely, due to their in-trial demeanor. In-trial dress, demeanor, and behavior can disproportionately influence verdict size.

When your client's family is sitting back in the gallery during trial, have a paralegal monitor their behavior and even their facial expressions. Family members can do more harm than good. Their bad behavior can minimize damages and even cost you liability. Scowling, smiling at inappropriate places, snoozing, having too good a time, facially "acting out" reactions, staring at jurors, or any of a wide variety of other common behaviors can dampen juror willingness to help your client. Except in extraordinary circumstances, limit the attendance of family and friends to a very small number, two or three—and even then your paralegal must keep a frequent eye on them. If there are problems, the paralegal should report to you, so you can correct the problem or get rid of the offenders.

One problem with family members at trial is that jurors often conclude that they are there because they are hoping for a bunch of money to come into the family, and that they'll get a cut of the pie: "I was there when you needed me, so. . . . "

The way jurors feel about the kind of person your client is and the way she comes across is one reason you cannot reliably gauge the value of your case in advance by comparing it to similar cases. No two clients are alike, so no two cases are alike. You must factor in—sometimes heavily—the impressions all parties will strike the jury.

Sometimes attorneys do not make necessary changes in the way a plaintiff dresses or, say, does her hair, because they fear that the opposition attorney will call attention to the changes. It is better to make necessary changes anyway. Your client is one of your most emphatic visual exhibits. You want that emphasis to work in your favor. Your opponent's snide remarks about the changed appearance of your client are momentary. The client's appearance is stage center beginning to end.[2] If the defense attorney makes any such comment, your client should explain that because this trial is critical to him, he felt obligated to look his best.

---

2. In many cases, it is better for your client never to come into the courtroom. See 7.11.

Juror reaction in terms of verdict size is affected not just by the kind of person the plaintiff is, but even by things the plaintiff might have done that were not related to the case. For example: Sally had an abortion ten years ago. No one claims the abortion had anything to do with the events of this case. But some jurors will not help a woman who had an abortion. Some will even believe that the harm the defendant negligently caused was inspired by God: "That's why this normally good doctor made such a terrible mistake. So rewarding this plaintiff with money would be counter to God's will."

Often you can keep such information out, but defense attorneys frequently find ways to make it seem material. In certain situations and with the right kind of jury, you can make the jury see just how cynical and unjustified this is. That can ignite some juror anger or disgust with the defense.

2.10
To Reward and Support Persistence

Fighting spirit. Jurors are motivated to give money when a plaintiff keeps fighting her situation no matter how hard or hopeless it is. Americans love a fighting spirit that refuses to give in to overwhelming adversity.

But the plaintiff's fighting spirit can be masked when you show that the situation is so bad that all hope is gone and the plaintiff has given up. No hope means no reason for jurors to provide much money.

So find and encourage your client's striving and hope. No matter how little she can do, point out ways in which she tried or is trying to do more, even when they fail. For example, show how she struggled back to work despite bad pain. The Little-Engine-that-Could did not get to the top by whining and crying "It's hopeless." He said "I think I can" and he worked at it.

So don't focus only on your client's limitations and ailments. Focus as much on how she is trying to transcend them.

Even with a minor injury, show how your client tried to cope and overcome, not just lie down and wait to get better. (Be careful not to turn this into her harming herself by trying to do too much too soon.)

Emphasize everything your client did or is doing to fight her situation. In a wrongful death case, show how the family is striving to survive the loss, not just stew in its misery.

Even jurors who are generally bad plaintiff's jurors—such as those who say we all must play the hand we're dealt, those who do not want people relying on others for care, and those who factor emotion out of their decision-making—often come to the support of a plaintiff who shows persistence. So don't emphasize hopelessness even in a hopeless situation. Emphasize your client's striving to overcome it, futile or not. Think "The Little Engine that Could," not Sartre. Americans cherish strivers and survivors, not whiners or quitters. God and juries help those who help themselves—even a little.

Defendant's exacerbation. It is particularly useful to show how your client's efforts have been made harder because she has lacked the resources and help she needs—and has lacked them because of the defendant's refusal to meet his responsibility. Show how that refusal has impeded the plaintiff's struggle to overcome. Jurors who value persistence will get angry at anything that makes the plaintiff's struggle unnecessarily harder. They see it as mean.

Active and passive. On liability, show that the defendants were the *active* parties, with your client the passive recipient of the defendants' negligent *actions.* But reverse the active role when it comes to harm and damages. Put your client into the action role: how heroically Sally strove to overcome the harms—while the defendant stood passively by and did nothing to help.

Past and present. If the harm is all past, show how your client strove. If the harm is continuing, counsel your client to engage right away in activities that are as optimistic and hopeful as possible, and that show a spirit of struggle. If the client cannot work, perhaps he can volunteer a few hours a week. If he cannot get out of the house, maybe he can use e-mail and the Internet to stay in touch with people and the world in general. He might be able to do something constructive on the Internet—such as helping others get through similar difficulties.[3] Counseling your client to strive in such ways will not only motivate jurors to give money; it will also improve the quality of your client's life.

Be sure your client does not fall into the opposite kinds of behavior, such as missing therapy sessions or quitting rehabilitation. That's a gift to the defense.

Caveat. Jurors become suspicious and angry when a plaintiff can do certain things that are harder than things she claims she cannot do. When she claims she cannot concentrate well enough to continue working but she still drives a car, jurors often conclude she is lying. "How can anyone drive without concentrating? And if she's really got brain damage, how dare she endanger the rest of us out on the highway!" Often it can be nearly impossible to make your client stop driving, because driving might be the last bit of freedom she has. But try. If you fail, at least be certain she does not drive to court—or anyplace else over the duration of trial. No need to turn your client's driving into an indelible demonstrative exhibit.

2.11
To Stop Wrongdoing

Punitive damages. Large punitive verdicts for a single bad act are rare because jurors see little need to "deter" an isolated, past incident. Large punitive verdicts are most often driven by patterns of continuing bad behavior. While jurors do punish an individual instance of wrongdoing, they go farther when the wrongdoing is habitual. So try to find patterns of the defendant's past, present, and likely future behavior that match the negligence in this case. (See Chapter 10 on punitive damages.)

2.12
To Be Important

Most people like to feel they are part of something important or that other people will see them as part of something important. When

3. But caution him not to counsel others on how to get an attorney to get money. Jurors might go to the Web site and interpret this advice in an unfriendly light.

jurors think a large verdict can make them part of something important but a defense verdict would not, they are more likely to come to a large verdict. This is because their personal motivation—their desire to be part of something important—drives them to perceive the evidence in the light most likely to make them a part of something important.

You can harness this to work in your favor. To do so, you need to employ one of the ultimate persuasion techniques in the arsenal: align what jurors personally want with what you want.

Aligning juror wants with yours. To illustrate this technique: In voir dire you *want* prospective jurors to open up and talk. The best way is to ask prospective jurors questions they will *want* to answer. Ask, for example, "What makes you good at your job?" Or "What makes you a good father?" Most jurors will eagerly await their turn to answer. The question invites them to show what makes them important, which is something most of them *want* to do. When they do it, you get what you want: information about the juror. You have *aligned* what you want (information) with what the juror wants (a chance for some stature in this neutering context of being a prospective juror). You both get what you want. And now that they have talked freely to you about something, they are more likely to talk freely in response to other questions you ask for the rest of voir dire.

(A valuable follow-up to "What makes you good at your job?" is "What would make you better at your job?")

Alignment and case outcome. How do you use this alignment technique in terms of case outcome? It works the same way: Identify something the jurors want, and show them how to get it by deciding in your favor. Align your want with theirs. It's not easy, but when you succeed the defense has no way to deal with it.

Example:

In a 1992 gas well case, when Kentucky attorney Gary C. Johnson got up to start jury voir dire, the first words he said were, "Folks, before I start my usual questions, there's something I've got to ask first. This case is likely to be the most important case you ever heard about. It may permanently change how things are done across the state, even across the country. It may change how outside corporations operate in

Kentucky and how we live here. There will probably be media coverage. Some reporters may try to talk to you after trial to find out why you decided the way you did. Now, you don't have to talk to them, you can say no—but some people don't want to be put in that position. And some people are uncomfortable being on a jury whose verdict could have such an important effect. So tell me this, and let me start with Mr. Jones here: How do you feel about being in a position like that?"

This is a legitimate information-seeking voir dire question. You need to find out how jurors feel about this, because importance-avoiding or limelight-avoiding jurors may keep a verdict low so they do not have to be part of such a situation.

But beyond gaining information, the question also aligns what you want (a large verdict) with what the jurors want (importance). As trial progresses and jurors come to understand what is at stake, they realize they can get what they want (their importance, their fifteen minutes of fame, or the chance to do something important) only by deciding the case the way you want. That means a large verdict.

When Gary Johnson asked that question, almost everyone—possibly excepting the defense attorneys—was suddenly eager to be on the jury. Prospective jurors who had earlier written five reasons why they could not possibly serve literally bounded into the jury box the instant their names were called, proud and primed and eager to serve. The judge asked one: "What about these problems you mentioned on the questionnaire?"

"Oh, I took care of all that. No problem."

Most of those dismissed for one reason or another were crushed. They wanted to be part of something important. They wanted to do something important. They wanted to be interviewed on TV.

At the end of voir dire, Attorney Johnson asked again, "Well, folks, now that you've had some time to think about it, is there anybody thinks they'd be uncomfortable on a jury that could be so important?" They all waved that off as a ridiculous possibility.

Over the course of trial, Johnson made sure the jurors understood that a very large verdict was necessary to make this an important trial. He aligned what he *wanted*—a large verdict—to what the jurors *wanted*: importance. The jurors got what they wanted, and the client got a full and fair verdict. The only one unhappy was the out-of-state company that had poisoned the groundwater all over eastern Kentucky.

The principle underlying this strategy is powerful: *When you align the jurors' personal wants with a good verdict, you are likely to get the good verdict.* This is an area of advocacy practice we are just starting to explore, so please share with me any strategies you come up with that are based on this principle.

Caveat. What people *personally* and *selfishly* want is not the same as what they believe or what they think is good. So don't rely on things such as "justice" or "fairness." Jurors can only give those things, not get them. The appeal must be to something they can *get*—such as importance, or feeling connected, or powerful.

CHAPTER THREE
MOTIVATIONS FOR NOT GIVING

This chapter describes juror motivations against providing money, especially non-economic damages.

3.1
Political Stance

By 2004, verdict size had become a full-fledged political issue—and will get fuller and fuller fledged well into the future. Political forces have made tort "reform" our most important problem.

The role and ethics of plaintiff's attorneys became grist for the political mill, not quite as salient as terrorism but significant enough to affect virtually every verdict. Many jurors with no previous strong attitudes or opinions either way adopted the tort-"reform" stances that insurance companies, chambers of commerce, and medical associations have been pushing for years.

With some such jurors this is not deep-seated. Such a juror's parroting of tort-"reform" slogans does not necessarily mean those slogans will affect his decision-making in trial.

But many jurors—as of early 2005, a quarter to a third in most areas—are now dangerous. They willingly and often eagerly nullify the law in order to minimize verdicts, thinking they are doing the right thing. This phenomenon is not new. Many pre-Civil War northern juries nullified by refusing to return slaves to their southern owners, despite the law. Many North Carolina juries refused to convict for bootlegging because they believed prohibition to be not merely unethical but inconvenient. In some states, jurors are still told it is up to them whether to follow the law, and until the 19th century, almost every jury had that right.

And now the tort "reformers" are seizing the opportunity. So in jury selection you must distinguish between jurors who are dangerous because their tort-"reform" attitudes run deep, versus those who are not necessarily dangerous because their tort-"reform" attitudes are shallow. Distinguish between mere slogans and the more dangerous substantive analysis. (Also see Chapter 5.)

Since you can rarely get everyone off the jury who is likely to keep your verdict low on the basis of tort-"reform" attitudes, a number of methods throughout this book will help you arm your friendly jurors to deal with tort-"reform" jurors in deliberations.

The direct result of tort "reform" is that more jurors than ever believe that verdicts are out of control: too high, too frequent, bad for business and the economy, responsible for high insurance and medical care costs, destructive of the local and national economy, and harmful to the national health, world peace, and eternal salvation—and ultimately paid for by individuals including themselves. If any of that seems to you like exaggeration, you have not been watching.

This is reinforced by talk shows and radio and TV commentators, late-night comedians, preachers, chambers of commerce, trade associations, insurance campaigns, presidents, lower-office politicians, conspiracy theorists, and others.

This has not affected every juror, and it is more pronounced in medical cases than others. But if affects enough jurors to sway every jury. And since the beginning of 2005, its effect on non-medical personal injury cases is pronounced and growing—often exponentially.

You cannot change these attitudes in a juror during trial. Trying will only harden and extend them. So do not, for example, try to justify any supposedly outrageous cases. You will lose the McDonald's battle every time even when you think you've convinced someone—and in the process you will convince some jurors that you are just another thief. ("That damned lawyer actually said the McDonald's case was legit!")

Use voir dire to identify and try to remove anti-litigation jurors. Be most wary of leaders with these attitudes (see 5.1), as well as jurors with these attitudes who seem stubborn, cynical or aggressively outspoken, or who like to show they are smarter than others. Such qualities often find their most pleasurable outlet by defeating "you and your kind" and bragging about it afterwards.

The good news is that tort-"reform" jurors rarely persuade jurors who disagree with them. The bad news is that even when heavily outnumbered, tort-"reform" jurors usually have more power than anyone else in deliberations when it comes to verdict size. The good news is that you can arm your favorable jurors with tools for deliberations to deal with the bad jurors. The bad news is that these tools must be used skillfully. The good news is that you will use them skillfully.

Don't Despair. There's more good news. Recent experience and a lot of jury research show that many jurors who seem in voir dire to be strongly anti-litigation often turn out to be high-dollar jurors. This is because many such jurors have a keen, energetic, and easily aroused sense of justice. This is why they get so angry about what they perceive as lawsuit abuse. If you get such jurors fired up about the defendant's bad acts, that same keen sense of justice often turns them into good plaintiff's jurors. If an anti-litigation juror has some favorable qualities—such as being a caring person, or leaning to the center or liberal side of the political and social spectra (see 5.37 on other such favorable qualities), then all is not lost.

So your job in voir dire is to differentiate between those with deep tort-"reform" attitudes and those whose anti-litigation attitudes are more shallow, or whose sense of justice can be turned to your favor. A juror can believe that lawsuits and verdicts are out of control, that runaway juries abound, and that the world is coming to an end because of lawsuits—but still believe that your case is different and deserves the money you ask for.

On the next page are the most common reasons jurors withhold money. They are explained in the sections following this one.

Avoid Criticism
Compromise
Blame the Plaintiff
Money not Necessary
Unclear Purpose
Future Medical Inventions
Come Back for More
Does Not Value the Plaintiff
Getting Along Fine Without Money
Hopeless Situation
Punitive Damages Do not Work
Making the Plaintiff Rich
Making Plaintiff's Lawyer Rich
Insurance Rates
Plaintiff's Insurance and Other Sources
Protect an Industry
Seen Worse
People Should Pay For Their Own Problems
Divine Punishment ("God is my co-juror.")
Revenge Against the Plaintiff
To Not Punish Defendant
Remorse
Inadvertent Wrongdoing
Speculation

3.2
Avoid Criticism

As some jurors draw closer to making a real decision, they start worrying about how people they know will react to their decision. A hospital secretary may start to worry that her colleagues and bosses at work, who resent lawsuits and plaintiff's attorneys, will resent her for being on a jury that has given a large verdict—even on a non-medical case. (People opposed to lawsuits in their own fields are often against good verdicts in any kind of personal injury case.)

Such jurors can tend to push for a defense liability verdict to avoid having to deal with the money problem. This is particularly true when the harm is so great that a verdict would be large if the jury decides the defendant is liable.

In voir dire, find out who the juror goes home to or back to work to. Might those people disapprove if this juror decides on a large verdict? So, for example, a juror whose wife runs a business that needs a lot of insurance can be a bad choice. Even if the juror does not think that large verdicts raise insurance rates, his wife might—and that is who he will have to deal with.

Ask jurors how lawsuits have affected the businesses or fields they work in, and how people at work feel about lawsuits. The more a juror feels that people at work (or at home or at his favorite hang-out) are anti-litigation, the more he is likely to resist a large verdict that could later expose him to criticism. This is usually true even he says it is not.

Focus groups, while helpful in many ways, cannot show how much this kind of thinking will affect your case. This is because focus jurors, unlike real jurors in open court, know that no one at work or home will know the outcome, so they do not worry about negative reactions. But real jurors feel exposed because the verdict will be public.

3.3
Compromise

Jurors who are only mildly supportive of liability often try to lower the verdict size. In a jurisdiction requiring unanimity, one such juror can lower the verdict significantly. She is in a powerful negotiating position because the others know if they insist on too large a verdict, she can reverse her liability vote and nothing will be given. In a non-unanimity jurisdiction, just two or three can do the same thing.

Unfortunately, this is no two-way street. Eleven high-money jurors have little power against a low-rolling minority of one. High-money jurors cannot get what they want by reversing their liability votes, so they can only accept the lower amount the minority wants to give.

To counter the power of low-money jurors, arm your favorable jurors with concrete ways to argue for money. (See Chapter 9.)

3.4
Blame the Plaintiff

Even with no plaintiff negligence, when a plaintiff's actions show a lack of responsibility, many jurors give less money. "She missed three doctor appointments. If she didn't care about her health, why should we give her all that money for pain and suffering?" When jurors believe your client shares responsibility, many assign a low absolute dollar value to the total losses and harms (no matter who caused them). This is because jurors do not like to reward irresponsibility.

Then, if asked to apportion contributory negligence, they further reduce that low amount by the proportion of blame they assign your client.

Finally, in some jurisdictions, the judge apportions again. You can be triple-dipped against. So explain in closing how the process works. Use the figures you are asking for, along with a modest admission of your client's negligence (say, 10%) as the basis for a demonstration of how the judge will apportion. (See 9.1)

3.5
Money not Necessary

Jurors usually think money requested for lost wages, medical care, and therapy is necessary, so they usually fund it. But some items in these categories can seem unnecessary.

For example, a life-care planner may specify a swimming pool for recreation and therapy. Even with explanation, some jurors will find it an unnecessary frill. That makes them suspicious of the whole minimum life-care plan.

With or without a minimum life-care plan, do not ask for anything that jurors can interpret as frivolous or as padding. It's rarely worth undermining the rest of the plan.

3.6
Unclear Purpose

Jurors are reluctant to pay for treatment and care they do not understand. It is not enough for an expert merely to say, "He needs muscle therapy." Explain:

- what it is
- how it works
- who does it
- why it is needed
- how it will help
- what will happen if it is not provided.

Show videos of the therapy, photos of the clinic, a video or model of the muscles the therapy will strengthen, and visuals to show what will happen if the care is not provided (such as an atrophied muscle). (See 6.8[g] and 7.7)

3.7
Future Medical Inventions

Some jurors think medical science will eventually develop a cure for the "permanent" problem, so why pay for it?

Turn this concern to your favor: Your experts should explain that if any "cure" is invented, it is not likely to be complete, that it is likely to be very costly, and that there is no money for it in the minimum life-care plan. So to make sure Jane can take advantage of whatever it is, the jurors need to add a significant amount to the minimum life-care plan. (You get past the preponderance requirement by explaining that Jane is worried right now how she'll pay for any such new treatment that might come along in her lifetime; added money can remove that worry, which unquestionably exists and thus meets the preponderance threshold.)

3.8
Come Back for More

Some jurors believe the plaintiff can come back for more money if necessary. Such jurors may withhold money for anything not needed for certain.

Make sure jurors know this is Jane's only opportunity, and that she should not have to gamble on whether or not certain things will be provided if the need for them arises. Again, the possibility of the need arising does not have to be more likely than not. Even if it's only a 10% chance, it is a 100% fact that Jane is worried about it right now—and it is the worry for which you are seeking compensation. Argue to the jury that: "There may be a 90% chance she will need it or just a 10% chance, but it is 100% certain that she worries right now about how she'll pay for it, because there's a 100% chance that if you don't include it in the verdict, she won't be able to pay for it. Your verdict can remove that worry."

3.9
Does Not Value the Plaintiff

If jurors think your client is not worth investing in, they give less money.

Jurors can feel this way for many reasons, some justifiable, some not. Your client might be physically unattractive, or a member of a minority, or old, or obese. Your client might be mean, or stupid, or irritating, or . . . it is a long list. And what makes some jurors value your client can make others devalue him.

Some things about your client can be improved, such as sloppiness, inappropriate clothing, or behaviors such as whining or being angry. When trying to change something, do not just tell your client to stop it. Suggest something to replace it. Say, "Tell us how your family helps you," not "Stop whining about yourself."

Try to improve just one behavior at a time. And consider using a trial consultant to work with your witness when there are particularly difficult problems.[1]

Sometimes the problem lies in something the plaintiff has done in the past that you cannot keep out, such as a forged check or spousal abuse. Once in a while you will have the facts to show that the check forger had acceptable motivations (he forged the check because his baby was sick). But usually not ("Who cares what her motivations were? Drunk driving is drunk driving!"). It then becomes primarily a jury selection issue, because you cannot change jurors' attitudes about it.

Negative stereotypes. Some jurors will think your client is not worth investing in if he falls into a devalued stereotype (minority member, old person, obese, foreigner, etc.). You cannot change a juror's stereotype beliefs, and can make matters worse by trying.

The National Jury Project's Susan Macpherson teaches that without challenging the jurors' beliefs about the stereotype, you need to show how your client is an *exception* to the stereotype. If the stereotype's characteristics include stupidity, dishonesty, and unreliability, have witnesses talk about his knowledge, honesty, and diligence. Have him testify in ways that show his knowledge and diligence. Showing how he is an exception to the stereotype can help jurors see him as having value.

3.10
Getting Along Fine Without Money

By refusing to settle, the defendants have been forcing your client to survive without money. Then they claim she is doing fine without money.

Even when the defense does not use this common and ignoble argument, some jurors think it up on their own. If you do not tell them that things are rough on your client in her present circumstances, they

1. See *Theater Tips and Strategies for Jury Trials, Third Edition,* by David Ball (NITA, 2003) for guidance in working with witnesses.

will think she has been doing fine, and provide less money. Show that your client has not been getting along well. Show the deprivations she has been living under, and how they will worsen in time.

Convey this in opening, or it can affect juror decision making throughout trial.

3.11
Hopeless Situation

Money cannot help hopeless situations, so jurors tend not to put money into them. Sometimes in your zeal to show how bad the harm is, you paint a totally bleak picture: unbearable, endless pain; no family; incapacity to do anything; no way anything can improve the situation. Result: no reason to give money. (See 2.10 for ways to show the hope in bleak situations.)

3.12
Punitive Damages Do Not Work

Some jurors believe punitive damages have no effect. This is usually because they believe that the defendant will pass the loss on to consumers. ("McDonald's coffee went up a nickel a cup after that verdict.")

See Chapter 10 for punitive damages strategies.

3.13
Making the Plaintiff Rich

Especially in the long shadow of tort "reform," some jurors hate the idea of making anyone rich—even someone they like—for having been harmed, no matter how grievously. This holds compensation down, particularly non-economic damages, and has an even worse effect on punitives when jurors know (as many do) that the money, or much of it, goes to the plaintiff.

Look for such jurors in jury selection. (See 5.32) And in closing, use arguments designed to contend with this problem (Chapter 9). See, for example, 1.7 about naming a trustee as a plaintiff when your client is a child.

3.14
Making Plaintiff's Lawyer Rich

Jurors assume you get a third or more of the verdict. This helps you if jurors decide to give the plaintiff a third more than they want to put into the plaintiff's hands, to cover your fee.

But some jurors give less because they hate making lawyers rich. And some jurors can have a particular problem giving money specifically to you. This can be because of the way you act, conduct yourself, dress, or look, or just because of bad chemistry between you and that juror.

Bad advertising. Sometimes jurors withhold money because the attorney has run offensive TV ads that revealed how greedy and unprincipled he is. That makes jurors suspicious of him and his case, and leaves them unwilling to enrich what they think are his already bulging coffers. Of course, some attorneys who run such ads have little intention of ever stepping inside a courtroom if they can help it. But if you plan to be in jury trials, take a hard look at whether your ads are undermining your credibility and likability. In one eastern city, a lawyer recently ran such an offensive ad campaign to attract people who had used a certain product that jurors not only ended up hating that attorney but also became deeply suspicious of every other attorney's case concerning the same product.

Attorneys who run such offensive ads are not likely to care how much they are feeding the fires of tort "reform," especially when the ads have brought in lots of clients. But these attorneys are poisoning the jury pool against themselves more effectively than the tort-"reform" forces could ever do. If people stick their fingers down their throats when they hear your name, you have poisoned the jury pool for yourself and others.

Jurors rarely admit they lowered a verdict because they disliked plaintiff's counsel. Often they do not even admit it to themselves. But once they start to dislike you for bad advertising or bad behavior in trial or for any other reason, they tend to see evidence, especially damages evidence, in the light least favorable to you. They want you to lose, so they are susceptible to the defense spin on each piece of evidence. They can believe they are making a fair decision on the facts, while actually allowing their feelings about you to taint every argument and piece of evidence.

Even when jurors like and trust you, some will not want you to get a lot of money just for coming to court for a few days or weeks. They don't know about your enormous investment of time and money or that if you lose you will probably have to pay the costs yourself because your client will never be in any position to pay you back.

Before and during trial you can minimize some of this resistance. (See Appendix A and Chapter 11.)[2] Pay close attention to the kind of person the jurors see that you are. Be particularly careful to show that you are motivated by caring, not greed. Do not suck up, but simply be as decent a person as you know how to be.

3.15

Insurance Rates

Fear of making insurance rates rise makes some jurors reluctant to give even modest compensation, and can affect liability decisions.

In jury selection, find out which jurors believe the verdict-to-insurance-cost connection. If necessary, you can do this without mentioning insurance yourself. Simply ask jurors what kinds of harm they worry about lawsuits causing. Some will mention insurance rates.

Be especially wary of jurors with a personal reason to worry about insurance rates, such as people whose situations require numerous personal or business insurance policies.

---

2. See *David Ball's Theater Tips and Strategies for Jury Trials, Third Edition,* Chap. 1 and Appendix H (NITA, 2003).

In some locales, everyone pays outlandishly high car insurance rates. Families spend a quarter of their income to insure their cars. Jurors in these areas who believe in the verdict-to-rate connection will have strong personal reason to keep the family's budget from being stretched even thinner.

In most venues, judges won't let you breathe the word "insurance." If this is discretionary, argue that not only is the insurance-rate bias damagingly powerful but is based on a misconception, so it leads to the worst kind of decision making: jurors factoring into their verdicts *a misconception that would be improper to use even if true.* It is juror nullification based on inaccurate information that an intentional campaign has inculcated. Since your client is now up against the results of that campaign, you should have the right to find out which jurors it has convinced.

3.16
Plaintiff's Insurance and Other Sources

Sometimes jurors give less money if they think the plaintiff has received insurance payments: "Why pay her medical expenses? She was a public school teacher and they have health insurance."

Sometimes jurors pay less on the grounds that there are services "our taxes already paid for" to take care of the plaintiff. Many jurors know people who are being cared for by the county or state, or who are on Social Security disability. This safety-net belief especially hurts with respect to future care.

In most jurisdictions, neither insurance nor public care services come up overtly during trial, so it is hard to argue against them. But they are frequently part of juror decision-making. So explain to jurors that their job "is to decide the *value of the losses,* and that it makes no difference if someone has a rich uncle someplace (and Sally does not) who's paid or will pay for medical care. All the jury has to do is decide the value of the losses, and not to guess how much money some 'rich uncle or someone' might be providing." This arms your favorable jurors in deliberations to deal with jurors who want to deduct from the verdict health insurance payments or other sources of money.

In some jurisdictions you can—and should—explain that money paid by insurance will come off the top of the verdict and go back to the insurance company.

This also helps your favorable jurors to argue for the full value of the loss even though Mom is providing the care. Explain that the dollar amount that goes on the care line is the total value—including the value of the care Mom provided, though of course she did not do it to get paid. Actual cost is not the point; *value* is, and should be compensated. Otherwise the defendant is using Mom to shoulder some of what should be the defendant's responsibility.

3.17
Protect an Industry

Jurors do not easily make decisions that hurt their self-interests, such as their potential dependence on the well-being of a defendant or a defendant's industry.

For example, some rural jurors will not want to decide on a large verdict against their only local hospital. Faced with having to choose between harming their families' only source of health care and giving a plaintiff what is deserved, some jurors understandably will sacrifice the plaintiff by holding damages down. Further, many jurors in such situations do not want to believe that their only hospital could be negligent. The possibility is personally frightening. And many jurors have been led to believe that med mal verdicts drive doctors away and discourage new ones from coming.

Jurors can also be protective of any business or industry important to the local economy. In a tourism area, jurors can fear that bad publicity resulting from a large premises-liability verdict against a popular hotel will hurt the incomes of many local people.[3]

If you cannot file in a different jurisdiction, a judge might consider a venue change if you contrast for her the attitudes towards the parties in the current jurisdiction versus those an alternative one. Professional

3. For an in-depth view of how this works, see Henrik Ibsen's play *An Enemy of the People,* in which almost everyone in a resort town hides the danger that all its tourists are in.

surveys can quantify such differences. They can show the judge that a typical venire in the current jurisdiction will perceive its interests to be the same as the defendant's—and that this is not the situation in an alternative venue.

Explain that staying in that jurisdiction will force you to exercise strikes on the basis of that bias, leaving you without the strikes you need for other problems—a problem the defense does not have. The judge is likely to respond, "Well, let's see how it goes." If it goes as you predicted, point this out and ask for extra strikes, or a more lenient granting of cause dismissals on the basis of this bias, or a change of venue.

3.18
Seen Worse

Jurors compare harms in the case to harms they have seen before. This can hurt you, especially when the harmed person they know gets along without the money you say your client needs.

Further, jurors who know people with harms similar to your client's will probably be less shocked by your client's harm. "My uncle is blind and he manages well." That takes away a juror's motivation to give much money.

Jurors tend to see how well people they know *seem* to cope. They are often unaware of the real difficulties involved. They see the smile on someone's face but not the pain their heart.

3.19
People Should Pay for their Own Problems

There are several reasons some jurors believe that people should pay for their own problems.

Some jurors believe life is a gamble, so when something bad happens, "that's the breaks and it's up to you to suffer through." These "deal with it" jurors also tend to believe that human beings should not be expected to take care of each other. (See Chapter 5.)

Some jurors may have been badly harmed themselves and received no compensation or assistance. Many of these "I didn't get anything" jurors see little reason why others should be compensated or helped.

Other jurors may have overcome different kinds of serious difficulties on their own, without the aid of others. For example, recovering alcoholics may have had AA support, but had to conquer their demons on their own. These "*I* managed!" jurors tend to demand the same of others.

The National Jury Project's Susan Macpherson observes that some jurors will think the plaintiff should be forced to struggle to get by with little money because it builds character and strength. Such tough-love jurors think it "makes for more disability to hand someone a ton of money. Better to have to make their way without it."

This attitude disappears the instant that juror himself is hurt. But that is not likely to happen unless he's run over in the courthouse parking lot.

3.20
Divine Punishment ("God is my co-juror")

"It's God's will!" Some jurors believe that serious illness or injury is likely the result of unrelated wrongs the victim committed earlier in life—even when they don't know anything about any such wrongs. ("If he got hurt like that, there had to be a reason for it. There always is.") Consequently, such jurors can believe that giving verdict money would be contrary to God's plan. You need to spot these jurors in jury voir dire. (See Chapter 5.)

3.21
To Not Punish Defendant

Some jurors see all compensation as punishment, and do not want to punish the defendant. This is especially potent with money for "pain and suffering," a phrase you should never utter except in jury selection because it is a buzz-phrase of tort "reform." Many jurors believe any verdict beyond medical and lost income expenses to be "punitive."

You can help this somewhat by making sure from the start of trial that jurors understand that none of the money is intended to punish; it is only to fix what can be fixed, help what can be helped, and make up for what cannot be fixed or helped. Always explain that no one is going to jail, no licenses will be revoked, and no one will lose his career. This is especially important with medical defendants.

Show that an under-compensating verdict punishes your client. "Compensate" means "to balance" (literally, to hang on the same level). A verdict that does not fully balance is as bad as an employer under-compensating an employee for a day's work. (See 9.9)

3.22
Remorse

Americans love remorse. A death-penalty jury is far more likely to give life than death if they see the murderer is remorseful. In the same way, civil jurors give less money in the rare instances when they see the defendant is remorseful for her wrongdoing.

Fortunately for plaintiffs, defendants rarely express remorse. Their attorneys say, "We're sorry Mr. Jones will never walk again," but not, "My client is sorry for being negligent." Weirdly, even when the defense stipulates liability, the defendant almost never looks at the plaintiff in trial and says, "I am so sorry for what I did to you." If more defendants said it and showed that they meant it, it would lower many verdicts.

But in itself, stipulating liability can make a defendant *seem* remorseful. Use the following arguments in closing:

> The defendant is saying, 'I'm sorry I did it, but don't ask me to fix it, don't ask me to make up for it.'
>
> There can be no remorse without responsibility.
>
> He did it and he doesn't care.

> Despite admitting it he is compounding the original harms by forcing Andrea to do without help and forcing her through the difficulties of a trial.

Such arguments can offset juror willingness to be forgiving. The American ideal is to admit responsibility and offer to make up for it without haggling over the price. We don't like: "Gee, Mrs. Williams, I'm sorry I broke your picture window; really really sorry; I'll pay for part of it."

3.23
Inadvertent Wrongdoing

Many jurors believe that inadvertent error should be responded to mildly—meaning with a smaller verdict.

This is why you should refer to everything the defendant did as a choice or decision. (See 1.5)

3.24
Speculation

Because calculating intangible damages is not based on anything concrete, some jurors withhold money because they feel that any figure would be speculative—and the judge tells them not to speculate. To deal with this common problem, use arguments such as the scales argument in 9.14.

CHAPTER FOUR

NON-ECONOMIC DAMAGES[1]

Intangible damages are hard to get for two primary reasons: Jurors rarely see what purpose the money can serve, and jurors never know how to figure out how much to give. When they say during jury selection, "Well, I wouldn't know how to do it," plaintiff's counsel usually gives them the worst possible response: "Well, you know, now I can't tell you how to do that. Nobody can, not even Her Honor the judge can tell you how. You'll just have to use your own life experiences and your common sense." This is the litigator's equivalent of shooting yourself in the foot.

What life experience can jurors use to help them decide how much they should give in non-economic damages? How can common sense possibly help? If you cannot tell them how to do it, and if the judge cannot tell them how to do it, and if no one in the world can, the only conclusions they can draw are that (1) it can't be done right and (2) since no one knows how to do it, it should not be done.

You make matters worse later in trial when you say, "We submit the figure should be $________." This is wretched in terms of language, and it does not help the jurors unless you explain why that specific amount is appropriate. The fact that you propose it does not make it appropriate. In fact, an unsupported proposal is more likely to create resistance.

If you offer no figure at all, you are leaving jurors with no guidance whatsoever. Even in venues where you cannot ask for a specific figure, you need to tell jurors how to arrive at one. (See, for example, 9.14, "Scales.")

1. Sorry for the repetition, but please remember never to use the term "non-economic damages" in front of a jury. You may see this same reminder in yet another footnote.

Jurors have less trouble calculating and giving economic damages.[2] Jurors see worthwhile purposes in paying medical expenses and—even if to a slightly lesser extent—lost wages. They rarely have trouble figuring out those amounts. But non-economic damages are harder, so jurors grasp at straws. This chapter and many suggestions throughout this book will help you provide the jurors with something more substantial than straws.

Some defense attorneys routinely argue that "all that money for pain and suffering can do no good because it won't make the pain or suffering go away." If you're faced with that, file *in limine* to prevent any such argument, because it's an overt appeal for jurors to nullify. Only four states still recognize nullification as proper (Maryland, Georgia, Oregon, Indiana), and even there you can move against allowing defense counsel to argue overtly for it.

4.1
Economic Damages as Benchmark

Jurors usually arrive at a non-economic damages figure by using the economic damages total as a benchmark. They often calculate intangible damages as a proportion, multiple, or equivalent of the tangibles figure.

For example, if medical bills and lost wages total $125,000, jurors will likely use $125,000 as an anchor for non-economic damages. In deliberations, jurors will argue that the plaintiff should get *half* that amount, or *double*, or the amount exactly, or just "a little more" or "not as much as." They begin with the anchor of the economic damages figure and argue to adjust it one way or the other.

In many venues where you cannot suggest specific figures for non-economic damages, you can still call the non-economic damages "the greatest harm in the case." Point out that "the money for medical care all goes to other people to help take care of John, so John never gets a cent of it; and the money for lost wages only makes John even with where he'd have been if the wrongdoing had never happened—so none of that money makes up for the biggest losses, John's human

2. Don't use that phrase either.

losses." This encourages your favorable jurors to see non-economic harms as requiring a larger figure than the economic harms.

Anchors that work against you. With a small medical figure, jurors may think there was not much harm—and thus provide little money for non-economic harms. If you still choose to seek compensation for medical care, explain that the figure is so small because "Medical science could do little for this kind of injury." But also consider dropping your claim for medical expenses. If your client deserves millions for what this has done to his life but the medical expenses are only $35,000, you might do better ignoring the medicals. Why float a comparatively tiny figure? An anchor of minimal proportions can drag down the verdict. There are ways to argue for non-economic damages that do not require an economic damages anchor. (See Chapter 9.)

Family caretakers. Money for family caretaking is usually hard to get. Instead, focus on replacing the family with professional caretakers—trained, if that's what's needed. This can significantly bolster your economic damages figure. You'll need to show five things:

1. **Forcing the family to provide care for harms the defendant caused is unfair.** The family does not begrudge doing it and will do it as long as necessary, but the defendant's responsibility is to relieve the family of that burden and return the family to being family members, not permanent care givers. You can do this even with no consortium claims if your client is deeply bothered by having his family forced into the position of care givers. This is harm to him and the jury can remove it by providing for paid, professional care.

2. **Show that family-provided care diminishes a husband-wife (or whatever) relationship into a care giver-patient relationship.** Show how specifics of the care (such as help toileting) limits and destroys many of the appropriate family values of the husband-wife relationship. A good social worker or marriage counselor is well worth the cost of providing testimony about this.

3. **Show that family-provided care is not good care, no matter how hard the family tries.** Trained professionals provide better care; that is the effect of training. Even when a family member is a professional care giver, an expert or treating physician or therapist can explain why non-family care is always preferable. In part, this is because an outsider's objectivity is unimpeded by long-term emotional attachments. Give examples of why this is important.

   For instance, a family member can be reluctant to put the patient through enough discomfort during home physical therapy to reap the therapy's benefits. This is because the family member, even when a professional care giver, is less likely than professionals to have the emotional fortitude or inter-personal authority to push the patient to do what needs to be done.

4. **Show that family-based care is not safe.** As Virginia lawyer Jeffrey Breit so effectively tells juries, professionals are trained to spot problems that untrained family cannot. By the time a family member recognizes the problem it can be too late. Thus, allowing the family to continue as the caretakers unnecessarily endangers your client. This is a particularly powerful point, since jurors do not consider safety a frill.

5. **Argue in closing that the verdict money is solely to make sure that the right people are providing the care.** This is a powerful argument if you have effectively taken care of numbers one through four during testimony.

In asking for money to pay the family for care provided so far, tread warily. Many jurors find it offensive that a wife, for example, would ask for money to care for her husband. Explain in opening that you are citing the family's number of hours and the value of those hours only so the jury can understand the enormity of the job involved in caring for anyone with these injuries. Then explain that the family members are not asking to be paid. It is your client who feels badly at this intrusion on their lives, so he wants them to be paid. This positions your client as grateful, rather than positioning the family as greedy.

If your client is unaware of the care his family is providing (as might be the case with severe brain damage), then make clear it is not the family members who are asking for money for their work. It is you as the protector of their legal rights, because you are required to do all that the law allows to help them.

Client's time: working for the defendant. Total up the number of extra hours your client is forced to spend on the usual daily tasks of living such as dressing, eating, washing, toileting, getting to and from medical and therapy appointments, shopping for special needs items, etc. If brushing his teeth used to take him three minutes but now requires six, and he brushes three times a day, that's nine extra minutes a day just to brush his teeth. If that was for eight weeks with a cast on his arm, it's nine minutes times seven days times eight weeks, totaling more than eight hours—just for brushing his teeth.

If the injury is permanent and there's a 35-year remaining life expectancy, the total is nearly 2,000 hours.

Add this to all the other time your client is forced to do work required solely by the defendant's negligence. Multiply that by whatever his average earning capacity was or would have been. You will be pleased with the results.

And remember: this is *economic* damage: compensation for actual hours put in. There is nothing intangible about it. So you may be able to use this method even in venues where you cannot suggest a non-economic figure. It gives jurors a larger economic damages anchor to use as their basis for considering money for intangibles.

This is usually more effective than hourly or *per diem* or *per annum* calculations of pain or suffering. Jurors sometimes go along with *per diem* arguments, but usually such arguments help only a little with overcoming juror resistance to giving money for pain or suffering. Jurors—even tort-"reform" jurors—are more likely to go along with money for the hours a client has actually put into "working" for the defendant.

In venues where *per diem* or *per annum* arguments are not allowed, hourly pay for actual time spent managing the injury is not a per diem argument.

Avoid suspicion. As you build your economic damages figures, don't let jurors think you are padding or exaggerating. Don't stretch any points, don't exaggerate. The total economic damages figure works as a powerful anchor for non-economic damages—but only if jurors perceive your economic figures to be solid and fair.

4.2
Time Is Tangible

Jurors have trouble with intangible losses largely because it is hard to place a value on something that cannot be measured. But as with extra time required to deal with the normal tasks of living, time is a primary component of every intangible loss. Time is readily and precisely measurable, so can be easily valued.

Proportion. The measurability of time is a basis for effective proportionality arguments. See, for example, "Scales," a powerful damages argument, in section 9.14.

Who would take this job? Less effective but sometimes useful is the "who would take this job?" argument: Counsel asks jurors how much a normal person would have to be paid per hour, twenty-four hours a day for the next ___ years, to take the "job" of suffering the plaintiff's plight: the pain, the emotional distress, the indignities, and the disabilities measured out over the time the plaintiff had or will have them. Like *per diem* arguments, unfortunately, many jurors are often unaffected by the "who-would-take-this-job?" argument. But it does not hurt to try them, except for the possibility of dissipating the impact of your better arguments.

Services. In many jurisdictions, one loss is described as "loss of services." Because such services are time and market based, you can easily valuate those services around the home that your client usually did but could not or cannot do due to the injuries. Dad used to mow the lawn and paint the garage, but now someone else has to do it. An economist can attach a figure to these tasks, or you can total the hours and multiply by the minimum hourly wage.

If a family member now does some of these tasks, use the argument suggested above under "*Family caretakers.*"

The most effective way to seek money for lost services is to show payment receipts for having the work done. Jurors' resistance to requests for services money diminishes when you show that someone was actually hired and paid for those services. And those amounts can provide the necessary anchors for the cost of future services.

When the family has no money to pay for these services, things may have fallen into a state of disrepair. This adds to the money you can claim: First for the value of the lost service, and second for the family having to live in a situation where those tasks go undone.

4.3
Worthwhile Purposes

Sometimes you can find unique worthwhile uses for money. For example, the family of a daughter killed in a traffic accident might find solace in starting and raising money for a charitable service foundation named for their daughter. The foundation would serve the purpose of finding better ways to teach traffic safety, "so that her death will mean something." You may need to be creative to let jurors know about it, but it can be done. Even a voir dire question is enough: "Has anyone ever heard of the Sally Frances Smith Road Safety Foundation? It's a . . . ."

You cannot ask jurors to include money for the foundation in their verdict. But they can hear about it in voir dire and in testimony ("Mrs. Smith, how have you been trying to come to terms with the death of your daughter?" "Well, it has helped that we started this foundation we're trying to get money for; we're hoping it will . . . ."). Once jurors hear about the foundation, they will assume some verdict money will go to it, and factor it into their verdict. Giving jurors this kind of worthwhile purpose helps overcome many of the powerful reasons they have for withholding money. (See Chapter 3.)

See 7.3 and Chapter 9 for other ways to show that money for non-economic damages can serve worthwhile purposes.

CHAPTER FIVE

WITH *OR WITHOUT* JURY VOIR DIRE

Even if you get little or no voir dire, many of this chapter's principles are essential for other elements of trial. So don't skip this chapter.

5.1
Voir Dire Limitations

Many judges allow the leeway for all of this chapter's jury voir dire strategies and questions. If your judge poses limitations, don't passively accept them. If you don't wait until the last moment, most judges will consider well-written, well-reasoned, well-researched motions for voir dire improvements. When trial consultants say this, many attorneys say: "Oh no, you don't know the judges around here." But we do know them. We know you can't win every motion, but we know by repeated experience that gradual—and sometimes not so gradual—improvements can be made. Two hours instead of one for questioning. A pre-voir-dire written questionnaire. Attorney-conducted voir dire where usually there is none. More of your questions being allowed. More and better follow-ups.

Given the importance of voir dire, a failure to seek improvements when necessary cheats your client. The failure most often stems from how busy you are just before trial, so the often futile attempt at some voir dire improvements can seem low priority. But given the juror climate, the priority is very high.

There are many ways to improve the chances of a voir-dire improvement motion being granted. For example, make your motions case-specific: Explain why the improvement is needed for this particular case, not in general, so that judges can accept it without having to worry about setting a personal precedent they might be pressured to follow in later trials. For many other experience-proven suggestions on seeking improvements, and for sample motions, see:

- *Jurywork* (Westgroup)
- *Jury Trial Innovations* (National Center for State Courts)
- *Blue's Guide to Jury Selection* (Thomson/West)

Not just for jury selection, but for many reasons all three books are must reading.

Also see the *ABA*'s *Principles for Juries & Jury Trials,* principle 11 (abanet.org/juryprojectstandards/home.html).

5.2
Primacy and Persistence

Your work in jury voir dire is crucial, particularly for damages. This is largely due to two psychological mechanisms: "primacy" and "persistence." "Primacy" is not what you may think.

Primacy. "Primacy" is the tendency to continue to believe that which one first believes. Belief has momentum: it continues until something stops or reverses it.[1] So in trial, whatever jurors first come to believe, they tend to continue believing. Once they believe something, it colors how they hear everything that follows.

So by the end of voir dire and opening, you want jurors to believe that the trial is about harm and damages: How much money will make up for what happened? You do not want jurors believing that the trial is mainly about liability.

If trial is stopped at the end of voir dire or opening and jurors are asked, "Okay folks, what do you think the trial is about?" you want them to answer, "It's about how much it will take to make up for what the truck driver did to the plaintiff." If they say, "It's about whether the truck driver went through the red light," you might not have done what you should have.

---

1. Primacy does not mean that we best remember or most notice or are most affected by what we hear first. This is how primacy is usually taught and it is dead wrong. In any oral presentation longer than a paragraph, placing something first subordinates it, makes it less noticeable, less memorable, and less effective. **Primacy has nothing to do with what is said at the start. It means that someone has started to *believe* something.**

This chapter and the next tell you how to inculcate the primacy belief you need. It is one of your most important tasks.

Persistence. "Persistence" is the mechanism by which primacy works. Persistence is the tendency to process new information in ways that support what we already believe. When we encounter new, non-supporting information, we distort it into something that supports our existing belief. We give disproportionate weight to new information that supports our existing belief. We downplay and reject—or simply ignore—new information that contradicts our existing belief.

Jurors do this all the time. We all do. People who believed O. J. Simpson guilty saw the glove display as proving his guilt. People who believed O. J. innocent saw the same glove display as proving innocence. This is primacy and persistence at work. Once a belief takes hold, the strong tendency is to use any new information to support that belief.

So what does this have to do with damages?

What the juror believes the trial to be about—liability? or harm and damages?—is of extraordinary importance. Based on their belief, jurors unconsciously choose which evidence to notice, how to weigh it, and how to use it in decision making. When you allow jurors to believe that a trial is mainly about liability, they hardly notice harm and damages. When you show harms, since they think the trial is about liability, they often distort your message into something that supports their belief that the trial is mainly about liability. For example, they'll think you're showing the harms in order to tug at their heartstrings so they'll decide liability in your favor. This makes them resent and mistrust you. They are no longer likely to trust your liability case. *And they will ignore or outright resent your harm and damages information.* So even if you squeak out a liability win, they are likely to provide little money because they never let your damages case get through to them.

Before you start your case-in-chief, you want jurors believing that the case is mainly about how much money it will take to make up for what happened to your client. Many damages verdicts are minimized because of counsel's failure to do this or do it well. Of course an excellent defense can offset the belief that the case is about harm and damages, but it's better for you to fight an equal battle than to just let jurors think the case is mainly about liability.

Remember that a trial or an opening or a jury voir dire is about whatever it spends its time being about (see 1.4). By spending a good proportion of well-positioned time in voir dire and opening on harm and damages—and doing it in the right way—you have a better chance of getting jurors to believe what you want them to believe: that this trial is about harm and damages.

Some advocacy teachers say that by the end of opening, 65% of the jurors make up their minds about ultimate issues. This is not true. At most, by the end of opening some jurors are leaning one way or the other. Few if any have reached decisions or even think they have. But jurors have reached firm—and possibly final—beliefs as to what the trial is about. You want that to be harm and damages.

Jurors naturally assume that your voir dire questions reflect what the trial is about. So unless most of your voir dire questions (as well as those on any questionnaire) deal with harm and damages, jurors will believe the trial is mainly about liability. This means they will not hear your damages case the way you want them to.

The same is true for opening. Unless most of your opening's second half deals with harm and damages, the jurors' first important belief, firmly in place before testimony begins, will be that the case is mainly about liability. That can doom you to a small verdict. As long as jurors believe the trial to be mainly about liability, they will believe that their main job is to judge who is right and who is wrong, not what it will take to make up for the harm. So they will pay attention mainly to the liability part of the case and ignore the rest.

Among other benefits: If you make jurors believe that the trial is mainly about harm and damages, they will hear your liability information with their attention where you want it: *How*—not whether—negligence caused harm.

To accomplish this, whether you have 20 minutes for jury voir dire or two weeks, half your time should be taken up with questions about harm and damages. Jurors tend to believe that the trial is about whatever voir dire and opening spend time being about.

5.3
How To Ask

Good voir dire questions gather information on which to base your peremptory and cause challenges. Do not ask questions that only condition or persuade. Particularly in today's climate, such questions can alienate. Moreover, questions that attempt to condition or persuade, and especially questions that try to get commitments from jurors, often backfire by setting up counter-arguments or resentment in the jurors' minds. And of course such questions are prone to defense objections.

So to establish the proper primacy of belief, and to gather the information you need for selection, you need a different way of asking questions.

Some decades ago, the National Jury Project's Diane Wiley pioneered the use of open-ended questions for jury voir dire. Open-ended questions are those that cannot be answered in a word or phrase. The closed-ended "Will you be able to award[2] money for pain and suffering?" gets only a yes or no. "Yes" often masks the real answer because jurors tend to answer closed-ended questions as they think you want them to. Even if they answer frankly, the answer does not provide much information.

Instead, ask open-ended questions such as, "What trouble would you have including money in your verdict for pain and suffering?"

If you are required to ask a group question before individual questions, it has to be a closed-ended question such as, "Who here has—or knows anyone who has—ever been seriously injured?" or "Who here thinks—or knows anyone who thinks—that lawsuits are causing problems these days?" In response, hands go up. Now you can start your open-ended, individual juror questioning to each juror whose hand went up.

Design your group questions to get as many hands raised as possible. So don't ask, "Who here will be unable to follow the judge's instructions on the law about money for pain and suffering?" Many jurors who will have trouble won't raise their hands, because your

2. Except here in voir dire to elicit bad responses, you should never use the word "award." It sounds like a prize. Use it in voir dire to lower the barrier to getting bad responses from bad jurors. The rest of the time talk about "money compensation," not "award."

question elevates the barrier to an answer: Jurors can be uncomfortable admitting they will have trouble following the law. You have to cajole it out of them. So for the group question, ask, for example,

> Many people would have a little trouble giving money for pain and suffering[3] because it doesn't make the pain and suffering go away. Other people think money for pain and suffering is okay. How many of you are a little closer to people who think money for pain and suffering is okay?

Some hands go up. Then ask,

> How many of you are closer to the people who would have a little trouble giving money for pain and suffering because it can't make the pain and suffering go away?

Hands go up. You can now talk individually to both sets of jurors. Ask each the all-purpose follow-up open-ended question: "Mr. Jones, please *tell me about that.*" And now—for the first time—you begin to hear what you need in order to make intelligent selection decisions. When you ask, "Please tell me about [whatever]," you are using an open-ended question that gets the juror talking.

If any jurors did not raise their hands in response to either question ("Who here does?" and "Who does not?"), ask them: "Miss Smith, I did not see your hand; are you closer to ____ or closer to _____?" This teaches jurors they cannot escape talking by not raising their hands. And when the judge wants you to start with group questions, you can still get to ask individual open-ended questions of every juror.

So there's usually no need to waste the tool of open-ended questioning.

3. "Pain and suffering" is a tort-"reform" buzzword. So the only time to use it is in voir dire to lower the barrier to bad responses.

5.4
Rewording Juror Responses

One quick way for you to get jurors to stop expressing themselves freely—and to make them think you are insulting them—is to reword their answers: "So what you're trying to say, Mrs. Juror, is that _____, right?"—and you put what she said into your own words. The only time to reword a juror's answer is in the later stages of pursuing a challenge for cause. ("So I understand you to say that if you become a juror you won't be able to set your hatred of plaintiff's lawyers aside?")

Rewording juror answers suppresses information you need. Most jurors will not correct any error. They won't like your putting words in their mouth. It can shut them up. Some will think you find what they have to say inadequate, and that you think you are smarter and sharper than they are.

Worst, you'll often reword inaccurately. So you'll end up thinking the juror has said something she did not say, and she will probably think you are rude and not too bright.

In jury selection—and in life—let people speak for themselves. Don't act as if you think you're the only biped who knows how to talk. If you are not sure what a juror means, ask her to say it again or to say it another way. You will often learn something you need to know that you will not learn if you reword answers.

5.5
Tort "Reform"

Ask jurors how they feel about lawsuits and tort "reform." Then get out of the way and let them talk. Follow up when they stop talking. You are looking for the ones who express their tort "reform" opinions the strongest. Encourage them to say as much about it as they have to say. Then say, "Tell me more about that." The most vociferous and angry jurors are the ones to get rid of. But you cannot find this out unless you lower the barriers to their being vociferous and angry.

My experience as of this writing is that 20% to 30% of any jury pool will be vehement about tort "reform." Work them carefully for a cause challenge. (See Appendix A.) Failing that, put them high on your list of possible peremptories. Be careful to distinguish between a juror's shallow or short-term opinions and his deep-seated attitudes. The more you get the jurors to talk, the easier it is to see the difference by means of tone, emphasis, strength of opinion.

If you have very little time for jury selection—enough, say, for just one or two questions—the tort-"reform" question is one of them.

5.6
Caps

Texas political and trial consultant Richard Jensen suggests this effective question:

> How do you feel about whether there should be upper or lower limits on the amount of money jurors should be allowed to give?

You can divide this into two questions:

> How do you feel about whether there should be upper limits on the amount of money jurors can give?
>
> On the other side of the coin, how do you feel about whether there should be lower limits on the amount of money jurors can give?

Whatever they say in response to any voir dire question, it's not enough. You need to know what's behind it. So say, "Tell me more," and "What else?"

5.7
Gerry Spence Technique Applied to Damages

One of Gerry Spence's more effective methods is called, "I'll show you mine if you show me yours." It involves your frank confession at the start of jury voir dire about your greatest vulnerability in the case. Lay it on the line and invite the jury to talk about it.

This works only if you are truly vulnerable and do not mask it. Your lawyer-mask or your professional in-control and authoritative tone of voice will discourage useful juror responses.

When using this technique, do not talk about what *you* think. Your intention—as with almost every voir dire question—is not to give information but to gather it.

> Good morning folks, I'm Joe Smith, one of the attorneys. This is when I get to ask you some questions for jury selection. But before the usual questions, something's worrying me I need to ask you about. We've all been hearing a lot lately about legal reform, tort reform, verdicts being too high, lawyers taking advantage, frivolous lawsuits, verdicts hurting business, hurting medical care, all those things.
>
> We need to know how people feel about those things. Mr. Jones—what are your thoughts? Tell me about lawsuits and lawyers these days. What bothers you about what's going on?

If you are required to ask a group question before you are allowed to follow up individually, ask:

"How many of you have been hearing about any of this?" And then, "How many of you have not?" And then, "Mrs. Johnson, I did not see your hand; what have you heard about these things?" Or, if necessary, "Have you heard about any of these things?" Then follow up as above. (On any topic, when you have to ask group questions before following up individually, this same method of "who has" versus "who has not?" works.)

Once you ask what a juror's thoughts are, let him talk. Do not interrupt. Do not argue. Do not show signs of disapproval or disagreement. *Keep quiet. Listen. Nod slowly.* Colorado trial consultant Mary Ryan points out that a lot of good information is lost in jury selections because lawyers nod curtly—which tells the juror you have heard all you want to, please shut up now. And they do. So nod slowly. Gesture for more. And follow up whatever the juror says by asking, "What else?" or "Please tell me more." When that juror has nothing more to say on that topic, go on to other jurors.

Since it is the start of voir dire, begin with a juror you think will be talkative. This helps set the standard for others. The more you get jurors talking, and the more you follow up, the easier it is to distinguish between jurors with deep-seated anti-litigation attitudes that can hurt you and jurors who have merely some recently-developed, comparatively shallow opinions that will not be as dangerous. The words of both are similar, but the juror's manner and vigor of expression will show you the difference.

If the judge allows only a brief time for jury selection, don't be afraid to ask for more to cover this topic. Argue that forces outside your control have created the current jury climate in which many potential jurors have been poisoned. Explain that you need to find out who those jurors might be so you can intelligently exercise your peremptories, and so that the judge can seat a fair jury. Remind the judge that a juror's ability to follow the law relates only to cause, not peremptory strikes—so you need to go beyond whether they can follow the law.

Once all the jurors have talked as much as you can get them to talk (or as much as you have time for), you should have a pretty good idea of who your problem jurors are likely to be.

5.8

Base Money only on Harm (No Impure Thoughts)

This is your most important theme: having jurors decide money based solely on the amount of harm. The intent of the following question is to uncover jurors likely to take improper factors into account.

> One of the questions on your verdict form will be how much money Sally should get. When figuring this out, some folks feel you should consider only the amount of harm. Other folks feel it's important to consider other things, such as how sorry they might feel for the plaintiff, or the fact that money cannot make the pain go away, or the fact that enough money to equal the harm might make prices go up for things or services we have to buy, or how much you like the plaintiff, or whether enough money to equal the harm would be too much money for one person, or seem like a

> windfall—or any other considerations other than the amount of harm. Mr. Juror, do you might be a little closer to folks who'd base their verdict amount only on the amount of harm? Or a little closer to folks who think it's important to take those other things into account at least a little?

Whatever they say—especially if they want to include considerations other than the amount of harm—respond with, "Tell me about that." When they finish, say "Tell me more," or as Michigan trial consultant Eric Oliver suggests, "What else?" Either way, keep the juror talking as long as you can. The more they say the more likely you can get rid of them for cause, so keep them talking until they start repeating themselves.

Generally, jurors who respond by saying "It depends on the case" are not likely to be good damages jurors. If they say "it depends," go through each improper factor one at a time (without saying they're improper) and ask if that's one they might factor in a little. If yes, say, "Tell me a little about that." Common improper factors include:

- Whether the money would do any good.
- Whether there's insurance.
- Whether it might harm any profession or business.
- Whether it might raise insurance rates.
- Whether the defendant can afford it.
- Whether it seems too much for one person.
- Whether it might be a windfall.
- Whether it might change the plaintiff's lifestyle.

Don't worry about suggesting anything they would not have thought of. They will think of these things without you. Your job here is to find out who will have the most trouble factoring them out. If you get jurors talking freely on this subject, you will have the information you need on which to base peremptory and cause challenges.

Once you have all the information you are likely to get, tell the jurors what they are supposed to do and ask who might have a little trouble doing it:

> I asked about that because everyone here—me, Mr. Defense Attorney, and Judge Wormer—all expect you to figure out your dollar verdict based *only on the amount of harm.* Nothing else. Now knowing that, who might still have a little trouble factoring out everything except the amount of harm? Mr. Williams?

This theme—deciding on verdict size based solely on the level of harm, and factoring all else out—is essential to seeking damages in the age of tort "reform." Carry this theme into opening as discussed in 6.8. In testimony go back to this theme whenever you can, as with, "Doctor, all we need to know is how much harm. With that in mind, please tell us what the impact did to Sally's brain cells." And see 9.9 for culminating this theme in closing.

5.9
Experience with Tragedy

In cases of major harm, ask:

> Who here has—or knows anyone who has—ever had anything tragic or nearly tragic happen to them?

And follow up:

> Please tell me about that.

Jurors who know people whose experiences are as bad as or worse than your client are often low-dollar jurors. So find out who they are. The defense usually strikes them fearing that their familiarity with serious injury will lead them to give more money. But the reverse is more often the case, so it's usually safe to leave them to the defense to strike.

5.10

Harms Lists

What should you ask about harm and damages? Start by preparing four lists of your client's harms:

Harms List 1: Mechanism of injury, and the immediate injuries (broken arm, death, brain damage, etc.).

Harms List 2: Problems caused by the immediate injuries (pain, limited motion, arm weakness).

Harms List 3: Consequences of the problems on List 2 (missed work, lost income, can't lift child so needs help bathing the babies, etc.).

Harms List 4: Fixes, helps: Measures taken or to be taken to try to offset the harms (surgery, pain medication).

When first compiling these lists, do not confine yourself to areas of recoverable harm. This is because you should be allowed to ask about non-recoverable harms in jury voir dire even if you cannot claim compensation for them—because a juror's attitudes about recoverable harms can be shaped by their attitudes and experiences concerning non-recoverable harms. To argue this to a reluctant judge, give an example: If the family's client saw him being burned in a wreck, the family's excruciating emotional distress may not be recoverable. But jurors who have had a similar kind of experience are likely to have strong feelings and opinions about, for example, victim pain, which is recoverable. Those strong feelings can affect their decision making about your client's pain. So you need to find out about them.

5.11

Harms List One: Immediate Injuries

List each immediate injury (broken wrist) and the mechanism of what caused it (hit the windshield). Examples:

> "When the truck hit head on, John was trying to steer out of the way. He was thrown forward so violently that

it *crushed the big bones in both arms and cracked the smaller bones in his wrists into tiny pieces.*"

Or, "*Internal bleeding reduced his brain's blood supply, killing brain cells* and resulting in permanent brain damage."

Or, "The machine collapsed, dropping 80 pounds of steel that *broke through his spine in three places,* paralyzing him for life."

"The baby's brain got *no oxygen, so brain cells that control movement were killed,* causing permanent cerebral palsy."

"The electricity went through him, *stopping his heart* long enough to kill him."

Except for death or the name of the permanent injury (brain damage, paralysis), do not go beyond the immediate injury. The consequences come in Harms List Two.

5.12

Harms List Two: Consequences of the Immediate Harms

List Two includes everything directly caused by each item on List One. List One's smashed wrists are permanently *painful, weak, and limited in movement*—so Harms List Two contains wrist pain, weakness, and limited movement.

Be thorough. Even in small cases, each immediate injury can cause many problems. Every such problem goes on List Two.

5.13

Harms List Three: Disabilities and Difficulties

List every disability or difficulty caused by each problem on List Two. His wrists' weakness keeps him from lifting, *so he cannot do his job*. Being unable to do his job, he *lost income*. Without income, he *could not afford his medical care*. So his *arm healed badly*. His badly healed arm means the *weakness is permanent*. Etc.

Don't limit this just to his job. His wrists' weakness also means he *cannot care for his children, play the sports he used to, work around the house and yard*, etc. List all the things he cannot do as a result of his wrist weakness.

Here's the list so far, though we're just scratching the surface:

- *could not work*
- *lost income*
- *could not afford medical care*
- *wrists healed badly*
- *weakness permanent*
- *cannot care for his children*
- *cannot play sports*
- *cannot do house or yard work*

Be thorough. List Three is the heart of your damages case. When you think it is complete, show it to your client, the family (including the kids), their friends, the doctors and therapists, and everyone else who might have something to add. List Three is much of what you are asking the jury to compensate for.

In a death case, list the survivor's losses (financial support, guidance, companionship, etc.) and the deceased's losses (not seeing his children grow up, not enjoying his retirement, etc.). Then list the consequences of those losses, such as problems caused by the loss of the deceased's income, or the emotional difficulties resulting from the loss of the deceased's companionship, etc.

Harms List Three should be exhaustive, containing dozens, sometimes many dozens of bad things resulting from each immediate injury. Do not worry about including more than you can use in trial. List everything anyone can think of. If there are too many, you will later select the more important.

To create List Three, get the help of everyone who knows or can learn what happened to your client and the consequences. These information sources need not all be people who will testify. They can be next door neighbors, relatives, ministers, teachers, acquaintances, doctors, therapists, hospital nurses, hospital roommates, people at work—anyone who has observed your client's harms.

In a recent wrongful death case, Indiana attorney Steven L. Langer was faced with the common problem that the deceased's widow had remarried—making it difficult to show the depth of her loss. Langer visited the grave with the widow. He learned in the most moving way the depth of her loss—and on the way out got an unexpected bonus: The graveyard caretaker took him aside and told him that the widow had been coming there alone every week for the two years since the funeral. Mr. Langer knew this would be persuasive testimony from a neutral witness that the widow had by no means gotten over the loss of her husband.

Harms consultants. Consult experts in fields related to your client's kinds of harm. These experts may or may not become witnesses. You can use them just to provide you with ways to better understand the harms and how to explain them to jurors. Or you can bring them in to testify.

For example, as Virginia attorney Robert T. Hall advises, in wrongful death cases you need a grief counselor to study and report on the kinds of harms the surviving family has suffered and will continue to suffer. (See 7.6)

Physicians and therapists who are specialists in pain can help you show jurors the full range of the consequences of pain. Social workers, physicians, therapists, mental health care specialists, and others can help you find and explain to jurors the consequences of every kind of mental, emotional, and physical injury. For just one example, it would take a grief counselor to come up with "Think what happens when a fully paralyzed person has a terrifying nightmare." This involves being unable to move upon waking, inability to call for comfort, etc. Can't even roll over and pull up the covers. In cases of permanent harm with long-term care consequences, use a geriatric disability specialist, such as a physician or social worker, who will know how your client's injuries will affect him and what kinds of care he will need as he goes into old age. Jurors usually think that if you take care of current problems, things will get better in time. You need to show that things will actually get worse over time and require more care—and that the consequences of not getting proper care will grow more and more serious as your client ages.

In selecting such counselors and specialists, you are looking for those who can provide credible portraits of the plight of the harmed —without being one of those hyper-sympathetic semi-hysterics who are likely to lovingly break into group hand-holding at any minute. You want a clinical report of human suffering, not a soap opera.

5.14

Harms List Four: Treatments (Measures To Fix or Help)

Harms List Four includes medical procedures, medications, therapies, hospital confinements, nursing care, assistance with daily living, appliances such as wheelchairs and braces—everything your client needs, has needed, and will need.

In a wrongful death case, Harms List Four would include therapy for the survivors. When there are ongoing problems, separate past from future measures. Harms List Four should include everything money can or has paid for.

Your four harms lists will be the basis for many voir dire questions, as described below (see 5.16). The four lists will also guide opening, testimony, and closing. Thorough preparation and use of these lists will help prevent liability concerns from overshadowing your focus on harm and money.

5.15

Voir Dire Questions

Harm-causing event. Before asking questions from the four harms list, ask about the harm-causing event itself: the wreck, or a medical error, or whatever.

> Who here has—or knows anyone who has—ever been *hit by a motor vehicle*?
>
> Who here has—or knows anyone who has—ever had a *doctor do something wrong to you*?
>
> Who here has—or knows anyone who has—ever had part of their body *caught in a machine of any kind*?

Follow up with open-ended questions. Your first follow-up question should almost always be: "Please tell me about it." You don't start learning anything useful until the second or third follow up. The fact that a juror has been hit by a car does not make that juror good or bad for you. You need to know the details: what happened, whose fault, how the juror feels about it, and so forth.

Questions about the harms-causing event can reveal material attitudes toward the wrongdoing in this case, its causes, and its consequences. A juror might say, "My cousin was in a wreck and the car was totaled, smashed flat, and he walked away just fine." Since your client's car was barely damaged yet she is claiming severe injuries, you have a concern about this juror.

Caveat. *Do not relate the harms-causing event or the harms on the four harms lists to your case.* Don't say, "A car hit my client, John Smith, so please tell me who here has ever been hit by a car." Connecting the question to your client makes voir dire adversarial, thus undermining your ability to get frank answers from many jurors. It can also start some jurors into deciding against you before they even know what happened in the case.

The jurors will figure out without your telling them that your harms questions apply to your client. If you ask those questions genuinely trying to get information from the jurors, and not to make any points to help your case, you can present your entire damages case in voir dire without arousing juror resistance, not even from the tort "reformers."

In a climate of tort "reform" you must not turn into an advocate too early. This means not until mid-opening.

5.16
Harms Lists Questions

Insofar as you have time, ask a separate question about each important item on each harms list. Examples:

> Who here has—or knows anyone who has—been run down by any kind of motor vehicle?
>
> Who here has—or knows anyone who has—ever had a broken bone?
>
> Who here has—or knows anyone who has—ever had several bones broken at the same time?
>
> Who here has—or knows anyone who has—ever had to have three or more surgeries within a few months?
>
> Who here has—or knows anyone who has—ever had to have eight or more surgeries within twelve months?
>
> Who here has—or knows anyone who has—ever had any kind of serious injury to the head?

Your harms lists should be the basis for many dozens of such questions. Ask jurors who have experienced any of the harms to tell you about it. Get them to tell you how it happened, whose fault it was, how bad it was, how long it lasted, and how they (or the harmed person) felt about it. But start by just asking them to tell you about it.

> Q: Who here has—or knows anyone who has—ever had to be in a wheelchair for any length of time?

Juror Berger raises her hand.

Q: Tell me about that, please.

A: Well, my uncle broke both legs so they had him in a wheelchair for a few months.

Q: Tell me about that.

A: He wasn't happy about it at first. But after a few weeks he seemed fine. Didn't have to go to work, spent the whole time fishing except when he was home with his buddies drinking beer and playing poker. I never saw a happier man, actually. I think he was sad to get up and walk again.

Probably not the juror you want if part of your client's problem is being confined to a wheelchair. This juror is likely to think it's not so bad. If you're not sure, get more information by asking what landed her uncle in the wheelchair, whose fault it was, and how he feels about those things.

It's best not to combine items into one question, but if your time is limited you may have to group similar items. Combine, say, broken arm, broken leg, and broken rib into "broken bones." As you ask follow-up questions, jurors will get specific: "Grandpa Dylan had to stop working the farm for a few weeks." Since you are trying to find out whether or not a juror regards the harm as serious, ask: "How did Grandpa Dylan feel about that?" The juror might answer: "Hated it. He couldn't pay his mortgage that month." Or he might say, "Loved it! Got a few days off and went fishing." If the latter, this juror might not think the harm to your client was such a bad thing. You need to know which jurors think that the particular harm is no big deal.

A surprising number of jurors see certain kinds of immediate harm—even serious ones—as relatively insignificant. This is partly why jurors who know people with harms similar to those in your case can be bad for the plaintiff. They've observed how Uncle Joe *seemed* to successfully and cheerfully cope with his harm. They may not know about Uncle Joe's suffering, because Joe kept it hidden: "If being in a wheelchair didn't bother Uncle Joe, why should it bother this guy?" And worse: "Uncle Joe got along fine," the juror may say in deliberations, "so this plaintiff's got to be lying about not being able to work."

Jurors who have the same harm themselves, or harm as serious, can also be bad plaintiff's jurors: "No one ever gave me money for my broken arm; why should this guy get any for his broken legs?" and "I didn't get to stay home for a month like this guy. I had to tough it out, what's he whining about?"

Not every juror who knows someone with a similar harm or who has himself had a similar harm will be bad for you. Jurors' decisions are made less on the basis of life experiences than on how jurors feel about those experiences. That is why the heart of your voir dire questioning consists of follow-ups. You cannot tell a thing about how a juror is likely to respond to your case on the basis of just knowing, say, that he's been in a car wreck. You have to learn the situation, the context, the consequences, and most importantly his reaction to those things. (His "feelings" about it, though some judges do not like that word.)

When a juror has reason for undervaluing any of the important (and sometimes even the unimportant) harms in your case, he may be bad not just for damages but also for liability. A juror who has seen Uncle Joe cope so apparently easily with his broken arm can think that broken arms are not a big deal. She can think you are exaggerating your client's problems in order to get money. That costs you credibility with that juror, and can poison how she perceives your liability case.

1. **Cover every immediate harm.** Broken arm, broken leg, and cracked teeth are three different immediate harms. Ask about each. (Do not get overly specific. "Six cracked teeth" is enough. Do not separate them into two cracked incisors, two cracked molars, and two cracked wisdom teeth.)

2. **Generalize.** Once you have gotten the jurors to say all they have to say about the harms (such as "broken ankle bone"), generalize:

   "How many of you have ever had any broken bones at all?"

And follow up.

Then,

> "Who knows anyone who's broken any bones?"

And follow up.

Then generalize a step more:

> "Who here has—or knows anyone who has—ever been seriously injured in any way?" Follow up.

3. **Final harms-list question.** Your final harms-list question:

   > "Who here has—or knows anyone who has—ever had to deal with as many different kinds of harms and treatments at the same time as all those I have just asked you about?"

If anyone says yes, follow it up.

Questions based on your harms lists fulfill the first requirement for any jury voir dire question:

- They seek information you need to make challenge decisions.

They serve other purposes:

- They help you spend half your voir dire time on harm and money.
- They teach jurors your client's immediate harms.
- They get jurors thinking about similar harms in relation to themselves and people they know.

5.17

Placement of Harm and Damages Questions

Don't start voir dire with any harm and damages questions. Save them for the second half—and if you have a time limit, make sure you don't run out of time. First ask questions that get jurors talking to you (see Appendix A), then ask about liability and other topics.

Do the same even when questioning just one or a few replacement jurors. You may be tempted to rush, especially at the end of a long day. But every juror is important—and those in the gallery were not listening even though they say they were.

5.18
Intangible Damages: Spotting Problem Jurors

Even a single juror who resists non-economic damages can drastically reduce verdict size. She can even cost you the case, because she is likely to be suspicious of plaintiffs, plaintiff's lawyers, and lawsuits that try to get non-economic damages.

You learn little in voir dire by asking useless questions such as, "How many of you have problems with giving money for pain and suffering?" Most jurors—especially some of the most dangerous—will not tell you. Instead, ask the questions suggested below. They will help you spot such jurors.

Go slowly (the " // " mark means to pause). Start with:

> Ms. Juror, we'll show you John's medical bills. // If you decide the truck driver's carelessness caused John's medical bills, // what trouble would you have—//even a little—// including money in your verdict for those medical bills?[4]

If possible, ask this question, and those that follow, of each individual juror rather than as a group question.

Please note five things about this question:

1. **It asks about the most concrete economic loss in the case.**

4. While this question does not "stake out" the juror, some judges might think it does. If so, back off of asking about your specific case. Generalize: "Mr. Juror, often when jurors are hearing a case, they see medical bills. // If you were a juror in such a case—not this one, but some other case, any case—// and if you decided that a defendant's carelessness caused those medical bills, // what trouble would you have—// even a little—// with including money for them in your verdict?" You can't be accused of staking out jurors about your case if your question is not about your case.

2. **The word "award" does not appear in the question.** "Award" is legalese, a term of art. In normal parlance it means a prize. No amount of explaining or redefining will get jurors to hear it any other way. So just as there are no "accidents" for plaintiffs, there are no "awards." (Don't use the word "damages" either. Or "economic damages" or "non-economic damages." They all mean different things to jurors than to you. Please see 5.50 on the destructiveness of using legalese, particularly in the age of advanced tort "reform.")

3. **The question above is open-ended.** "What trouble would you have . . . ?" not "Would you have trouble . . . ?"

4. **Its wording overtly assumes the juror will indeed have problems.** "What trouble *would you have . . . including* money for the medical bills in your verdict?" This makes jurors feel that you expect problems and that it's okay to have problems. So they'll more easily talk about them.

5. **The question asks about even little problems, not just major problems or inabilities.** This lowers the threshold to getting the bad answers you need to hear. Except in the end-stages of pursuing a challenge for cause, never ask anything like, "Would you have a really hard time doing such and such?" Instead, ask, "What trouble would you have—even a little—doing such-and-such?"

After the juror answers the medical care question (usually by saying, "No trouble at all"), ask her the same question about another tangible loss, such as past wages.

> Ms. Juror, you'll see John's wage statements from before he was hurt. At the end of the trial, if you decide the truck driver's carelessness caused John to lose wages, what trouble—even a little–will you have including money in your verdict for the wages he lost?

(Do not get complicated here with "earning capacity." This is about learning juror attitudes about non-economic damages, not about the tricky job of teaching what earning capacity means and why it is a legitimate loss.)

Virtually every juror will respond to the medical question that they'll have no trouble. Most will say they'll have no trouble with lost wages—though some will worry that there's no way to know for certain that your client would have worked; he might have gotten laid off or sick, for example. Jurors who think that way might be revealing a reluctance to give money for any harm that is less than 110% certain.

But the answers so far are not the important part of this sequence. Instead, as each juror answers your questions, focus carefully on her specific word choice, and on her vocal and physical demeanor: tone, body position, where she's looking as she answers, etc. The way she answers the medical and wage questions is her baseline physical and vocal demeanor for how she responds when she is comfortable with these damages elements. You will use this baseline shortly.

If you are not sensitive to subtle changes in demeanor and tone, bring someone with you to trial who is. It can be a partner, a paralegal, a consultant—but it need not be anyone involved in law. It can be someone such as your teenage daughter, if she's good at it. Just give her this section to read so she knows what you are trying to find.

5.19

Future Lost Wages: Your Next Question

> Ms. Juror, you'll see how much John will lose in wages over the next ___ years. What trouble would you have—even a little—including money for those lost wages in your verdict?

Some jurors may have trouble with future lost wages. This is not uncommon in times or locales of uncertain future work, or when a juror has worked in vocations with insecure employment futures: "Well, I don't know; how do we know he would have worked until he was 65? Some people retire early. My neighbor did. Or maybe he'd get hit by a car. Or laid off or something. Who knows? It's speculative." This can signal a general intangible damages problem, but do not strike a juror solely on this basis. She may be favorable in every other way, and you have only a few peremptories. To deal with such concerns, during trial (*not* during jury voir dire) show evidence that your client would have remained employed until retirement: He was good at his job and had always been a good worker; he was reliable, diligent, never missed work; he had good reports in his personnel file; he was a favorite at work; he would always have had many other job possibilities if anything had happened to this one; those possibilities would have existed well into the future; in bad times he'd have been among the last to be let go. And show the high percentage of people in his field who work until age 65. Show it is speculative to think he would *not* have worked until age 65.

Once you have asked about the economic losses (medical costs, lost wages), go on to the non-economics.

5.20
Non-Economics: The Revealing Questions

The next question is about non-economic damages.

> Mr. Juror, now we come to some harder questions. During the trial, we'll tell you about John's pain and suffering.[5] But there's nothing on paper with prices attached, like there are with medical bills and wage statements. So I need to ask you this: If you decide that the truck driver's carelessness caused John's pain and suffering, what problems will you have—even little ones—including money in your verdict for that pain and suffering, even though that money can't make the pain and suffering go away?

In a wrongful death case the next question is:

> . . . What problems will you have—even little ones—including money in your verdict for the family's loss of Mary even though money won't bring her back?

5. Remember that is the only time in trial you will use the phrase "pain and suffering."

Some jurors will give answers different from those to your questions about economic harms. A juror who was comfortable with economic damages but resists non-economics is a problem juror.

Often you will get answers of similar words as that juror's earlier answers, but delivered in very different ways. If a juror sounds or looks different—if his or her vocal or physical demeanor seems different—it's a red flag. So as jurors answer, compare their tone, choice of words, body positions, everything you can spot, with the way they were when responding about medical bills. (This is where you may want to enlist someone more sensitive than you to these things.)

For example, if a juror earlier answered your medical expenses question by firmly saying: "Medical expenses? Well sure, no problem!" Beware if his answer to your pain and suffering question is a tentative: "Pain and suffering . . . ? Mmmm . . . sure . . . no problem. . . ."

Or if a juror nods agreeably and comfortably when talking about money for medical costs, but shifts and looks away or changes in other ways when talking about money for pain and suffering, she could be a problem juror.

Be wary of jurors who sidestep answering questions on non-economic damages by saying "I would have to know more." You did not ask anything that requires them to know more; you merely asked if they decided there had been pain and suffering, what trouble would they have including money for it in their verdict. They don't need anything more in order to answer. When they say "I'd need more information," they could be harboring negative attitudes. Follow up: "What kinds of information would create greater problems for you in compensating pain and suffering?" and "What kinds of information would make it easier?" And follow up on whatever they say.

5.21
No Advocacy

Resist the temptation to load these information-seeking questions with information-giving facts: "In addition to the past medical expenses there will also be a lot of medical expenses in the future, too. So . . . " Your only goal here is spot jurors who might have problems with non-economic damages. Anything else you try to do—such as educate the jurors as to the extent of the claims—will interfere.

5.22
Wording

Note that the pain and suffering question, like the others, is worded to lower the barriers to bad responses. To do the opposite, such as by putting on your advocate's hat and saying, "Mr. Juror, the judge will tell you that the law of this state says that pain and suffering are to be compensated. . . ." buries information instead of unearthing it. Few jurors will say, "Well, Mr. Lawyer, the hell with the law and the hell with the state and the hell with the judge. I won't compensate for pain and suffering." Even jurors who despise such damages will often want to be seen as responding in a law-abiding way, so you will never know what they really think. They'll say: "I can follow the law."

So you get no information and lose the chance of removing this juror for cause. So keep the barriers to bad answers low. Do not validate the "good" answer by saying anything like, ". . . the law of this state says ___________, so will you do it?" In voir dire, advocacy and persuasion are more often counter-productive than helpful.

Once you ask about money for pain and suffering, continue with, "Mr. Jones, I'm asking this because my own mother thinks money for pain and suffering should never be given, because it does not make the pain or suffering go away. Other people think it's okay. I'm just asking which way you lean—closer to my mother who won't do it or closer to the people who will?" (Don't say "closer to the people who think it's okay because it's the law" or "because it's fair" or anything else that erects a barrier to a bad answer. Citing your mother *lowers* the barrier by giving jurors permission to give you bad answers. And in jury selection, you want to hear the bad answers.)

Some jurors may be more responsive to "Some people have some philosophical or moral oppositions to money for pain and suffering. Others don't. Where do you fall between them?"

5.23
Follow-Ups

As with all voir dire questions, success lies in how you follow up, especially when trying to lead unfavorable jurors into cause dismissals. ("Please tell me about that . . . "; "What makes you say . . . ?" etc.) Your success in trial can be directly proportional to your follow-up skill in pursuing cause challenges, especially over intangible damages. (See Appendix A.25)

If you use follow-ups well, you can also get jurors debating each other during voir dire. ("Mr. Jones, what's your feeling about that?" i.e., what Mr. Green just said.) This can show you how the jurors will act in deliberations, and which jurors are likely to be the most influential.

5.24
"Poisoning" Jurors

Do not worry about poisoning jurors by saying such things as your mother is against money for pain and suffering, or by letting jurors hear bad answers from other jurors. Jurors are not that easily influenced. They do not say to themselves, "Oh my goodness, I've been wrong all these years. I'm so glad this delightfully helpful juror has made me see the error of my ways." Bad attitudes do not poison good attitudes in voir dire (or vice-versa). Bad attitudes poison only deliberations.

Information jurors glean from your information-seeking questions can affect juror thinking about the case—mainly, what the case is about. But exposing jurors to bad attitudes is not dangerous unless the answer includes inadmissible evidence. ("Yeah, I heard about this case before—your client is the lady who forges checks and stole medicine from the old folks' home.")

5.25

Promise To Explain How To Calculate Non-Economic Damages

In answering your questions about non-economics, some jurors will say, "I wouldn't know how to put a price on it." This does not mean they're bad jurors. It just means they don't know how to decide how much.

Unfortunately, when jurors say they don't know how to put a price on, say, pain, plaintiff's attorneys often give the worst possible answer, "No one can tell you how to arrive at an amount of money for pain and suffering. I cannot tell you. The judge cannot. No one in the world can tell you how to do it. You have to use your common sense and your best judgment." Once you have said that even the judge does not know how to do it, some jurors will think there must be no proper way to do it—so there must be something wrong with it.

So never say, "No one can tell you how to do it."

Instead, when a juror says she would not know how to decide how much, tell her, "I'm not asking if you know how to do it; I'll show how later in the trial. (See 9.14) All I'm asking right now is what trouble think you might have—even a little—doing it *once you know how.* I'm asking because some people—like my own mother, for example—would have a lot of trouble with it because they believe the money doesn't make the pain go away, so why give it? So all I'm asking is, are you a little closer to my mother, or a little closer to people who say it's okay?"

No matter their answer, follow up.

A: I guess I'm somewhere in the middle.

Q: Please tell me about that.

5.26

Intangibles: Using the Jury Instructions

Jury instructions usually itemize the various kinds of intangible losses (physical pain, emotional suffering, loss of use of a body part, humiliation, inconvenience, loss of quality of life, etc.). Without relating them to the case, ask voir dire questions about each. Do not lump any two together. The more line-items, the better.

If you have time, ask jurors about their life experiences and situations regarding each item. (E.g., "What kinds of advice or guidance do your adult children ask you for?" Or "How do you rely on your parents for advice or guidance?") This helps you determine whether a juror has reason to value that loss element. This helps you decide if you want that juror. And during the process, the jurors all learn what those elements are, start to relate them to their own memories and experiences, and are sensitized to them as they will come up in trial.

The multiplicity of line-item damage elements helps arm your favorable jurors with bargaining chips in deliberations. A defense-leaning juror can get the satisfaction of making the jury give zero for one item, and in return allow the jury to give money for other items. ("Okay, $50,000 for lost advice, but not a nickle for those lost services.")

When jurors can compromise over multiple line-items, they usually give more than when they can compromise only over a grand total. So even if the verdict sheet asks only a grand total, introduce the line-items in voir dire, reinforce them through trial, and show them in closing as you fill them in. You want jurors thinking about and calculating damages line by line so that they consider each element separately.

5.27
Differentiation

In many jurisdictions, wrongful death damages include loss of:

Services	Companionship	Care
Protection	Comfort	Guidance
Kindly offices	Advice	Society
Assistance		

This list is a great advantage for plaintiffs. But plaintiff's attorneys usually read it off so fast (if they read it off at all) that it sounds like one mucuously amorphous glob: "Loss-of-services-protection-care-assistance-society-companionship-comfort-guidance-kindly-offices-and advice . . . whew!"

This turns your advantageous line-itemized list into mush—so jurors fall back onto trying to decide how much to pay for a death. Usually that's and time not much. So make each item separate from all the others.

There are also separate elements of loss for living clients: physical pain, emotional suffering, loss of use of body part, etc.[6]

Starting in voir dire, make jurors consider each line-item separately. This starts with you thinking about, researching, and proving each one separately. Think about what each means. What is the difference between "advice" and "guidance" and how does that difference apply to the losses in your case? And where "kindly offices" is listed, know what it means. Jurors have to be told what every line-item means, how each is different from the others, and how each applies to the losses in this case.

Start this process in voir dire by explaining what the first element means, then asking about it:

1. Have they known anyone or have they themselves had any ***loss of services*** from a family member for any reason? If yes, follow up.

2. Ask the next juror about ***loss of services*** and follow up. When every juror has responded, go to the next element.

3. Explain what it means, then ask if they known anyone or have they themselves ever had any ***loss of protection*** that had been provided by a family member? Do every element. You should have the right and you certainly have the need to uncover jurors with problems with any of these that apply to your case.

4. Explain each element so the jurors can see the differences: "advice" is different from "guidance," etc.

6. If one of your damages elements is hedonistic losses, please explain carefully what it means. To many jurors it sounds like doing things that would land a person in jail.

5.28
Tolerance for Pain

When pain is a factor in damages, ask jurors what their tolerance for pain is. Jurors who think they are able to resist pain are not likely to give as much money as jurors who are pain-sensitive.

And ask jurors about the worst pain they've ever had: What caused it, what it was like, and how bad was it?

5.29
Making the Intangible Tangible

Jurors have difficulty pricing pain, suffering, loss of life, and other intangibles. Jurors cannot easily find anything about those things to concretely measure. ("If you can't measure it, you can't price it.")

But *time* can be measured. Every juror has life experiences of paying and being paid for time. We are paid for our time at work. We pay for time when we hire a babysitter, a plumber, or a defense attorney.

And time is almost always a component of intangible losses.

Thus, in voir dire, emphasize the time component of intangible losses by asking jurors how long their own pains and disabilities have lasted—and how they felt about it. Later in trial you will base some of your damages arguments on the time component. (See 4.2 and 9.29)

5.30
Asking For a Specific Figure

In some jurisdictions, you cannot specify an amount for non-economic damages. But in such jurisdictions, you can usually imply a non-economic amount by reference to the proportion it ought to be. "The medical expenses and lost income total $75,000. The biggest losses are the human losses."

Even when giving a figure is allowed, some attorneys don't. Some hold off until closing. But in almost every case, the earlier you give a figure, the better. Jurors make more use of information they hear early than late. When they hear a dollar figure early, it becomes a factor in how they view the rest of the case. It's in their minds as they hear the bad things the defendant did. So they attach it to your liability case and tend to incorporate it into their thinking throughout trial.

In deliberations, favorable jurors more readily fight for the amount you want if that amount is an old idea to them. They more easily relinquish an amount they heard for the first time in closing. Jurors are more likely to have sticker shock when they hear the amount for the first time near the end of the trial. Sticker shock at the start of trial is more likely to wear off. So provide a dollar amount—or the best indication of it you are allowed to give—either late in voir dire or at the end of your opening.

In jury voir dire, there is wide variation in what judges allow in terms of your giving a specific figure. You can sometimes incorporate the amount into a legitimate information-seeking question, such as, "What problems would you have with being on a jury that's asked for a verdict of $400,000 or $500,000?" Jurors assume that your questions are relevant to the case, so they will conclude that $400,000 or $500,000 is the range you're looking for. Where you cannot specify an amount that includes intangibles, try, "Medical bills and lost wages are $95,000, but the human losses are many times greater. What problems will you have being a juror if that's the kind of money we're talking about?"

You might be able to head off a "staking-out" objection by adding: "I'm not asking if you'd give it, but only what problems you'll have if you decide it's the right amount. Some people have problems giving that much. Mr. Jones, how do you feel about it?" Or, "If you were a juror in some other case—not this one but any case—and the attorney there was asking for nearly $100,000 for medical care and lost income, and many times that for the loss of quality of life, what problems would you have with that?"

Some judges bar such questions, despite such questions being so important in seeking out common biases in the current climate. Find out in advance what your judge will let you ask. If she is restrictive, argue that merely asking if jurors have a figure in mind is insufficient, since few jurors have ever thought about it. The only way to find out if they can follow the law is to suggest a figure and see if they find it too high.

Do not easily give up. You are trying to do two important things: primarily to spot jurors with upper dollar limits, and secondarily to let jurors know the amount you are asking for.

Here is another approach: "Mr. Juror, at the end of this trial, if you think it will take just $50 to make up for what happened to John—but if you know John wants much more than $50—what trouble would you have ignoring what John wants and deciding on a verdict of only fifty dollars, if that's what you think is fair, in spite of feeling sorry for John?" Jurors will say they will have no trouble.

Then ask: "Now here's the other side of that question. If you decide it will take, say, half a million dollars to make up for what happened to John, what trouble would you have—even a little —in deciding on a verdict like that if you thought it was fair, in spite of feeling sorry for the defendant, who'll want it to be much less?"

If the judge will not allow that, try: "Mr. Jones, some people think there should be a limit on how much money a jury should be allowed to give. Do you ever feel that way?" and "Why?" and "Tell me more," etc.

This does not convey your amount, but it can reveal jurors with upper limits in mind. Ask, "What kind of amounts have you heard about that you think are too much?" If his amount is higher than what you are after, you can say, "So if a case requires, say, half the amount you just mentioned as too high, what trouble would you have with that?" You have now conveyed the range you are asking for.

When you cannot get the amount into voir dire, specify it at the end of your opening. Since you open first, that is almost as good as working it into voir dire.

In response to questions about dollar limits, jurors answers sometimes reveal deep-seated attitudes that can endanger your damages verdict. But just as often, their answers reflect shallowly held opinions that will have no effect of that juror's decision making. For example:

Q: Mr. Johnson, do you think there should be an upper limit on how much a jury is allowed to award?

A: Sure.

Q: And may I ask what that limit should be?

A: A million dollars.

With that, you can't yet tell whether this juror will be good or bad for your $5 million damages case. His opinion may be deep seated, making him bad. Or maybe he just never thought about it before, and just throws out an answer. You can find out by following up his "A million dollars" answer. Simply say, "Please tell me about that." You may have to listen to a few of his answers and ask your question a few times, but as he talks you will be able to tell by his words and tone the degree of importance this has to him. If it's not important, don't give it much weight. Jurors like this one give good verdicts all the time. But if this seems deeply important to him, pull the lever that opens the floor under his seat.

5.31
Punitive Damages

Before shaping your voir dire questions on punitive damages, read *State Farm v. Campbell* (538 U.S. 408, 2003) along with other Federal cases and those of your state. Do not let your punitive damages voir dire questions or your later arguments and evidence run afoul of case law. Courts will be looking closely at punitive verdicts that seem out of proportion to compensation. So this book's methods of seeking full and fair compensation become crucially important to punitive damages.

Since these waters are still being charted, read the cases conservatively. In our rapidly accelerating tort-"reform" situation, courts often seek out any reason they can find to reduce or eliminate large verdicts.

With tort "reform" continuing to tighten its grip, more and more jurors are becoming less and less willing to give punitive damages. Some believe that punitive damages have little effect: "It would just be part of the normal cost of doing business, it wouldn't make them do anything differently," and "The company will just pass the costs on to the rest of us."

To deal with this during trial see Chapter 10. But you still want to identify the anti-punitives people in jury selection.

Some jurors, even when furious with the defendant, do not want to make the plaintiff rich: "As far as I'm concerned, the company should be put out of business—burn it down! But I'm not going to make this family rich." (Because of this common attitude, in jurisdictions where punitive money goes mostly to the state—and when jurors know it—punitive verdicts are likely to be larger.)

In jury selection, probe for juror attitudes, beliefs, and opinions that hold punitives down. Begin with general questions that allow anti-punitive jurors to vent, such as by asking, "Mr. Juror, why do you think so many people are angry about juries giving big punitive damages verdicts these days?"

This may seem a dangerous question (why let these people spout their harmful opinions?), but remember that jurors do not poison each other, and this question encourages anti-punitive jurors to speak up.

> Mr. Juror, compensation is money is to balance harm. Punitive damages are to punish whoever did the harm and to stop their wrongdoing and the wrongdoing of others from now on. Some folks believe that works. Others think punitive damages don't work because the company just passes the loss onto its customers. What is your best guess about it? Which way do you lean?

Follow up whatever they answer with: "Tell me about that."

5.32

Who Gets the Money?

In years past, few jurors were aware that punitive damages money goes to the plaintiff. But punitive damages have now long been a frequent topic on radio talk shows and prime time TV shows, so while some jurors may still not know who gets the money, many do. And in deliberations, they tell those who do not know.[7] This means you should ask about it in voir dire:

Ask,

> If you think it'll take, say, $1 million or some other very large amount to make the company stop doing what we say it did and to keep other companies from doing it, how would you feel about all that money going to John?

Many jurors will be against it. Use cause challenges (see Appendix A) on the grounds that such a juror is impaired from following the law: She will factor into her decisions her resistance to giving John enough money to make punitives accomplish their intended purpose. Her problem is not how much money, but who gets it—and that will keep her verdict lower than if she considered only the law and the evidence.

Whether or not your cause challenge fails, in closing you can use the judge's or defense's rehabilitation to arm your favorable jurors for deliberations. For example, in rehabilitating a juror, the judge or defense counsel might ask, "Mr. Juror, you'll follow the law and set aside your reluctance to give Mr. Plaintiff enough money to accomplish the purposes of punitive damages, won't you?" So in closing, remind them what he said in jury selection, and say:

"So in deliberations, if anyone says they don't want to give John that much money, remind them that Mr. Defense Counsel already said, and the judge will soon tell you, that the only thing to consider is how much it will take to make Acme and every other manufacturer put guards on their machines—and not whether one person should get all that money." Your favorable jurors will use this in deliberations. (Citing cause challenge rehabilitations can work on every topic, not just on making John rich.)

7. In some states, part of punitive damages goes to the state. If possible, make sure jurors know this. In fact, income tax rates are high enough to ensure that a significant part of punitive damages goes to the government. You probably cannot tell the jurors this. But an effective anti-tort "reform" campaign would ensure that the public knows it.

Another punitives strategy in voir dire is to ask jurors how they punish(ed) their children, or what consequences they imposed for their children's misbehavior. Ask what makes punishment or consequences deserved or necessary, how the jurors decide the severity of the consequences, and what the jurors consider the "ultimate" punishment or consequence for their children—and why it works.

5.33
Differentiation

Ask jurors the differences between things a child just needs to fix (such as wiping up spilled milk) versus things he needs to be punished for (such as dangling his baby sister for the third time out a window). Ask what makes the difference: why is fixing the harm enough in one situation, while punishment and deterrence are needed in the other? You will hear some responses that you can incorporate into your punitive damages case and closing argument.

5.34
Jobs

Some jurors work in occupations where fines or other forms of discipline are imposed. Where appropriate, ask what kind of behavior is punished. What kinds of fines or discipline? Effective or ineffective—and why? Fair or unfair—and why?

Questioning jurors about punishment practices at home and at work reveals life experiences and attitudes that can affect how they will think and act about punitives in this case.

5.35
Juror Characteristics Affecting Damages

You cannot select a jury on the basis of demographics. Members of any particular demographic group (age, race, nationality, religion, sex, income level, etc.) are not similar enough to each other for you to use their grouping as a marker for jury selection.

For example, black people do not all have the same attitudes and do not all make the same decisions. Nor do old people, Asians, young men, older women, GenXers, Baby Boomers, any other kind of generational "cohort," rich people, bald guys, or any other demographic group. In the absence of extensive research on your specific case, choosing jurors on the basis of demographics is based on the same kind of bad thinking that underlies racism. It does not help you select a good jury. It more often will lead you astray.

In other words, *Batson*[8] and its progeny did you a favor. Both legally and in terms of effective strategy, you need demographic-neutral criteria for jury selection.

If choosing jurors by demographic grouping worked, every trial consultant would insist you do it. But the good ones do not. It is easy so it is tempting, but it does not work. You can't judge a book by its cover. Demographic groupings often work for marketing by being based on enormous banks of data. And to be useful in marketing they need to show only mild tendencies, as low as 5% or 10%. That means 90% or 95% wrong—fine in marketing, but not in jury selection.

However, there is a good use for demographic groupings: they help you identify common experiences some jurors might have. Poor people are more likely to have had difficulty getting medical services for their families. Find out in voir dire which ones have had such difficulties; such jurors can be more likely to decide cases against the medical establishment.

The fact that someone is in a very low-income demographic can alert you to the *possibility* or even probability of a common experience. But you have to ask each juror questions and look at non-demographic factors to make sure she actually has had that common experience, and that it has had the same effect on her as on most other people. For example, you may assume that a domestic worker has poor access to health care—but if her employer is a doctor, that assumption may be wrong.

You must look at jurors' individual experiences, attitudes, opinions, and beliefs (and how strongly jurors cling to them) as they relate to the issues and personalities in your case. You discover these things by using the kinds of questions suggested in Appendix A and in this chapter.

8. *Batson v. Kentucky* 476 US 79 (1986).

5.36
Personality Traits

There are certain personality traits you can spot in voir dire that can reveal whether a juror is likely to be bad or good on damages.

These personality traits affect juror giving, especially for non-economic damages. So during voir dire, try to discover where each prospective juror falls on each of the following continua:

Optimist/Pessimist scale

Caretaker/Non-Caretaker scale

Emotion/Non-Emotion scale

Insider Dispossessed scale

Content/Malcontent scale

These scales are detailed in the next five sections.

5.37
Optimist/Pessimist Scale

Optimists more readily provide money than pessimists do. This is because optimists are more likely to think that money can do some worthwhile good. (Remember the importance of juror perception of the worthwhileness of money; See Chapter 2.) You can see where a juror lies on the Optimist/Pessimist scale by her answers throughout voir dire. When a juror mentions any problem or bad situation, ask how she feels it is likely to work out, and why.

See if there is a difference between the juror's background/training/experience and what she is actually doing. A Ph.D. waiting tables, or a parent of a family with many problems, could well be more embittered than optimistic.

Ask if the juror feels she has done better in life than she had hoped, or if some things held her back. Ask how she feels about her future: are things likely to get better for her? Or stay about the same? Or get worse? Ask what she'd like to do next and if she thinks she'll get to do it. And follow up: "How?" and "Why?"

Ask how jurors feel their children will do as the years go on: better than the parents? Worse? How? Why?

Even a juror's demeanor is revealing. This is true not only when he is speaking, but also when he is listening to other jurors. If you are a good people-watcher, or have one with you, you will be able to differentiate.

5.38
Caretaker/Non-Caretaker Scale

Caretakers more readily provide verdict money than do non-caretakers. Caretakers feel it is right to help people who need help. "Caretaker" in this sense means an attitude, not a forced situation. Someone forced to care for a family member may or may not be a caretaker in spirit. Someone in a caretaking job may or may not be a caretaker by nature.

Non-caretakers believe it is better for people to take care of themselves than to be taken care of; that people can and should be self-sufficient; that each person is responsible for himself, so others should not be expected to help shoulder his burdens; that life is a gamble and you have to play the hand you are dealt without relying on others; or that people are usually partly at fault for their own problems, so do not deserve help.

In voir dire, you can distinguish caretakers from non-caretakers in several ways. Some of these ways also give you other useful information.

For example, ask jurors what they think are the most important values to teach children. Jurors who respond with values aimed at taking care of other people (such as "help those less fortunate") are likely to be caretakers themselves. Jurors who focus on values like "be strong" or "self-reliance" may be non-caretakers. Follow up by asking why they name the values they do, and how they put them into practice.

Another example: Explain that you understand that most people don't have time to do much for others outside their families, but you'd like to know: "Who here is involved in things intended to help other people—people outside your own family?"

Ask what organizations and clubs jurors belong(ed) to, and where they do (or did) volunteer work—and why. A person who belongs to a garden club, a bridge club, and a book club may or may not be a caretaker. A person who volunteers for Meals on Wheels is probably a caretaker. If a juror mentions a group or club that is not obviously care-oriented, or if you do not know the group, ask its purpose, what the juror's involvement is, and why. "We get together at Kiwanis for lunch to catch up with old friends" is different from "We at Kiwanis raise money for the hospital." The group may serve both purposes, but the way a juror chooses to describe it can tell you why she is in it.

If a juror used to do charitable or volunteer work but no longer does, ask why she stopped and what would make her go back.

Find out which charities the jurors support. Do they send money only to their alma mater or also to the local soup kitchen? And ask, "If someone offers to send money to the charity of your choice, which would you choose?" And follow up: "What do you like about that one?"

Since it is useful to spot leaders (see 5.34), find out which jurors are officers in any groups or clubs, and be on the lookout for any such groups that are caretaking in nature (do they build hospitals or do they build stock-market accounts?).

Ask about activities outside work: "What do you do evenings after work?" and "What do you do Saturdays?" and "What do you do Sundays?" Follow up. If a juror says he spends Sunday afternoons in church, say, "Tell me about that." Look for caretaking activities: things they do to help other people. (However, be wary. A few church folks spend time caring for others but are really interested in furthering the goals of their church, or their own chances of getting into Heaven, or just being seen as a good person. This kind of self-serving caretaking does not show they are on the good end of the caretaking scale.)

An excellent voir dire question that separates caretakers from non-caretakers (and good plaintiff's jurors from bad): "What should be done about the homeless?" The non-caretaker's knee-jerk reaction is something like, "Get them to work." The caretaker's knee-jerk response is to want to help. Most people answer somewhere between, so note which way they lean—and follow up.

Another way to distinguish caretakers from non-caretakers is to ask how help from other people has figured in their lives or in the lives of people they know—and how they feel about that: "How have you gotten through your most serious problems?" Answers that emphasize the personal strengths of the person who needed help probably come from non-caretakers. Caretakers are more likely to emphasize the value of the help received.

The goal is to discover whether or not each particular juror will be concerned about another's problems and be motivated to help.

To field objections to caretaker questions, explain to the judge that many jurors are reluctant to help others, and so are less likely to compensate fully and fairly. Explain that jurors whose attitudes and activities reveal a willingness to help those in need are more likely to use nothing but the evidence as the basis for their verdict, rather than incorporate their reluctance to help despite the evidence. Remind the judge that a juror's reluctance to help others does not have to rise to the level of a cause dismissal for it to be of great importance to a peremptory challenge.

5.39
Emotion/Non-Emotion Scale

Jurors who are comfortable with their own and others' emotions as a palpable and normal part of living and decision making tend to see emotional harm as worthy of compensation. Such jurors are likely to see that emotional harm is a component (sometimes the primary one) of almost all intangible harms: sadness, feelings of loss, worry, anxiety, fear, frustration, despair, loneliness, etc.

Jurors less at home with emotion tend to dismiss or not recognize emotional harms, so are less likely to compensate for them.

The distinction can be difficult to make with an abbreviated voir dire. One useful marker is whether a juror involves emotion in the way he answers your voir dire questions: Does he base his thinking and responses mainly on logic? Or does he incorporate emotion? Listen to his choice of words. Phrases such as "I feel. . . " or "You could see the emotion in their faces" can reveal a person who is comfortable taking emotions into account.

Listen for how each juror talks about and feels about the experiences he talks about throughout voir dire. Are all his reactions centered on logic and practicality? Or does feeling play a role? Many jurors have jobs surrounded by strong emotions—such as hospitals. Find out how it has affected them. Have they become hardened to those emotions in order to cope with them? Or remained open to the impact of those emotions? A juror who is, say, an emergency room attendant may be highly sensitive to the kind of suffering your client has undergone. Or he may be hardened to it. (Even if he's open to it, he may find your client's emotional suffering to be minor by comparison to what he sees regularly at work—so this may not be a good juror for you.)

Extremes. One of the many pieces of advice I got long ago from the National Jury Project's Susan Macpherson—and that years of experience have long since proven correct—is that you need to distinguish between jurors who incorporate emotion into their decision-making, and those who are simply extremely emotional. The latter can be unpredictably dangerous, because there is no telling what or which side their extravagant emotions might attach to. Fortunately, the defense usually strikes that kind of juror.

5.40

Insiders/Dispossessed Scale

Jurors with no stake in the establishment often tend to give money more readily than do jurors whose lives are integrally involved with the establishment, or who aspire to such an involvement.

The dispossessed, the renegades, and those who stand outside society's mainstream are less likely to feel threatened by the impact of large verdicts on prices and insurance rates, or by other supposedly harmful effects to society of a large verdict. Even if they believe in such harmful effects, such jurors have less reason to be concerned about them.

Such jurors also tend to have an easier time deciding against an authority or establishment figure such as a doctor or corporation leader.

This does not mean that every such prospective juror is an automatic good choice. View each juror's outsider characteristics in the light of everything else you can learn about her. For example, some outsiders are outsiders because they care little about other people, which is a bad characteristic for a plaintiff's juror. And some outsiders will fight a large verdict solely on the grounds that the other jurors want it to be large. Some outsiders are outsiders because they are oppositional by nature: they automatically do the opposite of what others do. You don't want such jurors.

5.41
Content/Malcontent Scale

Jurors who seem content with their lot in life can go either way in any case. But jurors who are discontent with life due to the hand they have been dealt are not likely to worry about what has been handed to your client. A person living in what he perceives to be a highly successful and apparently happy society who is bitter about how his own life is turning out can have little sympathy for anyone but himself. He's likely to believe that he did not deserve the raw deal his life has been, and thus sees no reason to provide much help to someone else who has gotten a raw deal.

So, for example, pay special attention to whether you want the juror with a lot of advanced education who works menial jobs. Watch out for people with a couple of years of college who feel they went the extra mile to improve their condition, but still have to wait for the sales at Wal-Mart to buy what they want.

Discontented people usually have little reason to help make your client contented.

5.42
Religion Matters

Some jurors believe that harm is a divine punishment for some wrongdoing earlier in life. Ask about this belief in voir dire. You do not want a juror who thinks the defendant's negligence was God's retribution for the sins of your client.

Jurors can be tenacious in this belief. Aside from its religious basis, it is a comforting belief: "If I behave well, I'll never get hurt." And conversely, "The plaintiff was hurt, so she must have behaved badly earlier in life—so it was her own fault." Such a juror is unlikely to give up these comforting beliefs, as she would have to do in order to give your client much money.

Among those likely to share this belief are some religious fundamentalists, Islamic and Jewish as well as Christian, and others. Some religious fundamentalists can be good plaintiff's jurors, but you have to find and remove those who believe that calamity is probably the consequence of earlier wrongdoing, or that God decrees all things so a lawsuit is a challenge to God's will, or that decent people do not sue each other.

Fortunately, many such fundamentalists also believe God wants them to be honest, so you will have a good chance of spotting them and removing them for cause. But some have an elaborate rationale for dishonesty when used in the service of what they think God wants (such as "Get on this jury and keep the plaintiff from getting any money.")

5.43

Allowances for Inadvertent Wrongdoing

The law holds defendants responsible for unintentional wrongs. Many jurors do not, so they tend to reduce verdict size—and even decide on no liability—when they think the wrongdoing was inadvertent: "The truck driver didn't hurt him on purpose," or "The doctor didn't cut the wrong blood vessel on purpose."

A focus-group juror once said, "The machine operator was careless and stupid, and he killed the guy. But it wasn't negligence." This juror had been told clearly that negligence meant the failure to be careful. But he would not give up his notion that it meant doing something on purpose.

It makes sense. From childhood on, we are taught by example that we will not be punished, nor will others be punished, for doing something wrong "not on purpose." Little Sally cries, "Mommy, Mommy, Billy knocked me down!" And Mommy, ruining little Sally as a future plaintiff's juror, says: "I'm sure he didn't do it on purpose, dear. It was just an accident." But Sally is still on the ground. Her knee is still scraped. She is still hurting, angry, and upset. But Mommy does nothing to Billy because Billy did not do it on purpose. "Just an accident." In fact, Mommy probably even consoled little Billy to keep him from feeling bad about what happened.

The lesson learned at Mommy's knee? It is not fair to punish inadvertence. "It was an accident" and "I didn't mean it!" carries us through spilling milk in kindergarten as well as the rest of what we do in school, career, and family life. So expect it from jurors.

Jurors who believe that inadvertent harm should be compensated less will sometimes oppose you on liability, and often on intangible damages. Remove such jurors when you can. And reinforce throughout trial that inadvertence does not trump responsibility.

To identify such jurors, use the same structure as you did for questions concerning intangible damages:

> Mr. Juror, Dr. Hyde did not hurt Mr. Smith on purpose. Now, some people think it's unfair to make a doctor pay if what he did was not on purpose.[9] Others think a doctor should pay even if it was not on purpose. Which are you closer to?

Whatever they answer, follow up with: "Tell me more about that."

5.44
The Preponderance Technique

When there are no affirmative defenses, the Preponderance Technique is one of the most important things you can do. By teaching jurors to use preponderance in their decision making, and by arming them to insist that others do the same, the Preponderance Technique will win cases you would otherwise lose, and often result in significantly higher verdicts.

The Preponderance Technique fills a triple vacuum: First, that plaintiff's attorneys rarely tell jurors that preponderance applies to

9. Don't use the word "accident" when you're blaming someone for causing it.

damages decisions as well as liability. Since jurors never know this (not even if the judge tells them), they often give only as much money as they are convinced beyond reasonable doubt is right. That is likely to be less than if they used preponderance.

The second vacuum this technique fills is that many attorneys wait until closing to mention preponderance at all. Closing is too late. The vast majority of jurors do not know the real burden, so during testimony they gauge the evidence according to their default understanding: reasonable doubt. When they finally learn the real standard in closing, they cannot go back and re-weigh each piece of evidence in this new preponderance scale. So without an explanation of preponderance in voir dire or opening, jurors will decide the case—especially damages—on the basis of reasonable doubt.

The third vacuum this new technique fills is the most important. Until now there has been no effective way to get a jury to base decisions on preponderance. Even when counsel explains preponderance in voir dire, jurors almost always default to beyond reasonable doubt on every verdict question. "Well, I'm just not *entirely convinced beyond a doubt* that the verdict should be a hundred thousand dollars. So I can't do it." And favorable jurors who would like to give the full hundred thousand have no way to respond. So favorable jurors fold—even when a defense juror says: "Well yeah, probably the truck driver did it, but they didn't prove it, so I can't go along with it." By "prove" he means beyond doubt.

If every plaintiff's attorney regularly uses this new technique, his or her track record will markedly improve.

When you conduct your own voir dire, there are five parts to this technique: two in voir dire, one in opening, one in testimony, and one in closing (see 6.15 and 9.10). That makes it sound complicated but it is not. It is simply a matter of turning "more likely than not" into a major theme of your case—in the same way "reasonable doubt" should be (but often is not) a major theme of every criminal defense case. Remember that a trial is what it spends its time being about. So unless there are important affirmative defenses, you want to spend a lot of time in every trial on preponderance. (When you do not get to conduct your own voir dire, the preponderance technique still works by using it in opening, testimony, and closing.)

When using this technique, do not use the words "preponderance" or "burden." They confuse jurors. You must execute this technique with crystal clarity. You may want to slightly adapt the wording of what follows to align it more closely with your venue's instructions. But keep it clear and twelve-year-old-child simple.

Preponderance. Part One. Identify jurors who are likely to have trouble making their decisions based on preponderance. This cannot be done by asking: "How many of you will not follow the law as the judge gives it to you, which is to make us meet our burden of proof which is the preponderance, meaning greater weight, of the evidence?" Anything like this is doomed to failure because jurors will have no idea what you're talking about. Even if they do, few will admit they won't follow the law.

Start Part One by explaining the doctrine of preponderance. Just don't call it that. (" // " marks mean to pause.)

> In this kind of case // you decide based on whether we are more likely right // than wrong. // More likely right // than wrong.

Add no other information or explanation. Avoid the usual temptation to show you know more than the jurors by overexplaining. Clarity requires simplicity and brevity, not more talk.

Then say:

> You can have doubts on both sides. // As many doubts as you want. // As long as after you weigh all the doubts // you believe we are more likely right than wrong. // If we just tip the scales, even a little.

Use both hands to show the scales tipping slightly.

> Now, we expect to show far more than tipping the scales just a little.

Use both hands to show an enormous tipping of the scales. Be sure to say, "We expect to show far more than tipping the scales just a little." Without it, jurors will think you believe you have only preponderance. That will lead some to stop listening; they'll decide right then you should lose.

Then say:

> But all we have to do is tip the scales just a little.

Use hands.

> Is it more likely than not // that the truck driver was negligent and caused harm? // Is it more likely than not // that $75,000 is the right verdict?

Then:

> Since that's all we have to do, some folks think it's not enough because it makes it too hard on the other side, the defense. // Maybe even a little unfair. // Other folks think it's okay.[10] // Mr. Jones, are you closer to thinking it might be a little unfair? Or are you closer to the folks who think it's okay? Where do you come between the two?

Most jurors will be in the middle. Whatever each juror's answer, follow it up with, "Tell me about that." (If your judge requires you to start new topics with group questions, ask, "Who thinks it might be a little unfair?" When hands go up, follow up individually with, "Tell me about that." Then ask, "Have I missed anyone? Anyone else think it might be a little unfair?" Then ask, "And who is closer to folks who think it's okay?" Follow up.)

Stay with each juror until you can tell how important the "unfairness" of preponderance is to her. Some will say they cannot make decisions on that basis—and, possibly, that the courts should not either. Tort-"reform" jurors have probably never before thought about preponderance, but now that you bring it up they might start thinking, "Aha! That's what's wrong with the system! No one has to prove anything!" When you detect such attitudes, place that juror high on your possible peremptory challenge list. She will likely be rough for you on every issue in the case, not just on preponderance.

10. Do not say, "Other folks think it's okay *because that's the law and they will follow the law.*" You want to lower, not raise, the threshold to bad answers.

Pursue for cause those who express themselves strongly that it's unfair (see Appendix A.25, for one effective way to mount a cause challenge).

Some jurors will express weaker concerns about preponderance. If their concern is mild, you will probably overcome it by means of the rest of this technique. But follow up carefully with these "mild" attitudes. Make sure it is their feelings about preponderance, and not merely their way of expressing themselves, that is mild.

To make sure you don't miss anything, ask, "And who thinks it's okay?" Some hands will go up. No need to follow them up unless you have reason to be suspicious of any. If anyone's hand has not gone up for either answer, ask, "Mr. Thomas, what about you? I didn't see your hand." And follow up whatever he says. This way you will hear what every juror thinks about preponderance even if they did not initially understand your explanation and questions.

As you go from juror to juror, you may need to repeat your explanation because they will not remember your question. Repeat it with the same words. Do not get wordy, do not over-explain, and do not try different ways of explaining. Clarity comes from consistent simplicity, not shifting terms.

Before going to trial, try your intended explanation of preponderance on 14-year olds of average intelligence. (I know; that omits your kids. Sorry.) Until you can get three average-intelligence 14-year olds to quickly and fully understand the concept with no re-explanation necessary, you're not ready to do this in trial.

(If the judge will not allow these questions, ask instead under what circumstances the jurors make decisions in life on the basis of more likely than not. And ask the lowest percentage of likeliness they're comfortable with. Without realizing it, most people make the vast majority of their decisions on the basis of preponderance. You want to spot the jurors who most forcefully deny that.)

To seek cause dismissals, urge jurors along by asking if they could decide questions in the case (or in life) if they were less than 100% sure. If they say yes, ask what the minimum is they'd be willing to decide upon—90%? 75%? 65%? Get them to tell you their cut-off point, and see how firmly they hold to it. In this way, one attorney recently managed to remove for cause almost an entire panel of problem jurors. 60% is a higher standard than preponderance, so if the juror would have great difficulty going below 60%, he should not serve.

Preponderance. Part Two. Once you have sorted the good from bad jurors on the matter of preponderance, start Part Two. It's fast and simple. You say:

> Anyone else with any problems with 'more likely than not?' It's the way we all hope you'll make your decisions. *Mr. Defense Attorney agrees* you should decide the case on that basis no matter how many doubts you have, and the judge will tell you it's the law. So just to be sure, anyone else with even a small problem with that?

The key phrase is "*Mr. Defense Attorney agrees* . . . ." Do not say "Mr. Defense Attorney *wants* you to decide the case that way." He's an officer of the court so must *agree*, but he needn't want it.

Please see Section 6.15, for the next step of the Preponderance Technique, which will be in opening. (It will be the first step of the Technique when you cannot conduct your own jury voir dire.) Section 7.10 explains how to continue in testimony, and Section 9.29 covers the culmination: how to wrap this up in closing.

5.45
Leaders

Leaders are jurors with the persuasive skills, charisma, or other qualities that will influence other jurors during decision making. Leaders who are against you can be lethal. Leaders who are for you can lead the jury to your side and to a high verdict.

Some leaders can be excellent for liability, bad for non-economic damages, and good for punitives. A person who makes decisions based on the cold, hard logic of rules—no emotions, please; just concrete stuff like rules—might be a good juror for your liability case if the defendant violated standards or rules. But that juror will not change stripes when it comes to non-economics. She will still want to avoid emotion and instead base her decision on a concrete foundation. That makes her less likely to give much in intangible damages. Since she is a leader, she is likely to influence other jurors.

Yet she might be useful on punitive damages because she will tend to believe that the violation of standards can have serious consequences, and that assessing big money can change, say, corporate behavior.

Helpful leaders. Many attorneys and consultants believe you cannot get a large verdict without a strong leader on your side. But be extremely careful in allowing any leader to be seated. If you have any doubts about which way a strong leader is likely to go, do not gamble. You can win and even do well without a strong leader on your side, but it can be impossible to win or get much money with a strong leader against you. Persuasive leaders can change the minds of three or four jurors within just a few moments, after which the rest of the jury often follows. So when evaluating leaders in voir dire, get rid of them unless you are sure they will be with you. (See Appendix A.22 on how to identify potential leaders.)

5.46
Bifurcation or Trifurcation

The problem. In some jurisdictions you encounter bifurcation or trifurcation: a two or three-phase trial in which compensatory or punitive damages is not dealt with until the second or third phase. The jury submits its liability verdict before hearing evidence, argument, or instructions about compensatory damages or about any wrongdoing that might justify punitives.

This can be a defense advantage, because while the jurors are deciding liability, they know nothing about the harm the wrongdoing caused or (in punitives cases) the egregiousness of the wrongdoing. This makes it harder to win on liability, because the jurors have less reason to want to see the evidence in its best possible light for you.

Bifurcation also gives the defendant the opportunity to appear remorseful for his wrongdoing, a showing that can dramatically diminish verdict size. In single-phase trials, few defendants know how to credibly repent for wrongdoing while they are still denying that wrongdoing. But in the second phase of a bifurcated trial, after liability has been decided, a defendant can more easily appear credibly sorry. "I have seen the light and I repent" saves verdict money as well as souls.

Americans soften in the face of remorse, even in death penalty cases. If we do it with murderers, we can be even readier to do it with civil defendants.

5.47
Offsetting the Disadvantages of Bifurcation

Multi-phase trials can hurt you because jurors do not hear some of your strongest evidence until after the first phase. You can offset this disadvantage in voir dire.

In most places, since the same jury will hear every phase, you should have the right and obligation in jury selection to ask questions to uncover information that might impact how jurors decide every issue at trial, including second and third phase issues.

If the judge resists, argue that she cannot seat a fair jury without questions about matters that relate to all the issues to be decided in every phase. Even with a judge-conducted voir dire, you are entitled to have the jurors asked questions relating to every phase, not just the first.

Point out to the judge that death penalty cases, which are bifurcated, work the same way. Jury voir dire for both phases precedes phase one. Counsel asks about punishment issues that belong exclusively to phase two. The judge has no discretion to prevent it.

Argue that the necessity of a fair jury far outweighs any prejudicial effect on an early phase of voir dire questions related to a later phase.

5.48
Child Witnesses

Sometimes your most effective harm witness will be a child, such as a young son or daughter who can testify about the harm to your client. Sometimes the client will be a child, and under some circumstances that child will be a good witness.

But some jurors have problems with your bringing a child into court. Such jurors may resent you for it if they think you are doing it just to get sympathy at the expense of the child, who they believe should not be subjected to the courtroom.

Thus, either in voir dire or opening, you need to make clear why you have no choice but to bring in a child witness.

In voir dire, you can do three things to deal with this problem. First, learn who these jurors are. Second, explain why you have to bring in a child. Third, see if the explanation is sufficient.

> Mrs. Jones, as a juror your job will be to decide how much money it will take to fix the harms that can be fixed, to help the harms that can be helped, and to make up for the harms that cannot be fixed or helped. To do that, you need to know the harms. One family member who has closely seen the harm is John's nine-year-old daughter. So I have to bring her here to tell you about it. But that might not sit well with everyone, and I can understand that. What problems will you have with me for bringing that little girl in to testify?

5.49
Paid Experts

Some jurors will not believe paid testimony, and you need to find out who they are. Such a juror is not an equal disadvantage to both sides. You have the burden. If a juror believes no experts on either side, it is no draw; yours is the side that loses. Pointing this out can help you convince the judge to dismiss such jurors for cause.

Such jurors tend to be bad plaintiff's jurors for other reasons. They often feel that lawsuits are frivolous and that plaintiff's attorneys buy dishonest paid testimony to make themselves and their clients rich. Some jurors feel that trial attorneys have been paying legislators to vote against tort "reform," so that trial attorneys are the ones most likely to pay their experts to provide favorable opinions.

5.50

Legalese and Other Jargon

"Legalese" (and any other kind of technical language) is any word, phrase, or syntax that makes you sound like a lawyer. "Subsequent," "on or about," "approximately," "prejudice," "exited the vehicle," and "proximate" are legalese.

The end of this section contains what might be the most persuasive reason you have heard for not using such language in court. But do not skip down; read the other reasons first.

Using legalese—words, phrases, or syntax that make you sound like a lawyer—hurts everything you do in trial, especially in voir dire, and particularly when it comes to damages. This is partly because legalese dehumanizes you, making you less persuasive when it comes to damages. It is also because many jurors do not want to give money to lawyers. So the more you sound like a lawyer, the less those jurors will want to give you money.

In voir dire, legalese discourages jurors from talking freely with you. In opening, legalese makes jurors listen to you less and trust you less.

Legalese has so many other shortcomings that it is always a blunder to use it. Instead, talk to jurors the way you talk to your family and friends—or at least the way you talked to your family and friends before you went to law school.

Many jurors think using legalese is arrogant. Lawyers on TV don't talk that way, so why must you show off and make everyone else feel stupid?

Legalese is unclear to jurors. When you say "subsequent" instead of "after," jurors sit there trying to remember whether "subsequent" means before or after. Simultaneously, you say the rest of your sentence, so they never hear it though it was the most important part of the sentence.

Tort "reform" has created a stereotype: the greedy, dishonest raptor in a blue suit, highly trained to seem trustworthy so she can get rich off the misery of others by manipulating the gullibility of jurors. It is a hated and widely believed stereotype. When you use legal terms, syntax, and phrases, you emphasize that you are that stereotype.

Other jargon. Technical language from other fields is equally harmful and rarely necessary. For example:

> . . . the radiologic evidence of the linear line stopping at the hippocampus.

You can do the most complicated medical cases without more than two or three medical terms. Say "heart problem" not "cardiac problem," and "skin," not "epidermis." Often during the preparation of a case you hear and use technical terms so frequently that you forget that jurors do not know what they mean, or that jurors can think those terms mean something different. For example, jurors who hear that your permanently and totally disabled client is getting "occupational therapy" will think he is going back to work someday, so they will give you less money for future lost wages. That is what "occupational" means to jurors.

Every word you use should communicate. So, for example, don't use the metric system even though your experts will. "The tumor was three centimeters" means nothing in the United States. Some jurors will think it's the size of a pencil point; others will think it means nine feet. If your expert uses it on the stand, have her prepared to give the equivalent in plain English. Better yet, have her omit the metric system altogether.

You can never predict what jurors will think your technical terms and legalese mean, and the errors can hurt you. (Juror post-trial comment "Why did you keep telling us you wanted your client to 'recover?' He's dead!" Yes, a juror really said that.)

Hard language also makes jurors fear they will never understand your case. That makes them stop listening.

Sometimes jurors think you are using difficult language to cover up a bad case.

The most persuasive anti-legalese argument. Many post-trial interviews show that legalese makes many jurors think you are amateurish, even juvenile. So when you talk that way they either feel sorry for you or laugh at you. They make jokes about you with each other. They guffaw about you with their friends. During breaks they often do unflattering imitations of you for each other. When they come back and smile at you, it's not because they like you but because they can't stop laughing at you.

If you enjoy that, use legalese.

5.51
Client Presence

Usually your client should be in court throughout trial. But sometimes not. Sometimes you will have to bring up things in voir dire, opening, or testimony that might not be good or easy for your client to hear, or that might embarrass or harm him to hear. In such circumstances, consider not having your client there for that portion of voir dire or opening, or for the corresponding portions of testimony. This is not only for the sake of your client's feelings. It also prevents jurors from thinking you do not care about your client's feelings or well-being.

In addition, having a visibly harmed client there too much can allow jurors to become inured to the way her harms look. Even the worst of conditions, such as grotesque facial disfigurement, becomes less shocking—and thus less deserving of money—with familiarity. So consider carefully the effect your client's continual presence will have on the jury.

If you are seeking money for an injured child and the parents are in court the whole time, jurors will wonder how they can leave the poor child for all this time.

Brain damage and other "invisible" injuries. There is no stronger visual damages exhibit than your client. Don't let that strength backfire against you. Many brain damaged clients look and talk fine, so they should probably not be in trial—not even in jury voir dire or to testify, if you can avoid it. (Please see 7.11.)

Weigh the reasons for not having your client there during trial against the reasons in favor of her continual presence. Depending on the client, her presence can humanize her, and jurors who become familiar with her can have a harder time leaving her with a disappointing verdict. In other cases, the effect of her presence can minimize the verdict.

A focus group can help you decide whether your client should be there throughout trial or only at particular times or not at all. However, presenting your client to a focus group can raise serious issues of loss of confidentiality and other problems. Before proceeding, check on this with an experienced trial consultant.

If you decide your client should not be in court throughout trial, you need an explanation for the jury:

> Her doctor says it would be bad for her to hear testimony about how serious her injuries are and how they're going to get worse.

Then ask for juror reactions.

Spouse. If there is a spouse involved, have the spouse in court all the time. Having to explain that "Mr. Jones will only be here some of the time because he has to go to work" will not sit well with jurors missing their own jobs to be there.

5.52
Multiple Survivors

In a wrongful death case with multiple survivors entitled to seek damages, ask prospective jurors how they feel about compensating several people for the death of one person.

> Some folks feel that each survivor should be compensated for what he or she individually lost. Other folks feel the verdict should be the same whether there's one survivor or five. How do you feel about that, Mr. Jones?

And follow up.

This helps you spot jurors who are unlikely to compensate multiple survivors. It also begins the process (to be continued later with argument and the judge's instructions) of arming your favorable jurors to argue for you in deliberations that the jury is supposed to compensate each survivor's losses. You want the jurors aware of this as early as possible.

5.53
Voir Dire: Summary

Consider the powerful position your damages case will have achieved if you use the methods suggested in this chapter.

You will have seated jurors who are aware of every harm in the case and of what it will take to fix, help, and make up for those harms. Those jurors will also know that their job is to do the fixing, helping, and making up for.

If there is an issue of punitive damages, the seated jurors will know the causes, and they will know the purposes of punitives.

And you will have created a strong foundation from which to launch your opening statement. You will be a far cry from the usual weak position of starting opening with the jurors still a blank slate with respect to harm, damages, and their tasks as fixers.

CHAPTER SIX
OPENING STATEMENT

Bear in mind that you start out as the least believable person in the courtroom no matter how credible you think you are.

Jurors almost never decide the case in opening, though that remains a popular myth. But by the end of voir dire and opening, jurors have developed almost immutable beliefs as to what the trial is *about.* That belief governs how they handle everything else in trial: what they pay attention to, what they consider, remember, ignore, use; how they weigh each argument, opinion, and piece of evidence; what they think it means; what they will do with it all in their decision making and witness evaluation over the course of trial; and in what they say and finally decide in deliberations. And each of these things continually circles back and reinforces the initial belief as to what this trial is about.

Obviously your opening also has other important purposes. The kind of opening suggested in this chapter accomplishes them all.

Caveat. In this tort-"reform" era, at the start of your opening you have virtually no credibility. You cannot ask the jury to believe you about anything, and you cannot expect them to accept your accusations ("This is a case about a negligent doctor."). Unlike years ago, starting your opening this way can cost you the case. By using the opening statement structure this chapter outlines, you will avoid this trap. Even with this structure, you need to carefully discipline yourself to hold off being an advocate at least you get into the "Why We are Suing" part of opening—and at that point, slide into advocacy only gradually. Bear in mind that you start out as the least believable person the courtroom no matter how credible you think you are. These days many jurors believe that your so-called credibility is a result of meticulous training to help you mislead.

6.1

This Trial is *about* Harm and Damages

Do not allow your opening to imply that the jurors' main purpose is to decide liability: "Who is right, who is wrong?" If you do, throughout trial they will think, "This trial is about whether the defendant did something wrong. So that's where my attention will go." This makes jurors subordinate harm and damages to second place, often a distant second place. So they pay minimal attention to, and are minimally affected by, your harm and damages evidence. This leaves them unarmed and unmotivated to argue for much money in deliberations.

You want your voir dire and opening to make jurors realize from the start, "Ah! This trial is about what it will take to fix, help, and make up for the harm. Well, I'd better pay attention to everything I hear about that." You want that to be their firm belief before they hear your first witness, even if your first witness has strictly to do with liability.

6.2

Control the Time and Emphasis: Structure

Jurors decide what the trial is about largely by what you emphasize and spend time on. They pay little attention to those little last-minute afterthoughts that essentially say, "Oh yeah, and this trial's also about harm and money."

This means you must control time and emphasis. The key to doing this is structure. Good structure will help you progressively build the jurors' belief that the trial is about harm and money. Good structure does this by layering in one subject at a time in a carefully planned and managed sequence that focuses juror attention and concern where you want it.

"Stream-of-consciousness" openings rarely work. They are usually nothing but the stream of a lazy consciousness that does not feel like preparing. Worse, they are the stream of counsel's consciousness, not the jurors'. The most common juror comment about stream of consciousness openings is something like, "What was he talking about?" While a well-structured opening helps you control the way jurors think about the case, "stream-of-consciousness" openings make jurors wish you would just control yourself.

The structure outlined below works for virtually every case. Once you have used it a few times you will find that it takes you far less time to prepare your openings. Even the first time, your opening will present a coherent and complete picture of the case, jurors will listen to you more intently, and you will feel good while you're giving the opening.

And by the time you are finished, jurors will know that this trial is about harm and money.

During the first two-thirds of opening, this structure prepares the jury to hear damages by taking care of its other concerns in the proper order. By the time your opening gets to damages, damages will be the jurors' primary concern.

Here is the overall structure, part-by-part. The way to do each part is explained starting in section 6.4 below.

Part One.	Rule and consequence
Part Two.	Story (of what the defendant did)
Part Three.	Blame (Who we are suing and why)
Part Four.	Undermine (What is wrong with the liability defenses?)
Part Five.	Damages (What are the losses and harms?)
Part Six.	Money (What do you want?)

Stipulated negligence or liability. When negligence or liability is stipulated, you should still use as much of this as you are allowed to. If you are prevented from discussing anything about negligence or causation, skip from your Part One Rule ("When the negligence of a corporation [or whatever] causes harm, the corporation must pay money compensation equal to the amount of harm") to Part Five of the opening structure.

6.3
General Guidelines

Stay on topic. One basic principle of this structure is to layer in one topic at a time. Do not mix topics. The topic of Part One is the rule, so do not mention anything else. Do not talk about what happened, whose fault it was, who got hurt and how badly, or anything else. Do not refer to those things indirectly, or even imply that there are such things. Treat them as if they did not exist. You will bring them into existence soon enough, when they will help and not hurt you.

Maintain the same purity of topic for every part of the opening. This will focus juror attention on one topic at a time. That optimizes juror listening, and keeps you clear, informative, and persuasive.

No wasted beginnings. Do not begin opening with such attention-dissipating detours as thanking the jurors, or lecturing them on the importance of jury service, or talking about road maps. (Jurors do not think, "Oh boy! A road map! Golly, I can't wait!") Above all, do not say, "Nothing I say is evidence." Say good morning and get right to your first point: the Rule.

No wasted words. Do not waste the jurors' time by being wordy. Your opening must be concise: Every word—literally every single word —must be a word the jurors will find useful. In the 19th Century when lawyers, like novelists, were paid by the written word, they had motive to go on forever, and did. Because the pay-by-word policy has disappeared, today's novels are a lot shorter. But lawyers still use too many words, both when writing and when talking. Most often, what you say in twenty words is more effectively said in seven. Learn how to do that and make it habit. Jurors—along with everyone else—will like you a little better and listen to you with a lot more attention.

No wasted topics. Do not waste jurors' time with things they don't need. Jurors are not there for a liberal arts education or to see how much you know that they don't. They are listening to you solely to find out what this case is about and how to decide it. Give them nothing but that, and they will listen carefully. Give them even a little more and their listening rate steeply declines.

What* they *think they need. Jurors listen only when they fully understand why they need to know what you are saying. Do not leave jurors in the dark about the decision-making relevance of each thing you say. If you do, they simply do not listen, so you might as well not say it. "But they need to hear it!" you might think. But jurors will not listen to it unless they know why they need it. Good structure makes clear why the jurors need what you are saying. Without good structure, you have to stop and explain so often that no one can follow your overall message.

Go slowly. There is a density of important information at the start of opening, so go slowly. Give jurors time to absorb each point. If you happen to be a rapid speaker, it will be hard to slow yourself down. But you can easily pause between phrases (see "Sample Openings," Appendices C and D). In fact, even if you talk at a moderate speed, early in opening you should pause between phrases.

Do not be an advocate. Opening is too early for advocacy. Things have radically changed for plaintiff's attorneys: You are no longer believed or even respected as you would have been years ago. Early advocacy that once was effective now makes many jurors brand you as exactly what the tort-"reform" forces have been claiming. In opening, you want to be viewed primarily as an honest conveyer of true and important information. Postpone advocacy.

Don't ask jurors to take your word for anything. They won't. Ascribe everything you say to a witness, expert or lay, or a book, or anything else but yourself. Never forget that at this point you are probably the least credible person in the room, no matter how much the jurors *seem* to trust you.

6.4
Opening. Part One: Rule and Consequence

Tell jurors first what they want to hear first. Anything else gets less attention.

In today's climate, the old way of starting with unsupported assertions about why you should win the case ("This is a case about a doctor who read an X-ray too fast") or by stating themes containing unsupported conclusions ("This is a case about a careless driver") can sink your case before you launch it. It will make some jurors stop believing you from then on; they'll see you as the evil stereotype of greed and dishonesty that the tort-"reform" forces say you are. Even jurors unpersuaded by tort "reform" cannot trust you enough this early to accept your conclusions. Instead, your conclusions and unsupported assertions will arouse their suspicions.

So what do jurors want to hear first?

If your child comes home with a new board game, you open the box, spread out the pieces, and you ask "How do we do this? *What are the rules?*" That is the natural first question whether a person is new to a game or new to trials. So forget what *you* want to tell jurors first. Tell them what *they* want—and they'll listen. The rule tells them how to play and what to pay attention to.

> A driver has to watch the road and see what's there to be seen. If he does not and as a result hurts someone, the driver is responsible for the harm. Now let me tell you the story[1] of what happened in this case.

That is the whole of Part One of your opening. Don't elaborate. Don't cover every rule. Just pick one or two that are central.

> Whatever a company manufactures has to be safe to use. If it's not safe and it hurts someone, the company is responsible for the harm. Now let me tell you the story of what happened in this case.

The words "Now let me tell you the story of what happened in this case" accomplish two important tasks: First, it tells the jurors that you are going to give them the information they need so they can decide for themselves whether a rule was broken. Second, when you say you're going to tell a story, they lean forward to listen. If they think you're going to throw a bunch of facts at them, they turn down their listening. State the rule in non-legal words, style, and syntax. Say

1. For a long time many good advocacy teachers warned against using the word "story" because one of its meanings is for fiction. But it also commonly means a true narrative of events—such as a news story, or the story of, say, your life. When you say you're going to tell them the story of what happened, no juror ever thinks you mean you're going to tell them fiction. The context makes it 100% clear. Many words have multiple meanings; listeners know by context which meaning is intended and don't even think of the other meaning. That's why you can say "Everyone in this case agrees . . . " and no one thinks you're talking about people in a box. It doesn't even occur to them. You might still be trying to figure it out.

"careless," not "negligent." Say "hurts someone," not "is a cause of harm to someone." If you make it sound legal, you can draw an objection. Worse, you sound like a lawyer.

In venues where you cannot talk about the law in opening, you can still talk about anything a witness will say. So if your venue forbids mention of the law in opening, simply make sure a witness will talk about the rules. A physician can testify that he was taught in medical school that "A doctor is supposed to do what other doctors would do in the same situation." A driver can testify that he was taught that he is "supposed to watch where he's going because it would be his fault if he hits someone." This allows you to say those things in opening.

There is almost always a way to explain the rules in opening. It is important enough that you have to find that way and start your opening with it.

Juror attention. By giving jurors the rule and then promising to tell the story, you have given them an active task: to listen to see if the rule was broken. They will embrace that task. If you watch carefully, you will see that some jurors even relax into their role. That immediately makes them into excellent listeners.

Adhere to the structure. In Part One do not say or imply that the rule was broken. There's no way for jurors to believe that until after you tell them what happened. In Part Two you will explain what happened—i.e., what the defendant did—still without saying he broke the rules. This lets jurors feel that you're giving them the opportunity to draw their own conclusions about how the rules were broken. After that, you will explain it.

Length of Rules Section. In most cases the rule and consequence will be two sentences. But in some kinds of cases, the rule may need to be longer. For example, in a medical failure-to-diagnose case, the rule must encompass how a differential diagnosis works. This takes a few paragraphs. Much medical malpractice occurs because a health care provider chose not to use a differential diagnosis. Similarly, most failure-to-diagnose trials are lost primarily due to counsel's failure to clearly explain and focus on differential diagnosis. Please see Appendix C for how to explain differential diagnosis at the start of opening and how to build the case around it.

Here's a beginning to your opening. (" // " means short pause.)

> Good morning. //
>
> When we drive on the highway, // we have to watch where we're going and see what's there. // If we don't // and as a result hurt someone, // we're responsible for the harm. //
>
> Now let me tell you the story of what happened in this case.

6.5
Opening. Part Two: Story of What the Defendant Did

Once jurors know the rule(s), they want to know *what happened.* Almost invariably, nothing else will have much lasting effect on jurors until they know what happened. In fact, until you tell the jurors the story of what the defendant did, many jurors will think that the story of this case is that a plaintiff's lawyer is trying to get herself a bunch of money. Partly for that reason, until the jurors know the story of what the defendant did, they cannot believe any implication or outright accusation you make of wrongdoing on the defendant's part.

In other words, your task is to tell the story of what the defendant did *without your words or tone or demeanor even slightly implying any blame.* You can say, "Acme Truck Driver Deason was driving 75 miles per hour." But don't yet tell us the speed limit. That will come later when it will do you a lot more good. Don't even say "75 miles per hour" as if it was too fast. If you do, you'll shift the jurors' listening into "adversary" mode, and that circles right back to you as the predatory attorney.

Part Two of your opening is the story of what the defendant did that caused the harm. Jurors still do not want your opinions or conclusions, will resent hearing them, and are still likely to respond to them by disagreeing or becoming suspicious. Jurors know it is their job, not yours, to draw conclusions. They do not yet want you intruding on their territory. So in Part Two tell them what the defendant did and leave you and your opinions out of it.

Subordinate your client. Leave your client out of the story of what the defendant did. It is hard for some plaintiff's attorneys to accept that the story of what the defendant did must exclude the plaintiff as much as possible. It seems a counter-intuitive reversal of all they have ever learned. But it is essential. This is because jurors believe they are here to decide who did something wrong. To make their all-important first decisions about who did wrong, they will over-use the early information you give them. When your client is doing things in that information, the jury will infer that some of those things could have caused what happened to her. They will turn her most innocuous actions (a cup of coffee before driving to work) into negligence. When that becomes one of their first beliefs, you will find it hard and often impossible to dislodge it later. Don't give them anything to start them on that path.

So in the story of what the defendant did, the more you subordinate your client, the less the jurors will start blaming her. The story of your case is the story solely of what the defendant did. Until the jurors know the story of what the defendant did, you don't want them thinking about your client.

You don't want them thinking about anyone else, either. Only the defendant. Take a premises liability case: an assault in a motel room. Three vicious men beat an elderly couple in the couple's room. Do NOT start the story this way: "It's 3 A.M. January 12, 1998. Three Central Prison inmates shoot a prison guard through the head. The prisoners escape over the prison wall. They run. They get to an intersection. They surround a gray Buick. They pull the driver out. They shoot her in the chest. They drive off in her Buick. They lose their pursuers. They park behind the C'mon Inn Motel. They shove open the door to Room 123. They demand money from the couple inside in terror. One of them beats John while . . . ."

That is good storytelling. The jury will listen. They will get the full horror of what the *escapees* did to John and Jane. Jurors will get the point: these bad guys were really bad. And that will become the basis for their ultimate decisions. Unfortunately, this is a premises liability case against a motel owner who installed flimsy doors and who never told guests of any previous break-ins. Starting the story with the escapees leads jurors to blame the escapees, not the owner. By the time you get to what the motel owner did, the jurors will be irrevocably furious with and blaming the escapees. You have created your own competition.

Here is a better beginning:

> It's November 14, 1998. The owner of the C'mon Inn Motel, Ray Baker, goes into Home Depot. Mr. Baker looks at a selection of locks. He buys the three-dollar lock, the cheapest one. Mr. Baker goes back to his motel. Mr. Baker installs the three-dollar lock in the door to guest room 204.
>
> Two months later, nine in the evening. Mr. Baker is working the desk. Mr. Baker tells an elderly couple, 'Yes, our sign out front is true, this motel is absolutely safe. Never had a problem.' Mr. Baker checks them in. Six hours later, three in the morning, he hears screams in their room.

Same case, different story. By shining your narrative light on the actions of the motel owner, you make jurors blame the owner and not the escapees. The escapees are not in the story so they are not on the jurors' minds. You keep blame where you need it. (You might want to start such a story earlier, when Mr. Baker learns of each of the previous break-ins and attacks. "In 1996, Mr. Baker gets a call at the desk about a break-in in room 244," etc.)

Rule of thumb. After setting the scene (see below), the grammatical subject of every sentence in your story should be the name of the defendant. So don't say: "On April 12, 2002, Sally Smith comes to Dr. Wilson's clinic with a lump on her breast." Instead, say: "On April 12, 2002, *Dr. Wilson* is in his clinic. Dr. Wilson examines a patient for a breast lump. Dr. Wilson finds the lump where the patient described." This keeps focus on the doctor.

Try not to use pronouns for the defendant's name. Use the defendant's name or title: "Dr. Smith" or "the doctor." And in the story of what the defendant did, don't use your client's name at all. She is "the patient," "the pedestrian," "the homeowner," or whatever.

Set the scene. Start your story by saying, "*Let me take you back to* ____________." Then in a few short phrases, set the scene.

> Let me take you back to October 12, 2003. Hennepin Avenue, downtown Minneapolis. Clear weather, dry

> street. Two in the afternoon. Acme truck driver John Smith drives west across the Hennepin Avenue Bridge. He drives into downtown in his steel-blue 18-wheel tractor-trailer.

If the story has to start long before the catastrophe, simply start at an earlier point.

> Let me take you back to the winter of 1991. The main headquarters of Acme Trucking in Burlington, Vermont. The President's office. Nine in the morning. Acme's President, Alan A. Acme, calls a meeting of his staff to order. Mr. Acme says . . .

Now tell the story of the decision making that created the company's faulty hiring policy. As you tell the story of what the defendant did, please adhere to the following guidelines:

Short sentences. Keep your sentences short. Short sentences are easier and clearer to listen to. Avoid complex and compound sentences.

Present tense. Tell the story in the present tense. "Acme's truck driver turns right onto Second Street," instead of "Acme's driver turned right onto . . . ." Present tense creates immediacy, so your story registers more strongly on jurors.

One action per sentence. Every story is a sequence of *actions*. The story of what the defendant did is exactly that: *the actions the defendant did.* A story is not a compendium of facts, descriptions, or explanations. A story is all actions: one per sentence. "The wall is green" has no action. "John Smith paints the wall green" has an action: *paints*.

An action moves us forward in time—a spit second or a millennium, it makes no difference, as long as it moves us forward in time. This is not an arbitrary rule for storytelling. It is empirically based on what makes people listen. As soon as you stop moving us forward in time—even if only for a sentence or two—our attention plummets.

So once the scene is set, every sentence needs one action. Not zero, not two or three; one.

"The apple is green" contains no action; it is mere description. No one does anything, and nothing is done. So we barely listen. "John eats the green apple" contains an action—it moves us forward in time—from before John eats the apple until during or after. "John wakes up" contains an action: It takes us forward in time from when he was asleep. "John is awake" does not; it contains no action; it does not move us forward in time.

Exposition. "Exposition" is any sentence or phrase that does not move us forward in time. "I eat the apple" moves forward in time. "The apple is green" does not, so that sentence is exposition. The less exposition in your opening story, the better. Save it until later when it will do you some good. "I eat the apple" is fine. "The apple is from an orchard in the State of Washington" is not. Jurors won't pay much attention. Use it later when they have reason to hear it.

In a story, jurors pay attention mainly—if not only—to what someone does. They pay far less attention to something's state of being.

You can embed brief exposition within the actions: "I choose a green apple from the State of Washington. I eat it." But don't embed too much information or jurors stop listening. The action always needs to be the central point of each story sentence, so don't bury it in more than a point or two of exposition.

Each sentence is important. In telling the story, give each sentence its own importance. Do not subordinate or rush through a sentence to get to a more important sentence coming up. "I wake up. // I go to the window. // I open the shade. // I see that it's snowing." Give each sentence its own importance. Don't subordinate it. Otherwise jurors fall into the habit of listening carelessly, because they know by your own subordination that only some of what you say is important. So don't rush through preliminary sentences to a main point.

Tell the jury only what can be seen or heard. Joshua Karton, the near-legendary trial skills coach, consultant, and teacher, often finds successful ways to teach in workshops what the rest of us have been struggling to teach—such as including in your story only what can be seen or heard. If you are fortunate enough to attend a Karton workshop, ask him to do the exercise that gets you to do this.

It can be hard to limit yourself to what is seen or heard, because you'll want to provide information that cannot be seen ("The truck had been serviced by backyard mechanics") or go inside someone's head ("John sees the deer and thinks it's about to run in front of his truck") or talk about what someone did not do ("John had not checked the truck's brakes that morning") or provide information ("Deer cannot judge the speed of approaching vehicles.") You can't see or hear those things, so for now leave them out of your story no matter how important they are. At this early point they will barely be heard, because the jurors are still trying to get just an overview of *what happened.* So hold everything that cannot be seen or heard until later in opening.

Often you can find ways to talk about the omissions by showing what the defendant did instead. Instead of saying "John does not check his brakes," say, "John drives past the bay where brakes are checked." Or start the story earlier and you can talk about John bringing the truck to unlicensed mechanics. If you cannot do this or something similar to turn a piece of information into an action done by the defendant, leave it out of the story.

There are a number of reasons for this. First, a story is more believable, clearer, and more memorable when there's nothing in it except what can be seen or heard. Second, mentioning what someone did *not* do is almost always an accusation—and you do not want to turn your story openly adversarial. Third, providing information distracts jurors from the flow of events, so the jurors never get a clear idea of them.

Point no fingers of blame. Jurors are not ready yet for anything adversarial. If you mix the adversarial with telling what the defendant did, you will reduce the credibility and clarity of both. One thing at a time:

In the story: *what the defendant did.*

After the story: *blame.*

So in the story, don't even imply blame. You can say what happened ("After the first impact, Mr. Defendant speeds up") but don't criticize it ("After the first impact, Mr. Defendant *even* speeds up" or

"After the first impact, Mr. Defendant speeds up despite the ice on the road."). All we want here is the facts.

End of story. Your story of what the defendant did usually ends with the harm he caused. Give a one or two sentence report of what happened to your client. This is when to first use your client's name:

> The pedestrian—Jonathan Smith—was thrown against the concrete wall. The wall bounced him unconscious back into the highway. He lay there unconscious with his leg broken until the EMT people got there and put him in the ambulance.
>
> John's knees were broken and they'll never properly heal.
>
> Jack was killed.
>
> Allison's neck was injured and took a year and a half to get better.

Elaborate later.

That is the end of the story of the case, unless you can add:

> Meantime the Acme truck driver stayed in his truck. He called his boss on his cellphone. A passing motorist called 911.

The next thing the defendant did. During investigation and discovery, always try to find the next thing the defendant did right after doing the harm. Did the truck driver sit in his cab talking on his cell phone, and not get out to help your bleeding client on the side of the road? In a med mal case, did the hospital immediately send in a social worker to help the family deal with what had happened? Or instead did the hospital send in a risk manager? (Which, by the way, can be made to seem an implicit admission of negligence. Risk managers don't show up when a medical outcome is merely unfortunate. They materialize when the hospital knows there's a reason for someone to successfully sue. Why else?)

A tidbit such as the truck driver sitting in his cab or the risk manager showing up can end the story. Be careful to report such a tidbit in a non-advocate way. Just tell what happened. Don't make anything out of it; at this point all you want is jurors to infer, not you to imply.

Here is an example of a story, starting with the Part 1 rule. (The " // " marks are pauses.)

> Good morning. //
>
> A driver has to watch the road // and see what's there to be seen. // If he doesn't // and as a result he hurts someone // the driver is responsible for the harm. //
>
> Now let me tell you the story of what happened in this case. //
>
> Let me take you back to December 12, 2002. // Interstate Highway 85 in Durham. // Wet road. Rain and wind. // Just past midnight. // Acme Company truck driver Howard Littlejohn is driving south // in his eighteen-wheeler tractor trailer. // He passes the Gregson Street Exit. // The Acme Driver pushes in the cigarette lighter. // He feels around the seat for his cigarettes. // He leans over to feel around the floor. // He sits up with his pack of cigarettes in his hand. // The Acme driver looks back at the road. // He sees his truck has drifted to the right, partly onto the shoulder. // He sees a red flare. // The Acme driver sees a disabled pickup truck beyond the flare. // The Acme driver sees someone changing a tire on the right side of the pickup truck. // The Acme driver swerves left. // The Acme driver's front right corner clips the back of the pickup truck. // The Acme truck's impact knocks the pickup into the man changing the tire. //
>
> The man changing the tire is Jim Franklin. The impact breaks Jim's neck, leaving him permanently paralyzed from the neck down.

Please note several things. First, the story contains only what can be seen or heard. If something cannot be photographed with a camera or recorded by a sound recorder, keep it out of the story. Keep out anything that does not happen or is not done ("The driver failed to . . ."). Keep out actionless information. In movies and plays, this is called "exposition" ("The driver had been driving professionally for eighteen years."). No matter how important such things are, they will do you far more good later. So don't say that the Acme driver cannot find his cigarettes. Just say he looks for his cigarettes—because we can see him looking. Omit the fact that he had not checked his brakes earlier morning. Such things are unseeable: "He failed to look at the road" does not conjure up a mental picture. Worse, telling us an omission is pointing a finger of blame. Doing that this early, while jurors are still suspicious of you and before they know what happened, can create a lasting backlash against you.

In addition, what a defendant did ("feels around on the floor") instead of what a defendant failed to do ("fails to look at the road") is more believable and more memorable at this point because we can see the defendant doing it. It's closer to indelible—but it can be erased in a story containing omissions as well.

Second, in the sample story above, there is hardly any mention of the plaintiff. The story does not talk about how the plaintiff was driving, had a flat, carefully pulled over, carefully lit a flare, got out to change the tire, etc. We don't want the plaintiff or his choices on the jury's mind until after the jury knows what the defendant did.

Third, this sample story may not start in the best place. The better beginning of such a story may go back to the driver's morning routine and his long driving hours that day. Or it may go earlier still, back to Acme's meeting when they made the decisions about hiring that resulted in employing this driver.

Inevitability. When you start with the rule, you make no accusation. You merely state the rule. This keeps you from turning into an advocate too early. But the jurors infer that someone broke the rule and caused harm. After all, they know this is a trial.

As you tell your story, they will usually spot the rule-breaking. That will make the bad outcome seem inevitable to them. So when you finally tell them the outcome at the end of the story, you will just be confirming what they have already figured out. This is the best possible kind of persuasion—much better than saying anything like, "The defendant was negligent and hurt my client." It is always better to lead jurors to make their own conclusions. The story of what the defendant did, if told properly, almost always does exactly that.

This indelibly etches into the jurors' minds your version of what the defendant did. It becomes their truth of what happened, difficult for the defense to dislodge.

First person stories. A current trend of some trial advocacy teaching is to give your opening story in the first person. ("I" instead of "he.") But please be wary. Jurors smell gimmicks and tricks a mile off. To cynical jurors (about a quarter of them), first-person story telling in an opening—before you gain standing to be trusted—can seem like a gimmick or trick. They resent it.

Moreover, since your opening story should be the story only of what the *defendant* did, it's the defendant's story you'd have to tell in the first person. That lands you on potentially objectionable ground. You don't know how he saw things. Telling his story in the first person is putting words in his mouth and thoughts in his head. Besides, why give the defendant's point of view?

Finally, it is difficult to confine a first-person story solely to what is seen and heard, as your opening story should be. It is too easy to slide into what the first person thinks and feels. Opening is too early for that.

When advocacy workshops teach first-person storytelling, participants try it and everyone is often emotionally moved by the result, sometimes deeply. Afterwards there is hugging and tears. This is because no one in such a workshop has swallowed the tort-"reform" line, so everyone is in perfect alignment with the storyteller. It's preaching to the choir. So the participant who got the good response thinks, "They were all *so moved*; I've got to do it in front of my next jury." But jurors are not workshop participants. Some will be moved but others—especially the ones who are leaning against you—can easily think your first-person narration is a trick, a manipulation.

To have a chance with tort-"reform" jurors, you must start your opening by showing them you have facts and rationality, not the emotional gush of a first person story—especially not with your client as the first person. Save it for closing.

6.6
Opening. Part Three: Blame (Who We Are Suing and Why?)

First, explain *who* you are suing.

> We are suing truck driver Ed Littlejohn for three reasons. We are suing his employer, Acme Trucking, for two reasons.

Now you finally get to point some fingers of blame. Not before. You can now do it safely and with credibility, because by now the jurors know the rule, what the defendant did, and the harm it did. So far you have given the jurors no reason to mentally argue with anything you said. You are in pretty good standing with the jury—despite tort "reform." Things are not perfect, but you have done nothing to make jurors think you are one of the demons they have been warned about.

So the jurors are mentally ready to hear why you are suing. If you have stayed closely with the structure thus far and not added or omitted anything, the jurors will listen carefully and absorb an unusually large proportion of what you say. Jurors normally hear and absorb less than a quarter of what is said in trial. This structure significantly increases that.

Use the following paradigm for each thing the defendants did wrong or chose to omit.

A. What was the negligent act or choice to omit?

State in an affirmative way what the defendant did. Do not say it was negligent. Just describe the act or the choice to omit.

If whether or not he did it is in dispute, state how it is known he did it (e.g. cite a witness who saw it or an expert who figured it out).

> The first reason we're suing Acme's truck driver is that *he chose not to keep his eyes on the road.* A gas station attendant watched Acme's truck driver looking down at something next to him on the seat. Or,

> The first reason we're suing Dr. Akroyd is that he chose to ignore the possibility of bladder cancer.

"*Choose*": Do not say "He *failed* to keep his eyes on the road." Or "He *failed* to consider bladder cancer." Jurors forgive failures. We all have failures. Turn every omission into an affirmative act by using a form of the word "choose." Jurors are less forgiving of dangerous choices.

If whether the defendant did that act is in contention, add how it is known that he did it. Two witnesses saw it, or an expert's analysis reveals it, or whatever. If everyone agrees that that's what the defendant did, then there's no need to explain how it is known.

B. The general principle: What is wrong with it? How does it foreseeably cause harm?

Without mentioning this case, explain in principle what is wrong with doing what you mentioned in "A." Unless it's common sense, tell us who or what says it's wrong, and how it is—in general—a foreseeable cause of harm. Do not ask jurors to take your word for anything.

Even if it's common sense, try to cite a source for what's wrong with it. This is good persuasion and prevents objections that you're arguing.

> Peter Driver, who runs the Alamo School of Defensive Driving in San Antonio, will tell you that when a driver does not look at the road, it's likely that he's going to run into anything in his way. Or,
>
> Dr. Stephen Hyde who runs the Department of Urology at Earl University Medical Center will tell you that it violates the standard of care to ignore any reasonable possibilities. Ignoring any reasonable possibility allows it to go untreated, so it can get worse without anyone knowing.

Again, do not yet refer to your case. Separate principle from case. This allows the standard of care to stand on its own, giving it more authority.

C. What harm did it do in this case—and how did it do the harm?

Now explain how the wrongdoing in Part A harmed your client—and when possible, who says so or how else it is known (unless it's obvious).

> Because Acme's driver chose not to look at the road, he did not see Jim's pickup truck in time. So by the time Acme's driver finally saw Jim, the Acme driver was only 40 feet away and going too fast to stop or swerve. Or,
>
> In this case, Dr. Hyde will explain that Dr. Akroyd chose not to consider bladder cancer so did nothing to rule it out or treat it. By not treating it, Dr. Hyde reports, Dr. Akroyd allowed the cancer to spread to other organs. Dr. Hyde will explain to you why that cannot be cured, and why it killed Sally.

D. What should the defendant have done instead (and who says so, if it's not obvious)?

E. What good would that have done (and who says so, if it's not obvious?

Often you can put **D** and **E** together:

> Acme's driver should have kept his eyes on the road. If he had, he would not have drifted off the road onto the shoulder, and he would have seen Jim's pickup truck in plenty of time to avoid it.
>
> Dr. Hyde will testify that if Dr. Akroyd had considered bladder cancer, he'd have done the tests that would have shown it indeed was bladder cancer. If Dr. Akroyd had seen that by July, he'd have sent Sally to a cancer specialist. Dr. Alexander Herman, who runs the Cancer Center at the Bob Jones University School of Medicine, will show you the studies that prove more than 90% of bladder cancer patients who begin treatment at the point Sally was at in July 2000 are cured.

Expert opinions. When citing an expert's opinion in this or any other section of opening, explain the basis for the opinion. Be brief but complete. Never say, "Dr. Nebelthau, head of cancer research at the University of Minnesota, will tell you that if Dr. Larson had spotted the cancer in time, Sally would have lived." Jurors will not believe it just because Dr. Nebelthau says it, and some will think it less likely than if you had said nothing about it. So explain *how Dr. Barnes knows,* "Dr. Barnes will show you medical textbook diagrams of how fast this kind of tumor grows. We know its size when Sally died. We know its growth rate. So working backwards, Dr. Barnes easily calculated that when the defendant saw it in July of 2000, it was still small enough to be removed and leave no harm. Every doctor on both sides of this case will testify that this kind of tumor never does harm if it's removed before it's had a chance to spread the cancer."

Easy-to-have-done. The simpler and easier the defendant's proper action would have been, the better. Even in the most complex medical cases, you can almost always show how simple the right action would have been. "If the doctor had followed the rule," or "If the nurse had notified the doctor." In every case, you want the jury to believe that the right course of action was easy, simple, and commonplace: the *ordinary* thing to do in the circumstances. The simple, easy, and obvious norm. Start this "easy-to-have-done-right" theme here, carry it through testimony, and emphasize it in closing.

Now go on to the second reason you are suing the defendant. Use the same paradigm in the same way. This one will go faster because you can shorthand some things you have already explained. So:

(A) The second reason we are suing Acme's truck driver is that he admits that he chose not to check his brakes that morning.

(B) This violates Federal regulations. It is dangerous because, as trucking safety expert Alistaire Eunice will explain, the brakes on 18-wheelers can go from good to dangerous in just a matter of hours. This is why the Federal Regulations require drivers to check their brakes every day before leaving on their day's run, and after every work break—because if they don't check their brakes, they might not be able to stop in an emergency.

(C) In this case, because Acme's driver had not checked his brakes, he was driving with bad brakes and could not slow down enough to swerve away without hitting Jim's pickup truck.

(D) If Acme's driver had checked his brakes as required, he'd have known they were bad and would have had them replaced before leaving on his run. Accident reconstructionist Walter Moore will show you how easy it would have been for the Acme driver to slow down enough to swerve away if the brakes had not been bad.

(E) And that would have saved Jim.

Or,

(A) The second reason we are suing Dr. Akroyd is that when Sally came back two months later with the same symptoms, Dr. Akroyd still chose not to consider cancer.

(B) Dr. Hyde will explain that choosing not to consider a reasonable possibility violates the standard of care because it means the doctor will often miss urgently dangerous problems.

(C) Dr. Hyde will explain that Dr. Akroyd's conclusion that Sally had a bladder infection made it even more necessary for Dr. Akroyd to consider bladder cancer—because even if Sally had had a bladder infection, bladder infection is a sign of cancer. By not considering bladder cancer, Dr. Akroyd lost his last opportunity to get Sally surgery and start her on treatments to give her any chance of surviving.

(D) Dr. Hyde says if Dr. Akroyd had followed the rules and considered bladder cancer, he'd have sent Sally to a cancer specialist who would have been able to

(E) save her.

After you have run through every reason for suing each defendant, add one more reason for suing:

> The final reason for suing is that the defendants have refused to meet their responsibility, so we are forced to bring them to trial.

6.7

Opening. Part Four: Undermine (What Is Wrong with the Negligence Defenses?)

This part of your opening should provide your side of the story for every important defense negligence contention. (Undermining causation and damages contentions will come later.) If you do not do this, when jurors hear them first from the defense they will think you were trying to hide them because you are afraid of them. So with rare exception, everything important you do not want the jury to believe should be covered in this section.

Do this in a non-defensive way. It is defensive to say, "You will hear the defense tell you X, but . . . ." This wording makes jurors think the defense found things wrong with your case that you had not anticipated. Some jurors will wonder whether you'd have taken the case if you'd thought of those problems yourself.

So instead of saying, "You'll hear the defense tell you . . . ," explain that you took the initiative: that before deciding to come to trial, you considered and researched all the possibilities. Here's how:

First, say:

> Before we decided to come to trial, several things had to be determined.

Second, state a defense contention to undermine:

> For example, the Acme driver says there was ice, so he could not help skidding into Jim. So it had to be determined whether there was really any ice.

This shows you took the initiative to investigate.

Third, explain why this possibility had to be determined. If you lose the case if the jury believes this defense contention, say:

> Because ice would explain why the Acme driver hit Jim so *there'd be no reason for us to come to trial.*

But don't turn a non-pivotal defense contention into one that is pivotal. Once you say " . . . there'd be no reason for us to come to trial" you are making this issue case-pivotal even if it is not. So when a defense contention is not case-pivotal, simply say something like:

> Because ice would have been one reason the Acme driver hit Jim.

Fourth, explain what you did to determine the truth. Cite fact witnesses, experts, and whatever else you have:

> So we asked the two passing motorists who had stopped at the scene, as well as the state trooper and both EMT workers on the ambulance crew. All five will be here to tell you there was no ice. We also contacted the National Weather Bureau, and they're sending a meteorologist to bring temperature charts that show it never went below 35 degrees, several degrees too warm for ice.

Fifth, explain what the result means:

> That's how it was determined that there was no ice, so we could come to trial.

Sometimes there is only one defense negligence contention. Usually there are more, sometimes many more. Undermine them all. Any you omit will hurt you when the jurors hear them first from the defense. And when you let the defense bring up a defense claim first, they spin it their way—making that spin the jurors' first impression of it. Worse, you may not be able to respond until well into your case-in-chief. By then it can have already done permanent damage by coloring how jurors have heard your other evidence.

Intervention. There can be problems that the defense is not going to bring up, but that you should still deal with in this section anyway. One is the concept of cause. Some jurors will think, *The cause was that he had cancer; the doctor missing it did not cause it.* You and the judge and even the defense attorney can explain forever the doctor's duty to have intervened, but some jurors will still blame only the cancer.

Explain in opening that an expert will explain why a wrongful choice not to properly intervene is negligence—and thus one of the causes. Explain that proper intervention is the only reason the medical profession exists. Then return to, "If the lack of proper intervention allowed harm or led to harm, it's a cause." Say it twice. Then stop. An analogy will help with this in testimony or closing, but not in opening. Throughout trial you should make "intervention" a theme of the doctor's primary main duty.

Use the same language in testimony:

> Q: Doctor, how did Dr. Fell's choice not to intervene with a Caesarian section allow Jennie's cerebral palsy?

If that's the only wrongful cause, ask:

> Q: What else contributed to her cerebral palsy?
>
> A: Nothing but the things Dr. Fell should have intervened in and stopped.

Don't miss anything. Be thorough in examining the defense case to make sure you undermine everything the defense and the unfavorable jurors are likely to throw at you. Find ways to dismiss each one by referencing witnesses, experts, and whatever else you have. Length does not help you in this section. Keep everything as concise as you can.

When citing experts, never say, "Dr. Jones will tell you why he concludes that Dr. Fell caused Jenny's cerebral palsy." You need to tell us here in opening the basis for Dr. Jones's conclusion.

Do not undermine defense damages or causation contentions here. Do that as the topics come up in the next section.

6.8

Opening. Part Five. Damages (What Are the Losses and Harms?)

You are now half (or two-thirds at most) of the way through opening. The rest will be about losses and harms. (Technically you still are on liability, because causation is part of harms and you will cover it in this section.)

Remember throughout each part of opening to limit what you say exclusively to the topic of that part. So, for example, in "Why We're Suing" you should not talk about damages. Once you start talking about harm and damages here in Part Five, it is even more important to maintain this purity. While talking about harm, do not bring up anything related to negligence. Do not expect jurors to deal with two things at once.

Start Part Five by explaining—even if you already explained in jury voir dire—why you need to show the losses and harms, and that the reason has nothing to do with sympathy.

> One of the questions the judge will give you to deliberate on is how much money it will take to make up for the harm the truck driver did to Jim. When figuring that out, the *only* thing you are allowed to take into account is the amount of the losses and harms. Nothing else. No outside reasons. We'll show you later how to figure it out, so you'll see that you'll need to know all about the losses and harms.
>
> We're not showing you the losses and harms to get your sympathy. The time for sympathy is long over. We're here to get the money it will take to make up for John's losses and harms, the only things you can base your decision on.

Part Five of opening explains every important consequence of the immediate harms. "His broken knees kept him from climbing or standing, so he was out of work seventeen weeks. Here are the things he could not do with his knees broken. . . . And here are the kinds of pain he went through. . . . And here is what the lack of income did to his family. . . ."

Organize this into subparts.

A. Physical damage

B. Primary consequences of the physical damage (disabilities)

C. Nature, extent, and duration of the pain and suffering

D. Tasks of life and work your client could not or cannot do

E. Safety consequences of the harms

F. Before and after

G. Fixes and helps

H. Make up for

A. Physical Damage

What was the physical mechanism and extent of the damage? How did the arm get broken and how big is the break? When he hit the ground, what did the forces do to each part of his knee? What killed his brain cells? How much of his brain did it affect? How and how badly was his eyesight damaged? What were the forces that ripped apart the nerves? How much damage did the forces do? In a death case, take us step-by-step from the impact to the death: what was the mechanism of death?

Do not yet discuss disabilities, surgeries, medications, or anything else: just describe the physical process that caused the physical harm, and how much harm it caused.

Use your own body to show where each injury was. Don't point at the area; touch it. Run your finger along it.[2] When there is just one injury or very few, you can "anchor" the injury by touching that part of your body whenever you mention it during trial. This helps keep it physical and real. In deliberations the jurors will mimic the gesture. This is usually your most effective possible "exhibit"—and it's free.

When describing the mechanism and extent of the injuries, be detailed and clinical—but do not use technical language. Call a collarbone a "collarbone," not a "clavicle." Call a pool of blood a "pool

2. But use discretion. East of the Mississippi, running your finger along your crotch can be risky.

of blood," not a "hematoma." A brain bleed is a "brain bleed," not a "subdural hematoma." You can throw in a few technical terms to make the seriousness of the injury apparent, but you must immediately revert to plain English. "At the hospital they found that he had a cerebral hematoma; that means blood pooling inside his skull."

When your client has emotional harm caused by something physical, explain what that was. Explain in lay terms what caused the physical changes in the brain's chemistry. If an injury is permanent, explain the physical reason it cannot heal or get better.

Do all this with constant reference to the doctors who will testify about it. You still do not want to ask jurors to take your word for anything.

B. Primary Consequences of the Physical Damage (Disabilities)

What did or does the injury physically or mentally do to your client? What are the disabilities? Because his knees were shattered, he could not walk, kneel, stand for long, etc. Because millions of brain cells were killed, the areas of the brain that remember and make decisions were permanently damaged.

With mood disorders, explain how the physical changes in the brain's chemistry caused, say, the Post-Traumatic Stress Syndrome. Explain how the chemistry of the brain controls mood—and how that led to the depression in this case.

If the harms will extend into the future, explain what they are, and how, why, and when they will get worse.

Do not yet discuss the specific tasks the physical disabilities keep or kept your client from doing. That will come in part D, below. For now, focus on the body, mind, or emotional balance that was harmed. So explain here that he can't lift anything, but save for later his inability to lift his baby out of the crib or carry crates at work. Explain where her depression came from, but save for later what her depression keeps her from doing.

Take your time with this subpart. Make everything concrete and specific. Do not just parrot the clinical language of the medical reports. Describe the human consequences to the person.

C. Nature, Extent, and Duration of the Pain and Suffering

Pain. Be specific about physical pain. When, where, how often, and how intense? And what kind of pain is it?

"Nine on a scale of ten" is useful but does not say enough. Compare the pain to something jurors can readily identify with: "Like a bad stomach cramp that never goes away." "Like the chafing from a bad shoe." "Like slamming a finger in a car door."[3]

What is the nature of the pain? Burning? Sharp? Dull? Sore? With pain syndrome, explain step-by-step how this vicious cycle works.

Simple analogies are effective ways to convey the nature and intensity of pain.[4]

> If someone burns himself with a hot iron, that's how Jane's arm feels all the time.
>
> Lots of people get short-term pulled muscle that keep them from moving. That's how Jane's neck will feel for the rest of her life, whenever she turns her head or nods or even just sits still.

Use analogies from common experience. Not "It always feels like a nail being driven into someone's skull," but, "It always feels like someone in a kitchen standing up quickly and banging his head on the corner of a cabinet door."

Alternatively, use analogies jurors can identify with. "Like aiming a blowtorch onto her toes." That's not a common experience but it's easy to feel it.

Suffering. Be specific about mental and emotional suffering: What does it feel like? What makes it real? Why won't it go away if your client just "cheers up"? (If the defense is challenging these problems, you should undermine the challenge, but not here. See part "D" below.)

---

3. Be careful not to put jurors into your client's shoes by saying, "Like slamming *your* finger in a car door." This can result in a disruptive objection in opening. In closing it can reverse your case.
4. Analogies are useful in describing harms, but generally ineffective and sometimes counterproductive for liability.

How does the suffering differ in cause, type, and intensity from normal moods? How do we know? What does it interfere with? What does it feel like? How long does it last?

Find analogies. "Anyone who's ever awakened from a terrifying nightmare feels at that instant how John always feels whenever he hears a car horn." Or, "The most panicked anyone ever gets in an emergency is how Jane feels all the time."

D. Tasks of Life and Work Your Client Could Not or Cannot Do

How do the consequences of the immediate harms limit his activities? At work he cannot fill customer orders because he cannot walk, so he cannot earn an income; nor can he play with his children, or hunt, or shop for himself. He cannot remember or process information, so he cannot learn a new job or do his old one.

In a wrongful death case, if relevant, explain what has happened to the family since Dad was killed. In Connecticut and other venues where the only compensable losses are for what the deceased lost, describe those losses.

And as always, keep everything concrete and specific.

Do not let this section be clinical. Focus on the human consequences of the disabilities: Tell us the disabilities, then tell us what your client's life was like (or will be) for the duration of those disabilities. Missouri's Ed Hershewe teaches, "Don't show a condition; show a person."

That said, be sure jurors understand the mechanism of injury that causes anxiety or depression. This will show how anxiety and depression are involuntary, and caused by chemical and physical factors beyond the plaintiff's control.

Income and job losses. Once the jurors understand the causes and disabilities that prevent(ed) your client from working, you can describe what the loss of work means economically and emotionally. Include how the economic loss affects other things: standard of living, access to treatments.

With long-term or permanent disability that forces the client to change jobs, show how this means not just less money and the inability to do one's chosen work. It has also turned your client at, say, age 45 into an entry-level worker competing with workers less than half his age. And your client will never be able to climb as far as the younger workers because he doesn't have that many working years left. Show all that is lost by starting a new job path at age 45. If possible, describe what your economist will say about the lost value of your client's accumulated credentials that will no longer do any good.

E. Safety Consequences of the Harms

Safety concerns are persuasive to jurors. Show how your client's situation places him in danger. For example, a paraplegic living alone without assistance is a magnet for danger. People in the neighborhood know he is alone and he cannot escape or defend himself. Your client knows this is an open invitation to thieves. When he hears a noise at 2 A.M. at night, he cannot investigate. All he can do is lie there alone, helpless, and terrified. Even lesser disabilities can make escape from fire or other dangers difficult or impossible. Living with that terror is in itself a compensable harm.

And the only reason John had or still has to live with that terror is that the defendant's continuing refusal to accept responsibility and provide the necessary money to fix, help, and make up for the harm he has done. See "Interim Deprivation" below.

Separate this kind of harm into two compensable parts: first, the danger itself. Second, the measures to be taken (which you will describe in the section below on helps and fixes). Examine your client's situation carefully enough to spot all the dangers it presents and the level of worry and fear it caused or still causes. Ask your client and everyone familiar with your client's situation.

Brain damage. Brain damage cases often have special kinds of safety issues. Emphasize them, first because they often help jurors understand the nature and extent of the brain damage, and second because jurors tend to provide money for safety concerns. So, for example, when trying to get money for round-the-clock care, show that while your client now tests to have the mind of an eight-year old, at least an eight-year old knows not to wander out in traffic; your client does not know that.

Also point out that an eight-year-old child is capable of taking care of himself in some ways—but if you left him alone all night the Department of Social Services would intervene because it is not safe.

F. Before and after: Go backwards.

In cases of long-term harm, and even in some cases of limited-term damage, before-and-after comparisons are powerful. Focus on the distance your client has fallen: where he started versus where he is now. Explain that the height of that fall is the measure of fair compensation.

The traditional sequence of presentation—telling the "before" followed by the "after"—is not as effective as the reverse. By this point in opening, the jury knows the "after" story, so now contrast it with your client's life before.

Avoid generalities. Generalities are nearly worthless, such as "She used to be very energetic" or "He used to be happy." This has little effect. Instead, find mini-stories: Talk about a particular ball game when dad coached the kids, ran all over the place, and carried most of the gear to and from the van. Contrast that past event with a recent game Dad had to watch from the bleachers and leave early because of the pain. That's better than "He used to play with his kids and now he can't."

So don't say "He used to be an 'A' student but now can't remember anything he studies no matter how hard he works at it." Instead of saying it, tell a mini-story of how he worked all day, what he studied, how mom and sister helped that evening, and the heartbreak when he came home in tears after the test and said, "It all just went away." Then contrast that with a specific story from before: coming home one Spring day with his great report card.

Replace your generalized assertions with persuasive, concrete mini-stories of the facts. Jurors use them to make solid conclusions about your client's situation. Jurors do not do that with generalizations. Compared to the disappearing ink of generalizations, stories are indelible.

G. Fixes and Helps

Give the descriptions and costs of every important fix and help: medication, therapy, psychiatric care, rehabilitation, all other past and future treatments, equipment, replacement of lost wages, assistance in daily tasks, etc.

Explain what the jury can do to fix the harms that can be fixed: "The wage records show that John lost $18,000 in income. You can fix that loss by including that $18,000 in your verdict."

Be explicit about how to help the things that cannot be fixed: "John will never walk normally, but Dr. Brownlee says $2,000 a year will pay for the therapy to help him walk better than he can now."

Treatments cause pain. Emphasize the treatments that cause pain and extra disability. Surgery hurts as soon as the patient wakes up. Tell us how much it hurt, what the pain was like, how long it lasted. Surgery creates short-term but severe disabilities. Describe them.

Minimum life-care plan. A life-care plan, if you have one, is invaluable. If you have no formal life-care plan, make your own list of harms that can be (or were) fixed and helped. Explain the particular harm that each fixing or helping item dealt with or still deals with, and how much it cost(s).

But don't call it a "life-care plan." Tell your expert you want a *minimum* life-care plan. This does not mean the expert should take anything out. It simply means the expert should be able to explain (as you will do here in opening) that a *minimum life-care plan provides the minimum humane level of care, comfort, and safety*. In most venues, this lets you argue that " . . . two or three times the cost of the minimum life-care plan could be spent on the *best* available care, comfort, and safety." Give a few examples of what is not covered: "If in ten years the Mayo Clinic in Minnesota discovers a way to help Jack walk again, the cost of that treatment is not included in the minimum life-care plan." Throughout trial, call the plan the "minimum life-care plan." Your life-care expert should do the same. If she will not, replace her. Don't argue with her; just don't use her again.

Pay particular attention to safety. Jurors can be very willing to go beyond the minimum life-care plan to provide better safety. Such things as sophisticated alarm systems, night care, and conservative medical monitoring are likely to seem necessary at levels beyond the minimum life care plan.

"Minimum life-care plan" turns the ceiling of the life-care amount into a floor. (See also 7.7 and 9.6.)

Life expectancy. There is a second way to turn the life-care ceiling into a floor. Life-care plans are based on life expectancy. Explain in opening that your minimum life-care planner will testify that many people in this population group will live longer. Your life-care planner should study the life-expectancy tables. Often more, sometimes many more, than half your client's grouping will live longer. Many will live a lot longer. If more than half of your client's life-expectancy grouping will live longer than the average, use a spread-chart to visually show how many people out of every hundred will live longer than the average, and how much longer some will live. This is not only persuasive, but also gives you preponderance: your client is more likely than not to live longer. This lets you argue for more than the minimum life-care figure based on average life expectancy.

If fewer than half of your client's life-expectancy group live longer, you can still get preponderance. Your client is worried about what will happen if his life-care money runs out at that "expectancy" age of 82.6, just when he will be least able to get along without care. The reality of this worry turns the less-than-50% chance of longer life into a legitimate worry about what happens if he beats the average. That worry can be removed by providing the amount of money it will take to remove it.

In other words, this harm can be fixed. The jurors can fix it by providing money for as many years as they want beyond average life expectancy.

And remember this: If someone lives to her life expectancy, at that point she has a better-than-even chance of living another X years. If she makes it that extra X years, she has a better-than-even chance of living another X years. And so on.

Have your planner show a chart of how many people are expected to live an additional three years, six years, nine years, etc. And have your minimum life-care planner or your economist provide care cost figures for each additional three-year period.[5] And add, in closing, that the defense is arguing for an abbreviated life span or just an average life span in the desperate hope that the jury will provide no more than the amount for the minimum life-care plan.

California trial consultant Rodney Jew labels this theme, "What happens when the money runs out?" As with all of his suggestions, this one is extremely effective. He shows that it is even more effective when "What Happens When the Money Runs Out?" is the heading on a visual that illustrates the actual life-expectancy possibilities versus what the defense wants the jury to believe.

Geriatrics. Your minimum life-care planner should incorporate the expertise of a geriatric medical specialist who knows the increasing special needs of your client's later years. Health care providers untrained and inexperienced in geriatric needs will miss a lot that needs to be in the minimum life care plan.

Jurors tend to believe that even the worst needs and problems diminish in time. So tell the jurors that a geriatric specialist will explain how your client's needs will increase, how her plight will worsen as she ages, and how she will never "get used to" her situation because each time she gets used to it, things will get worse. Things will get worse in a series of downward plateaus. Do not rely on non-geriatricians for this kind of testimony. The strongest combination is a physician who specializes in geriatrics along with an experienced social worker who does the same. This can significantly increase the verdict for both economic and non-economic damages. Special geriatric clinics are a good source for this kind of expert.

Case manager. If there's a case manager in the life-care plan, make sure the jury understands why. A good case manager is not merely a clerk who arranges appointments, though that's usually how life-care

---

5. When using an economist, keep in mind that Americans are largely "economically illiterate." Few know or care what economists do, or how, or even why. What we do "know" is that economists rarely agree with each other. They seem even less reliable than weather forecasters. Whenever an economist's testimony invites or requires jurors to accept assumptions, it is an invitation for jurors to doubt. Since reduction to present-day value always involves assumptions over which economists can wildly differ, it is better when the figures—especially for the additional three-year periods—come from your minimum life-care planner. Your economist's role is best limited to confirming the minimum-life care planner's figures, and to explaining that the bottom line figure is the amount that will be used up, along with all the interest it can generate, by the end of the average life expectancy period.

planners explain it. Safety is also a factor: A case manager has the expertise to spot risks and problems in time to do something about them. Give examples.

Do not have your planner nominate herself for the job of case manager. Jurors can see this as a conflict of interest, and it can be. It gives a planner a motive for exaggerating the need for and the cost of the case manager as well as the entire minimum life-care plan. The planner must be positioned so that the jury's verdict cannot have any effect on her.

Empirical experience. Your planner should have experience in following up her earlier life-care plans to see how things are working. Explain this experience in opening. You want a planner who has gone out and monitored her previous plans over a long period of time. Otherwise she's just working on theories, not in-the-field experience. "I see how these things work out in the long run, and I used that information when I made up the plan for this case." And get a few examples.

Attribution. Attribute to other people, such as treating or expert physicians, your knowledge about each harm, fix, and help. This attribution keeps jurors from having to take your word about the losses. Jurors think your substantial cut of the verdict motivates you to exaggerate harms and costs. So do not say that Mary needs pills costing $1,000. Say that her physician says she needs them. As trial progresses, avoid the temptation to shorthand this into your assertion. Position yourself throughout trial as a messenger.

When no person is the source, cite the paper evidence, such as: "The wage records show that . . . ."

Future care costs versus past care costs. Beware of the common situation in which annual future care will cost significantly more than annual past care. Explain, for example, that actual past costs are low because the family had no money for proper care—which is the why you're in court. Explain that past medical costs were comparatively low because there was only so much that medical science could do—but that as a result, future care costs are high. Whatever the reasons for the disproportion, explain them in opening and again in closing. Otherwise jurors often think that past care costs are the fair measure of future costs.

Language. Here and elsewhere, do not use language that can be interpreted as exaggerated. Hyperbolic language, too often used by plaintiff's attorneys when describing harm, undermines your credibility. I recently heard a lawyer ask a jury to compensate his client for the "tragedy of her broken leg." Broken legs are painful but not tragic.

Understate. Allow the facts, not hyperbole, to do the intensifying.

Total. Provide a total cost of all the fixes and helps.

H. Make Up For

Explain that every cent of the money you just talked about goes to pay other people for John's care, treatment, medications, and equipment—except for the lost wages, money for which will only make John even with where he would have been if this had not happened. "None of that money makes up for the greatest part of the damage: what this did to John himself, his human losses." Give an example of the distinction: Paying for surgery for a broken arm is one kind of required compensation; money to make up for John's having to suffer with the pain of the broken arm and the pain of the surgery is another.

Base this on the jury instructions. They often detail intangible losses more specifically than merely "pain" or "suffering" or "death." Instructions commonly include "loss of use of a body part," "inconvenience," "humiliation," etc. In death cases, the instructions can list loss of services, advice, kindly offices, guidance, companionship, etc.

Even if your instructions have no such items, get lists from other jurisdictions. "Loss of use of a body part" and "humiliation," whether in your instructions or from the next state, are useful in explaining suffering.

Do not bunch these losses or rush through them. Each is a separate item of damage. With each, do two things:

First, explain each one separately and clearly. "Humiliation means feeling embarrassed, or disgraced, or disparaged, or reviled."

Second, relate it to this case.

> Sally's doctor says Sally feels that way a lot. Sally doesn't like to talk about this, but when she walks into a restaurant she feels like people are staring at her. She thinks she repulses them and that they want her to leave so she won't ruin their lunch. She thinks they talk about her when she leaves. Now, most people don't react that way, but some do, and people with scars on their faces feel like almost everyone does. That feeling gets inside you and never goes away. You want to run and hide. That's what the law means by humiliation, so it's one of the things you'll use money to make up for.

Each such intangible loss becomes a separate line-item in your request for money. Even if you have asked questions about them all in jury voir dire, in this sub-part of opening you should specifically relate each one to your client.

Do not limit this to a legal-sounding itemization. Focus on the human content of each item. For example, "kindly offices" really means "kindred offices," the things each of us does in the "office" we hold as a family member. That is legal sounding, so as soon as you explain it, give it human content: "It would have been John's job as a dad to teach John Jr. how to ride a bike, or in another few years to talk to him about girls."

Interim deprivation. One kind of harm can result in more money—especially when jurors do not like the defendant or defense counsel. This harm is caused by the defendant's refusal to meet his responsibility. It has forced your client to get along without the fixes and helps that could have made life safer and more bearable. So your client has had to endure months and years of extra unnecessary pain, danger, significant inconvenience, and discomfort. Show everything your client has had to go through that is due to the delay in getting money for fixing and helping.

In closing, explain that one way to figure out how much it will take to make up for this period of irresponsible and needless deprivation is to base it on the monthly cost of the life-care plan, or of the other kinds of care that will be needed. Apply that monthly rate to the months of deprivation—and double it, because it made life harder than it had to be.

6.9

Loss of Personal Image

An often ignored area of loss can have to do with your client's self-image. North Carolina's William O. Faison explains that the discrepancy between your client's self-image and the actuality now forced upon her is a loss because it is a source of suffering. Her life-long self image, until now, has not been that of a woman whose face is scarred and whose hand is useless. Deep inside she still thinks of herself as a normal-looking person who can do things with her hands. So every time she looks and sees what she really is, it wrenches her apart.

We begin constructing our personal self-image when we are very young children. We create it a piece at a time over the years and decades. It becomes the way we see ourselves in relation to the world. (Pain and disability counselors can help identify and describe the loss of personal image and its consequences.)

The issue of harm to self-image is not merely argument for closing. If your client or an expert or treating caretaker will testify about it, talk about it in opening.

6.10

Undermining Defense Damages Contentions

As you work your way through Part Five, undermine any minor defense damages or causation contentions as you come to the harm it is relevant to. Do it similarly to the way you undermined defense negligence contentions:

> Before deciding to seek compensation for lost income, it had to be determined whether the reason John was not working was that his company had layoffs. So we spoke with his boss, who will be here to tell you that they would never have laid off John, because John was one of the few who . . . .

Undermine any major defense damages and causation contentions—such as malingering and previous major conditions—after you have told the jury about all the harm and damages.

Malingering and symptom exaggeration. Cite each expert and lay witness who will testify that the pain or disability is real and not exaggerated. Explain how they know your client is telling the truth.

To prepare jurors for a malingering or exaggeration defense, have an expert testify (and preview it here in opening) that no doctor has any way of knowing when a patient is faking or exaggerating. Claiming otherwise is speculation based on junk science—and you want an expert who will explain that.

When your client will appear honest to the jury, a defense claim that she is malingering or exaggerating can be a gift to you. (See 9.23) But when your client is not particularly credible, move to bar defense mention of malingering or exaggeration. It has no real footing in science. Some judges will agree it has no place in trial. See Appendix F.

Also, if relevant, explain that symptom magnification is involuntary, and caused by chronic severe pain. Provide in opening your expert's explanation of the vicious cycle that causes symptom magnification. Explain how he knows the pain is as real and just like any other pain, except that painkillers often don't help.

Previous conditions. The defense often claims that all or part of the plaintiff's problems were there before, or come from previous causes. You must undermine this in opening as effectively as the evidence is going to allow you to do. When jurors clearly understand the mechanism of injury (each step from impact through the disability or pain), they more likely will decide this issue your way. You need to convey that clarity here in opening.

This is dangerous area. Jurors seeking ways to minimize damages often focus aggressively on previous problems. Some jurors will think your client is trying to get money for problems he had before.

When the defense is going to claim your client had some of the problems before, use this part of opening to distinguish clearly and frankly between any previous problems and those you are seeking money for. Make clear you are seeking money only for what the defendant caused, not for anything from before.

Previous problems chart. Use the same chart you will use in testimony: a simple, double-column chart with previous problems in the left ("Before") column, and new problems and aggravations[6] in the right ("After") column. Starting in opening, emphasize that you want no money for the left column. As you talk through each "After" item, cite your experts' or treating doctors[7] explanations of how they know the defendant caused it. Refer back to your earlier explanations of the mechanism of how it happened.

If there are grey areas, tell jurors not to provide money for them unless they decide the defendant "more likely than not" caused them. This adds to your credibility and bolsters your preponderance theme. (See 5.45)

6.11

What Can the Jury Do about It: Charging the Jury

> Everything we show you in trial is for you to see why John should be compensated, and how much money will equal the amount of harm the truck driver caused. By the end of trial you'll see why the evidence will force me to come back and ask you for a verdict of $______ ______. You'll see that that amount equals the amount of harm the truck driver caused: the medical costs, the lost income, and the greatest harm in the case: the harm to John himself. The medical costs, lost income, and the substantial harm to John are the only things you can take into account for figuring out the proper amount of money.

Say "thank you" and sit down. No need for a big finish. Keep things rational at this point, not emotional.

If you cannot give a non-economics figure, end your opening with,

---

6. Do not say "aggravate." To most people it means "annoy," not "worsen." So instead of "It aggravated her back pain," say, "It made her back pain worse." Wait until closing to say "aggravate," when you are massaging the instructions and can explain what it means after the jurors already understand the issue. See 9.7.
7. "Treating doctors" is an unfamiliar term to many jurors. Say, "John's own doctors."

> Everything we show you in trial is for you to see why John should be compensated, and how much money will equal the amount of harm the truck driver caused. By the end of trial, you'll see why the evidence will force me to ask you for $___________ for John's medical expenses and lost income. And you'll understand the substantial harm to John beyond just those costs. The judge will give you (a) question(s) asking how much money will *equal all the harm*—medical bills and lost income, plus money for [the greatest harm in the case:][8] the substantial harm to John himself. The medical bills, lost income, and the substantial harm to John himself are the only things you are allowed to use for figuring out the proper amount of money. (See 9.9 for how to continue this crucial theme in closing.)

There's a long-standing debate about whether or not to give a verdict figure in opening. The answer is yes. Jurors actually complain when you do not specify a figure. They want guidance. Give them that guidance when it will do you the most good: *before* your case-in-chief. You want your figure in the jurors' heads the whole time they are hearing testimony about what the defendant did wrong, how he caused harm, and how bad the harm was.

6.12
Stipulated Liability

With minor adjustments, the same structure for opening—somewhat abbreviated according to what will be admissible—works well when the defense stipulates negligence or liability.

Stipulated Liability Case. Part One. Rule and Consequence

Focus on money:

8. If you can say that, do. If you cannot make such a comparison, omit the bracketed words. Do it instead with your hands: Hand low, palm up to represent the $125,000 meds and lost income; hand much higher when you say, "the substantial harm to John himself." See Chapter 9, "Closing" for other suggestions.

When a truck driver's negligence harms a pedestrian, the pedestrian is entitled to an amount of money equal to the level of the harm.

Stipulated Liability Case. Part Two. Story (What The Defendant Did)

Tell as much of the bad stuff as allowed. Argue to get in as much as possible. For example, tell the judge that part of the harm is your client's vivid and painful memory of what happened. The traumatic memory of the defendant's truck careening at her across the median is causing her emotional harm now, so it is material to damages.

Often a plaintiff's anguish is exacerbated by knowing that this would not have happened if the defendant had just followed a few simple rules. A psychologist can validate this exacerbation. It makes the way the defendant violated the rules a material consideration for damages.

Stipulated Liability Case. Part Three. Blame (Who We Are Suing and Why?)

Again, include all you can get in. Try to cover each thing the defendant did wrong, why it was wrong, how it caused harm, what the defendant should have done, how easy that would have been, and how that would have prevented the harm. Technically this may or may not be material, but include as much as the judge will allow.

Stipulated Liability Case. Part Four. Undermine (What Is Wrong with the Liability Defenses?)

If the defendant's denial of negligence all along until the eve of trial can be seen as causing harm, it can add to your client's anguish that the defendant never accepted responsibility until it helped him with his trial strategy. "For three years, Jane had to live with the knowledge that the trucking company refused to admit its drunk driver did anything wrong—until the night before trial."

Stipulated Liability Case. Part Five. Damages (What Are the Harms and Fixes?)

Same as when nothing is stipulated.

Stipulated Liability Case. Part Six. Money (What Do You Want?)

Same as when nothing is stipulated.

When liability is stipulated, make sure that nothing excluded can unfairly prejudice jurors against your client. For example, a head injury can easily lead jurors to believe your client was not wearing her seat belt. So if she was wearing it, get it in if you can.

6.13

Keep Jurors Listening

With or without stipulations, the final parts of opening are about harm and money, so you want jurors listening intently.

Do not do anything to diminish their listening.

A common error late in opening, when you might feel jurors are growing restless, is to speed up or to skim. You should, of course, be sensitive to the restlessness of jurors. But the solution is not to omit things. And don't speed up or skim, because it makes jurors feel that what you are saying is unimportant—the worst possible impression when you are talking about harm and money.

Instead, slow down and speak to jurors more directly, conveying the impression that this is your most important topic. Take a step closer. Speak more quietly. Tell them this is your most important topic. Emphasize that they particularly need what you are now going to talk about.

To keep jurors listening through the end of your opening, you must keep the earlier parts of opening succinct. Not fast but succinct. Jurors listen less when you use five words where two will do, and when you repeat unimportant stuff over and over. Jurors resent it.

"Succinct" means using the fewest possible words. You must remove excess verbiage, and practice your opening out loud a number of times—each time paying attention to, among other things, speaking concisely. Most attorneys use two or three times more words than necessary. So jurors stop listening and get annoyed with the attorney and his case.

Speaking succinctly takes practice. It means overcoming five bad habits from law school:

1. **Do not use too many words to make each point.**

2. **Do not repeat obvious information.** "At approximately 8:45 P.M. late in the evening of October the twelfth, in the year nineteen hundred and ninety-seven . . ." can be said in seven words instead of 20. It need be said just once. After the first time, just say, "That night." Do not keep parroting time and place or any other such information, as if jurors are stupid. A juror told me that half-way through a recent trial she started keeping track of how many times "the idiot" repeated the entire date. Total: more than 100.

3. **Do not use the passive voice.** It uses more words than necessary, and it is less effective and interesting than the active voice. The passive voice "The car was hit by the truck" is 40% longer and 100% less emphatic than the active "The truck hit the car." "The truck hit the car" is five direct, effective words instead of seven boring, indirect, "legal speak" words.

4. **Do not give speeches.** Talk to jurors the way you talk in real life. Speeches entail a formality of demeanor and tone. Unlike half a century ago, jurors do not listen to speeches or trust them.

5. **Never be satisfied with semi-clarity in place of crystal clarity.** Express your points clearly enough to be understood by every juror the first time, not just by you.[9]

Too many words, repetition, passive voice, giving speeches, and lack of clarity: If you conquer these problems, jurors will still be listening when you get to the money parts of your opening. In fact, they will listen to you carefully throughout trial, and listen willingly in closing instead of thinking, "Is he *ever* gonna shut up?"

9. The test: Gather a group of eight or ten average-intelligence 14-year olds. Give them your opening. Then give them a written test to see how much they understood and absorbed. Anything they miss, the jurors will also miss.

6.14
Openings: Miscellaneous Points

Fear of not understanding. Even in "simple" cases, many jurors fear they will never be able to understand what they need to understand in order to make a decision. The National Jury Project's Susan Macpherson advises that you assure jurors early in opening (if not in voir dire) that everything will be clear. Demonstrate in all you say that you are their unfailing provider of clarity. This will help make them listen to you and trust you.

Showing them and assuring them you will be clear is especially important when the instructions or evidence are either complex or unfamiliar to everyday experience. For example, some jury instructions make the assignment and computation of damages sound impossibly complex or vague. From the first time you talk, and every time after that, show that you will make everything clear and concrete.

Think of yourself as the jurors' guide. Get them to think of you that way. If you establish yourself that way early, jurors will more likely still be listening intently as you get to the important damages parts at the end of opening, and even when you get to closing.

Ease of preventing the wrongdoing. Remember that jurors tend to give more money when they think the defendant could easily have avoided the wrongdoing. When avoiding the wrongdoing seems hard or complicated—or even difficult to understand—jurors tend to give less.

Show the right thing the defendant should have done and how easy and simple it would have been. Make the jurors feel that they themselves could easily have done the right thing in the defendant's place. Help them clearly understand the right thing, and its simplicity: "Stick the label here." "Follow this rule." "Give the test before giving the drug." "Look at what you're doing."

Remember: You cannot be clear when you use technical, medical, or legal language.

When jurors do not understand, say, the right way to have done the surgery, they think it was complicated and difficult. This makes them think a bad outcome was hard to avoid, so that the wrongdoing was inadvertent instead of the result of conscious choices that should not have been made.

In opening, in testimony, and in closing, explain in the simplest, clearest terms (and with the use of the clearest possible visuals) what should have been done. Jurors who clearly understand the right way are less forgiving of the wrong way. Argue, "One reason we're suing is because doing it the right way would have been so easy."

Motivations. This was one of the most important concepts in the first edition of this book—yet the most ignored. Let's try again, and *please* heed. Motivations are the foundation of belief. The most persuasive way to convince jurors that someone did what you claim is to show the motivations that led the person to do it. So if you want the jury to believe someone did something or chose not to, provide the person's motivations.

If you do not show motivations, jurors will make them up—and they may or may not drive the action or omission you are trying to prove. It is not enough to say the radiologist read the X-ray too fast. Many jurors do not easily believe a doctor would do such a thing. Some think "Why would someone who cared about helping people, who cared enough to go to all those years of medical school, who cared enough to study hard, who cared enough to invest years and lots of money, suddenly turn around and speed through reading an X-ray?" They are interpolating the motivation of "caring." Suggest a different motivation: His daughter's birthday party was at 6 P.M. that evening and he could not be late. So he was motivated to speed through his work in time to get to the party. It's not an evil motivation, but it is dangerous—and makes it easier for jurors to believe he did what you say he did. Sure, it excuses him a little, but better for the jurors to excuse him a little than to believe he did nothing that requires excusing.

Do not merely claim the driver was speeding. Show his motivation: Why he was in a hurry to get where he was going?

Do not merely claim the manufacturer chose not to put a necessary warning label on the chemistry set. Show how the manufacturer was motivated by the fear that a warning label would scare off buyers.

Money is one of the most common motivations for wrongdoing. The nurse had to work too fast because the hospital did not hire enough nurses—because the hospital wanted to save money. The manufacturer did not apply a warning label for fear it would discourage sales and thus result in less income. The truck was overloaded because more weight means more money.

Seek out what motivated the wrongdoing. Introduce the motivations in opening or (when possible) by jury voir dire questions (" . . . ever know anyone who . . . ?") Look for motivations during discovery. Find out where the defendant doctor was planning to go after the surgery. With every defendant, search for anything that can give clues to motivation. You do not need proof; you need only suggestions.

Motivations are the foundation of belief. They provide your favorable jurors with powerful tools to argue on your behalf in deliberations. And by showing why the defendant did something wrong, they make it easier for jurors to give significant money.

Caveat. Avoid making jurors think you lose the case if they do not believe your assertion of motivation. In closing, say: "We don't know why the radiologist sped through reading those X-rays. Because he had to be at a party at 6 P.M.? Or something else? We don't know and he's not telling. But *something* made him go too fast." This lets you suggest motivations the jurors will adopt—without losing if a juror disagrees.

Loss of consortium. Many jurors believe a spouse signs on "for better or for worse." When they hear your consortium claim, they wonder whether she read the marriage contract.

For a consortium claim to succeed, you have to show major, concrete harm to the spouse. Generalizations are not enough. You have to work as hard to show how the harm damaged the spouse as you do to show how it damaged the initial victim.

Tacking on a consortium claim as a brief afterthought results in little, if any, money. Worse, it harms your persuasive abilities for other issues—including compensation for the initial victim. Many consortium afterthought claims go like this: "And by the way, Mrs. Plaintiff should get some money too because she's a victim too. She has to take care of her husband and her sex life isn't what it used to be."

That is rarely enough to motivate jurors into giving her money. Instead, from the start and throughout the trial, position the harm to the spouse as among the most important harms in the case.

Often you do not need a consortium claim. When jurors understand how the spouse has been affected, they tend to take that into account when deciding verdict size. But pursuing the claim sometimes lets you to get more information into evidence about the harm to the spouse.

A useful strategy is to focus more on the harm to the spouse than on the harm to the injured person. This automatically encompasses the harm to the injured person because that is the source of the harm to the spouse. That magnifies the harm to the injured person while at the same time showing jurors the full degree of harm to the spouse.

6.15
Preponderance

The technique that began in jury voir dire of getting jurors to make their decisions on the basis of preponderance (see 5.44) should be continued in opening, or started in opening if you could not do it in voir dire.

> Dr. Simpson will tell you it's more likely than not that the truck was speeding. He'll also say it's certain, but first he'll use the phrase 'more likely than not' because we have to prove that it is more likely than not.

6.16

Delivering the Damages Message[10]

A trial is a human event. The more human you seem, the better. Following are some brief notes to help make you more human rather than less.

Talk like a human. During opening (and at all other times) do not talk like you went to law school. Use plain English, a normal conversational tone, and a warm but not ingratiating manner. Fake smiles are fake.

Go slowly. Everything is new to the jurors, so give them the chance to keep up with you.

Enunciate. Many jurors, more and more as time goes on, are of the age when hearing poorly-enunciated speech is difficult. This is especially true in the poor acoustics of most courtrooms. Speak clearly. The speech teacher at a local university theater department can give you easy exercises to help you better enunciate.

Speak up. Speaking quietly can seem dramatic—but not to jurors who can't hear it.

Eschew* PowerPoint *bullet points. PowerPoint has its effective uses but the display of bullet points during an opening or closing is not one of them. Especially in opening, keep the focus on yourself, not on brief phrases on a screen.

Dress approachably. Give away your black and your dark blue suits, or save them for funerals or when you're acting the part of a lawyer in a play. Blue suits and black suits not only place you squarely into the negative stereotype of trial lawyer (see Chapter 11), but they are power costumes. Jurors will relate to you better if you can be secure enough to seem approachable and modest, not distant and powerful. So wear browns, olive greens, grays, whatever you want—but no dark blue or black.

10. See *Theater Tips and Strategies for Jury Trials* by David Ball (NITA, 2003) for further guidance of this kind.

Decorate yourself modestly and moderately. No Rolex watches or the like. No expensive pens (send them to me for safekeeping).

Men, no expensive haircuts, and lose the toupee or leave it at home for the cat to play with. Do *not* send it to me. And don't peer at jurors over half-lens reading glasses.

Women, no expensive or attention-grabbing jewelry or other accouterments. If that engagement ring is an eye-popper, wear a surrogate in trial. And while there is no research to back this up, it is probably better not to change hair color before trial ends.

Talk for how long? Jurors will listen for as long as they think they need what you are saying. Don't talk longer because they won't listen.

But claims that modern Americans have short attention spans do not match experience. People read, and they watch movies, plays, and sporting events for hours without getting bored. The social scientists who say attention span is short are not showing their subjects anything very interesting or useful. Jurors listen as long as you are useful (or dancing, singing, and telling jokes). Openings using the structure outlined in this chapter will come across as useful for an hour or more, but only if necessary. Longer requires you be *very* useful, but if you stay strictly within the confines of the structure, you should be able to go longer effectively.

The rule of thumb is to aim for 40 to 45 minutes, and as you develop your opening see how much shorter or longer it needs to be.

Eye contact. Don't say anything unless you have eye contact with a juror. Move your eye contact from juror to juror frequently; no one likes to be stared at. And do not look at the floor or the wall behind the jurors or at your notes. None of those things vote.

Movement. Don't dance aimlessly back and forth. Stand in one place and talk to the jurors. Move when there's reason to. If you have a dancing or wandering problem, rehearse your opening wearing just one shoe.

Rehearse. Rehearse your opening a number of times, the more the better. But never rehearse in front of a mirror. Instead, videotape yourself so you can watch later and take notes for improvement.

For best results, rehearse two or three times in front of different "juries" made up of people you do not know and who are not in the legal profession. First run your jury voir dire on them, and then do your opening. Get their reactions afterwards. The nearer you can do this to the start of trial, the better. Do this live preview for one trial and you will always do it, because you'll see how much better you feel and do once trial starts.

Notes. Do not memorize anything or you will sound memorized, which means fake. Do not read your opening. Speak from skeletal notes typed large enough to see from a few feet away (18 in most fonts, and upper and lowercase, not all caps) so all you have to do is glance at them now and then.

Lighting. If the blinds are open behind the jury, shut them in advance so you can see the jurors and not just their silhouettes. If the blinds are open behind you, shut them for the same reason.

Courtroom technology. Remember at every moment in trial that *a trial is a human event.* Technology is not human. It can help, but do not make the trial about technology. Mom's Thanksgiving dinner is about mom and dinner, not the stove. Trial is about your client and you, not about a computer or projection equipment or remote controls. Use technology sparingly and relegate it to the background.

Mantra. "I'm a person and these jurors are people."

CHAPTER SEVEN

DIRECT EXAMINATION

Remember the damages goal: to spend half your time on harm and money. Among other things, this means you need more harms and damages witnesses than you may think. Early in the planning for trial, cast a wide net for possibilities.

7.1
Who and How Many?

Client. Try not to use your client as a main source of testimony about harms or he can seem like a whiner even if he does not whine. No one likes people who complain about their own problems. Jurors are motivated to give money when they hear others describe the problems and your client talks about how he tries to overcome them.

When there is permanent harm that seriously interferes with how your client lives her life, ask her what her long-term plans had been before she was hurt. Then ask her how she is pursuing the fragment of those plans she still can. This shows her to be unwilling to give up.

Spouse. A spouse, if there is one, should testify. But a spouse has an obvious interest in how the case turns out, so you need others to corroborate such as, in some circumstances, the children. More distant family members—those who do not stand to gain from the verdict—are effective. So are neighbors, coworkers, friends, clergy, and anyone else in a position to know the situation. Look for those who know the harm and can best communicate it. The obvious choice is not always the best. Audition your possibilities.

Effect witnesses. When the injuries have healed, you need witnesses to describe the effect the injuries had while they lasted.

Before-and-after-witnesses. Where the consequences of the injuries are ongoing, you need witnesses to describe your client's condition before the injury and witnesses who can talk about the way things are now. Some witnesses will be able to compare before with after, but others may be able to speak only to one or the other. Use both to present a comprehensive picture.

How many? There should be no fewer harms witnesses than liability witnesses. Three or four is okay for a small case. In larger or longer cases, ten or fifteen is better. Different people see different things about the situation, so no need for this to be repetitious.

7.2
Stories

Good harms testimony is story based. A witness who merely reports abstractly or in generalized conclusions ("She can't do much any more" or "She's unhappy now") is less effective than a witness who gives story illustrations.

A witness might say "She had incredible energy before; now she's tired all the time." Ask him, "Give us an example of her incredible energy," and "What have you seen since she was hurt that shows she's always tired now?"

"She's tired all the time" says little. "She's always hurting" is weak. Jurors barely notice such general stuff. They remember mini-stories. "We'd go shopping and she'd make me go into every store in the mall. During Christmas shopping the year before she got hurt, her sisters and me and the kids finally just dropped our packages and collapsed and couldn't move. She kept right on going. The kids called her the Energizer shopping bunny. But last week I took her to the mall and she was so exhausted from just getting there that she could only sit on a bench while I shopped."

There is little the defense can do to wipe out that mini-story or diminish its effectiveness.

In venues where wrongful death claims include losses to survivors, use witnesses to show the differences in the family before and after the death. Have the witnesses tell mini-stories to illustrate these differences. The jurors already know the general kind of loss any surviving family undergoes; you need mini-stories for specifics.

An effective mini-story to elicit in cases of severe injury or death is to have each affected person describe where they were and what they were doing when they first heard of the death, and how they reacted. The reaction should include what they did and why, as well as what they felt.

North Carolina attorney Don Beskind suggests getting family members to talk about your client's past role in specific family events, such as decorating the tree or carving the turkey—and what happened the first time your client could not do that, or was no longer alive to do it.

7.3
Witnesses as Sources for Worthwhileness

Your client, along with before-and-after witnesses and other people who may or may not actually testify, can serve an additional purpose. They can suggest worthwhile uses for money. Such uses can also be powerful additions to your opening.

Ask everyone who knows the situation—not just potential witnesses—what good money might do beyond paying care and living expenses. While most answers will not be useful, some will be persuasive.

I asked the neighbor of a West Virginia quadriplegic plaintiff, "He'll never heal, so what's the point of money beyond care and living expenses?" This neighbor was not going to be a witness. All he knew about the case was that the plaintiff was paralyzed. But he had an answer:

"Ed loved hunting. He never shot anything, I don't think, but he loved those woods. Now he's stuck inside this city apartment forever. If he had some money, his wife could buy a mountain place where she could wheel him onto the back porch every day and he'd be back out in the woods he loves."

Not many jurors would turn a deaf ear to that.

A New Jersey plaintiff had reflex sympathy dystrophy in her arm. The slightest touch was excruciating. I asked her, "What good can money do you? Your pain won't go away." "I miss my grandchildren," she said. "They live out west. They're too young to fly to see me, so I have to go there. But I never know from one day to the next when I'll be well enough to fly, so I can't get cheap advance-purchase tickets any more. Even if I could, the aisles on the plane are so narrow that I can't take the chance that the stewardess might bump my arm as she goes by. It's too painful and it happens all the time. Or whoever's sitting next to me could accidentally do it. If I had enough money for a wider seat up front, and if I didn't need an advance purchase cheap ticket but could buy the ticket on a day when I felt well enough to travel that day instead of having to guess weeks in advance, I could see my grandchildren a lot."

All by itself, this will not get you a huge verdict. But a few things like this can give a large intangibles damages request some worthwhile substance.

Spend time with family members. They will usually have no suggestions at first, but after some discussion they are likely to think of something "My husband lies awake. I ask him what's wrong and he says he's worrying about how to pay for college for the kids now that he can't work anymore."

There is no element of damages that goes to paying the kids' tuition. But because the husband's worry is a consequence of the wrongdoing, you can show what he is worried about. You can argue in closing that therapy cannot fix this particular harm—his worrying—but that the jury can fix it with money. College tuition for his kids may not be a recoverable item, but money to remove the worry is. Since it is money that serves a worthwhile purpose, jurors are likely to include it in their verdict.

It can take some creativity to get some of these ideas into evidence, but you can almost always do it. It is worth doing, because they show how money for your client is worthwhile.

7.4

Sequence of Witnesses: Weave in Harm and Money Witnesses

Weave in harm and money witnesses. Do not bunch all your harm and money witnesses at the end. Keep harm and money on the jurors' minds throughout your case-in-chief. Weave in harm testimony, followed by testimony about money (costs of care, lost income, etc.). Alternate between loss/harm/money witnesses and liability witnesses.

First witness. Your first witness should come as close as possible to meeting the following four criteria:

1. She should be able to tell some significant part (not necessarily the largest part) of the overall story: either what the defendant did or the results of what the defendant did. (Your first witness should not talk about what your client did. See Chapter 6 for a description of this principle in opening.)

   For example, your first witness can be someone who saw the defendant driver coming fast and swerving onto the sidewalk where your client was standing. This is a significant part of the story.

2. Your first witness should be able to speak at least a little to the harm that was done—such as seeing how hard the car hit your client.

3. Your first witness should have no stake in the outcome. If your client's spouse is first, he will likely be met with suspicion by some jurors because he has a stake in the outcome. Jurors likely will respond more positively to him later on, when his testimony will support what non-interested witnesses have already said.

4. Your first witness must be cross-proof. Your opponent's cross-examination of your first witness is the first time jurors see your case tested in the crucible of truth, cross-examination. Jurors have heard you make your claims and now for the first time see your credibility tested. They are primed to create their first belief about your credibility. Your trustworthiness is on the line.

If your witness holds up under cross, the jurors' initial belief will be that you are credible. If the cross-exam shows holes in your claims, the jurors' initial belief will be that you are not altogether credible.

Due to primacy (see 5.2), that initial belief will linger throughout trial. It can diminish everything you say and present. So no matter how much of an overview of your case a witness can provide, do not use her first if she can be impeached in any significant way.

7.5
Children

Often, good witnesses to a plaintiff's losses happen to be children, sometimes small children. This can make for effective testimony. But some jurors will have problems with your bringing a child to court. (See 7.5)

Be careful not to appear to be exploiting the child or to be putting the child through anything jurors might construe as hurtful or harmful. That makes them resent you and listen to the child less carefully. Treat that child in court as if it were your own and you were an excellent, gentle parent.

In some venues, wrongful death losses include, or are limited to, the dead person's losses, as opposed to the losses of the survivors. Connecticut's Ernie Teitel advises that in such a situation, it can be especially useful to bring in the deceased's children. But do not have them speak of their losses. Simply have them describe, in an upbeat way, what their lives are like: what they do at school, in sports, in clubs; what their achievements have been . . . all the things the deceased has missed out on. This can be excellent testimony because you can keep it entirely upbeat and positive, yet it goes to the heart of the losses.

7.6
Grief and Pain Counselors

Grief counselors, disability counselors, pain specialists and counselors, and other counselors and therapists who specialize in the emotional, psychological, and other consequences of suffering and loss can be excellent sources for information to help your damages case.

By studying your case, these experts can find and explain the real and hidden harms; provide concrete insights into the consequences of the injury, disabilities, pain, emotional suffering, and grieving that your client or the surviving family is dealing with; and the long-term consequences and how things will get worse instead of better. These experts provide you with information you cannot get from your clients, their acquaintances, other experts or treating physicians, or your own analysis. This information can be central to the jury's calculation of damages.

Merely saying, "It's ten on a scale of ten" does no more to describe pain than saying "dinner was good" describes dinner. Jurors need more to want to compensate your client. Grief and pain counselors will provide more.

You can use such a counselor as a witness or just as a pretrial resource to educate you about the losses. If one testifies, they can do so as experts or as treating therapists. Either way, they add professional and scientific authority—and thus tangibleness—to the subject of intangible losses.

7.7
Minimum Life-Care Plans (and Equivalents)

Jurors usually base their non-economic damages amount in large part on the economic amount. They use the economic damages amount as a benchmark, and then discuss non-economics as some degree or proportion more or less of that amount. Thus, the higher, the more concrete, and the more persuasive your economic damages figure is, the more money you are likely to get for non-economics as well. (See 4.1)

As a result, your most important damages asset can be the minimum life-care plan or an equivalent list. (In cases with no life-care plan, you can assemble a list: everything the treating physicians say will be—or was—necessary or helpful to treat and care for your client.)

Aside from helping get more money, such lists help jurors grasp the extent of the harm.

By effectively presenting the list in court, you will make the jurors accept it as valid and use it as their benchmark for determining an amount for non-economic damages.

The suggestions below assume the presence of a full-blown life-care plan. You can use many of the same strategies with a less formal list.

Some attorneys tend to rush testimony about the life-care plan because it seems tedious. It is quick and easy to describe a few representative examples of the items on the life-care plan, and then give a grand total. But that is what the defense hopes you will do. The defense does not want you to present your life-care plan carefully and concretely. The defense prefers you to leave the jury with only a vague idea of the life-care plan's content. This almost always results in jurors considering the life-care plan the way they think of non-economic damages: fuzzy stuff, something to be bargained over, a kind of prize for the plaintiff instead of a necessity.

Jurors with only a vague idea of the contents of the life-care plan often and easily compromise on its size.

Jurors tend to fight for giving the full amount of a life-care plan when they have concrete, specific knowledge of each item in it. This means they have to know:

a. What is it?

b. When was it invented?

c. What is it for?

d. How does it work?

e. Why is it necessary in this case?

f. How much does it cost
(per each and over the term of the plan)?

g. What happens if the plaintiff does not get it?

Do not worry if this takes a long time. You might want to explain in voir dire or opening that this section of trial will take a while because so much is needed to take care of your client—and the jurors need to know about all of it in order to figure out how much money to provide. Build that same point into an early question to your minimum life-care planner "These folks have to figure out what Sally needs and how much money to provide for it, so let me start by asking you . . . ."

Think of your life-care planner as your centerpiece. Put her on for the better part of a day. In long trials, continue her direct into a second day. You don't want her testimony buried.

Treat each important item on the life-care plan as a separate issue to be proven.

Show-and-tell. Turn your life-care planner's testimony into a magnificent show-and-tell. Have her bring things to court—the leg braces, the special dinnerware, the Velcro fasteners for clothing, the urinary catheter, etc. Pass these things around the jury.

Have your life-care planner teach the jury what these things are for, specifically how they are used, and what makes them work. Have her show videos of the kinds of therapy in her plan. Show a blow-up photo of the rehabilitation center.

Make every important item memorable. Do that not with words but with the objects themselves (pass them around), with pictures, with videos, with tactile demonstrations. These are important fixes and helps. Nothing is more important for the jurors to take with them into deliberations.

Words are never enough. Neither are tiny pictures from a medical supply catalog. Minimum life-care planners who do their jobs right probably need to drive large vans to haul all the stuff.

See 9.6 for how to follow up in closing on your minimum life-care planner's presentation or your informal list.

Warning. Before presenting a minimum life-care plan, edit it carefully. Omit anything that can seem unnecessary or frivolous. Even if there is good reason for that swimming pool, get rid of it. Some jurors will find it frivolous. That will undermine the rest of the plan's validity. It is crucial that jurors have total confidence in the validity and necessity of every part of the plan.

For the same reason, make sure the prices seem reasonable. Some items are expensive only when purchased from a medical supply house. That $250 canvas chair might cost $14.95 in a regular store. A minimum life-care plan with seemingly overpriced items undermines juror confidence in your entire case, including liability. So scrutinize for necessity and reasonable price. Your planner is the expert but you are the jury expert. You must override the minimum life-care planner's judgment and remove anything that seems frivolous or expensive, or that seems like padding—unless you can clearly show it to be essential and properly priced.

Please see 9.6 on how to bring your plan home in closing. It's an essential ingredient, and one of Don Keenan's brilliant additions to the store of plaintiff's advocacy skills.

7.8
Using other Witnesses for Damages

One of the dangers of fighting a difficult liability case is that jurors can go for hours, days, and sometimes weeks without hearing about harm or money. This seriously undermines your pursuit of one of the basic principles of damages: time proportion. Out of sight, out of mind. Using your liability experts for damages is an effective way to offset that problem.

Your liability expert who testifies why the light pole's location was dangerous can provide statistics about the number of severe injuries such placement has caused.

If your expert physician who testifies about standard of care can explain why that particular standard of care exists and the kind of harm it is intended to prevent, he can probably talk about the mechanism of the injury that results from the violation.

7.9
Day-in-the-Life Videos

Day-in-the-life videos are effective if they focus on the obstacles your client has to (or had to) face. But beware. When jurors see a day-in-the-life video, they often say "He's not as bad as they made it sound." Result: low verdict. So always test your day-in-the-life video in a focus group to see its effect.

"Staged!" Don't show anything that looks staged. One recent video showed a woman who had been disabled for two years struggling to open a jar of peanut butter. She had the use of only one arm. She tried several maneuvers that failed. Finally she discovered a way to do it. The camera caught it all

"Obviously staged!" said the jurors. And they were right. The woman did not actually discover how to open peanut butter while the camera just happened to be there and running. This undermined the juror's confidence in the video, the client's injuries, the attorney, and the case.

Videographer. A human being does not transform into a videographer just by buying a video camera. Before you use someone, look at samples of her work. Make sure she knows the basics—such as how to expose properly so that faces are easily visible. Make sure she knows the feel of a day-in-the-life video: emphasis on the obstacles, the pain, the difficult measures necessary to get through the day.

Time span. Videographers are often too literal about what "day-in-the-life" means. It need not end at the end of the day if there are night problems.

Principals. Many people are uncomfortable on camera for the first time. Often it is best to shoot over the course of several days. This also gives you more material to choose from.

Stranger in the house. Before the time the videographer begins to shoot, he should have spent a good amount of time with the client and family. This is partly to make them comfortable once they are on camera. It is also so the videographer can get familiar and comfortable with the things he's going to video.

Lighting. Avoid extra lighting for the camera unless absolutely necessary. Good video cameras produce good results even in very low light, especially with a videographer who knows how to take advantage of the light already present.

Windows. A videographer who puts his subjects between himself and a bright window will produce useless silhouettes, not striking images. A competent videographer does not do this. Look for this danger sign when you view a videographer's sample work before hiring.

Sound. If you are allowed sound in your video, it can be effective —or can undermine you. When watching the finished product, listen carefully to make sure the sound helps you. Dad cursing at the kids in the next room while mom lovingly helps the disabled child may not be the family image you wish to convey.

Background. Be careful what your video shows in the background or periphery. The injured child can be getting rehabilitative therapy in the living room on an exercise mat near a picture window. Very effective—unless the exercise mat is in front of the family's 84-inch projection-screen TV, which tells the jury that the last thing this family needs is money. (Especially with the matching Jaguars in the driveway outside the picture window.)

And regardless of the TV's size, turn it off. Even if people are listening in the next room, turn it off.

Jurors judge a family partly by its home. Make sure what the jurors see of the home on the video conveys the impression to you want. You need not show abject poverty. But if your day-in-the-life video shows an extravagant lifestyle, jurors will conclude that this family needs no money to take care of Junior.

Settlement conferences. A reliable day-in-the-life video (one that has been tested in front of lay strangers) can be powerful at a settlement conference—especially if the defendant and not just the defense attorneys and insurance adjusters are there. In fact, if the defendant has control over settlement, you should routinely demand he be there so he can feel the impact of your settlement presentation, and not just leave it to his lawyers and the insurance company.

Show a video that is 100 percent admissible. You can also have the commonly used kind of video made solely for the settlement conference that provides glimpses of what your case in trial will be like. But if your day-in-the-life video is a good one and will be admissible, it can provide strong ammunition for you at a settlement conference, because the defense knows the real jurors will see it.

7.10
Preponderance Technique

This is the continuation of the technique for getting jurors to make their decisions on the basis of preponderance. (See 5.45, 6.15, and 9.10.) Simply work the words "more likely than not" into your questions:

1. Q: Doctor, is your conclusion [never say "opinion"] that more likely than not the impact caused John's brain damage?

   A: Yes, more likely than not.

2. Q: Beyond that, is your conclusion to a reasonable degree of medical certainty?

   A: Yes.

3. Q: By "reasonable degree of certainty," you mean certainty based on reason?

   A: Yes.

4. Q: And beyond that, how sure are you?

   A: Absolutely sure.

Question 3 is necessary because to most jurors, "reasonable degree of certainty" sounds like "maybe." As North Carolina's Tracy K. Lischer points out, it is too easy to let an expert's opinion slide into being merely a supposition in the jurors' minds. Instead, work in the other direction, as shown above.

Do the same thing with fact witnesses:

1. Q: Miss Carlton, in your memory is it more likely than not that the light was green?

   A: Yes.

2. Q: And beyond that, how sure are you?

   A: I'm positive.

The goal is to use the phrase "more likely than not" as often as you can, and then follow it with, "How sure are you?"

7. 11
Should Your Client Be There?

One of the long-taught "basics" of trial advocacy is that your client should be present during trial. Often this is a bad idea. If your client looks better than she really is—as brain-damaged and a number of other kinds of clients often do—it is probably best that she never enter the courthouse. My research at JuryWatch shows that verdicts almost always go down when jurors see such clients.

For example, your brain-damaged client can do a great job on the stand and even withstand a forceful cross—despite your claim that she cannot think or remember well enough to keep a job. Jurors say, "She remembered all that stuff on direct and handled cross-examination better than I could. So her attorney and those 'experts' must be lying about brain damage."

In cases involving brain damage, intense pain, and other problems where much of the problem is invisible, do not automatically decide to bring your client to court. Keep her away unless you have good reason for bringing her in.

In weighing the factors, don't worry that the jury will "expect" her to be there, that they'll think if she's not there that she does not care about her case. When you explain that her doctors and family say it's better for her not to be in trial and have to relive everything all over again, the jurors will not fault her absence.

Keeping your client out of trial is an anti-intuitive concept. Many plaintiff's attorneys resist it. The proof of its effectiveness is that when the defense finds out, they try to get the judge to force her to be there. They do this because they know how powerful your client's appearance works against her.

In brain damage cases, the defense wants jurors to see that your client looks and sounds normal—even though how your client looks and sounds is a deceptive measure of her brain damage.

Some judges approve defense motions or subpoenas to force your client to be there. Be prepared to fight it. Argue that the defense has no right to inflict further harm on your client—the harm of having to re-live the trauma, the harm of her having to hear how hopeless her case is, and the harm of public humiliation. Have affidavits from her doctors specifying the harm this can cause. Argue that the defense knows that jurors will gauge her brain damage by the way she looks—something no expert in the world can do. The defense wants the judge to let the jury be misled. Have expert affidavits showing that non-experts will be misled by seeing her—so that her presence would misleadingly prejudice her case, and serve no probative purpose. Point out that there is no other reason the defense has to want her there.

Other than for testimony, the client's presence or absence is none of the defense's business, and really none of the judge's, either.

Juror Preparation. If the defense subpoenas your client to testify, or has her video deposition, have your experts explain to the jury in advance why she seems to be so much better than she really is. Do not position this defensively, but as a harm in itself. A person with brain damage or other harm that cannot be seen is constantly thrust into situations she cannot handle. The expectations people place on her—that she's normal and can do normal things—can result in painfully humiliating situations. No one expects a person missing a leg to walk or run. But people do expect a person missing millions of brain cells to think. This is one reason brain-damaged people tend to withdraw from society. They are in constant fear of being humiliated by being unable to do some commonplace thing such as remember how to get home from downtown.

Treat this as a compensable harm. Have your experts explain how anyone with brain damage can look good and talk cogently. Otherwise jurors will jump to erroneous conclusions when they see and listen to her in testimony. Their conclusions will be close to immutable. Explaining in advance can turn your client's later testimony into an illustration of the expert's explanation. But if your client testifies before anyone explains why she looks and sounds better than she really is, don't expect much money.

7.12
Client in and out of Trial

All the world's a stage—and the jurors are the audience. If the jury is ever going to see your client or even her picture, instruct your client that from the week before trial until the verdict is in, she has to assume that every time she goes out of her house jurors will see her. Smoking, drinking, rudeness, or anything else you would not want jurors to see in trial should be strictly avoided in public at all times—even in the next state, and no matter the time.

If your client is claiming she cannot work for a living again, she must not be seen driving. In fact, she probably should not be driving anyway. (See the caution note in 2.10.)

You should also be careful. Assume that there's a juror in every car you see. That includes the idiot who just cut in front of you and sharply slowed down. Before you give in to highway rage and begin flashing finger signals, consider that a juror (or judge) might be in that car. For the duration of trial, let motorists into your lane of traffic, don't steal anyone's parking space, and in every other way pretend to be a mature and generous adult when you're behind the wheel.

I'm collecting the horror stories that result when these simple guidelines are not followed. Please send me any true examples. And someday you'll hear the nightmare story of the foreperson and the drunk-driving plaintiff fighting to park their giant SUVs in the same space during a snowstorm.

7.13
The Best and the Cheapest

In every community, there is an ample supply of first-rate expert witnesses who can testify on a wide variety of topics. Explore this resource especially, but not exclusively, for smaller cases where you have no money to bring in the usual high-priced array. For between $50 and $100 an hour you can often solve some of the biggest problems in your case.

For example: A car hit the rear of your client's car at only five miles per hour. Barely made a dent. You know jurors will say things like "My Uncle Benny's car rolled over three times, it was flattened to a pancake, and Uncle Benny walked out just fine. So how can someone be hurt as bad as this lawyer says in a car that's got hardly a dent?"

You also know if you had the money to bring in an accident reconstructionist or a physicist, you could convince jurors that this little rear-ender can result in plenty of injury. But the case can't afford it, so you can't do it. Result? You win liability and get a verdict of a dollar or two.

So what do you do?

Bring in someone from the best repository of testifying experts you can find: high school teachers.

They need not provide opinions. All they have to do is explain (and perhaps demonstrate) a principle or a process. Good high school teachers know how to relate to the people they are teaching. They bring with them more credibility—especially locally—than many professional witnesses. And high school teachers are often more cooperative and easier to work with.

High school teachers are the world's experts on teaching complex concepts to people who know nothing about them and do not particularly want to learn.

A well-selected local high school physics teacher can explain how a six-mile-an-hour impact can leave barely any dent on the car but still injure your client inside. "You would never put your hand between those cars as they hit. There's too much force. Now, that force has to go someplace. It can't just disappear. Much of it goes into abruptly shoving the car forward. The less dent, the more forcefully it shoves the car forward, because making a dent would absorb more of the energy. So a smaller dent means the impact jars the car forward more forcefully. So forceful that it can bounce a head back and forth harder and sharper than anyone's neck can take. Here, look at this." And he shows his Mr. Wizard demonstration.

What "Mr. Wizard demonstration"? For a few hundred dollars, the teacher can devise and build a Mr. Wizard demonstration of how the force of impact goes from the back bumper to moving your client's neck. Such a show-and-tell demonstration makes it easier for jurors to believe that a low-speed rear impact can injure the driver.

You'll use that Mr. Wizard demonstration along with this high school teacher in case after case—for a fraction the cost of far less persuasive "professionals."

Another useful Mr. Wizard demonstration for a high school physics teacher to create: The mechanism of a contra-coup brain injury. Good animations do this well, but animations are not allowed in some venues, and even when allowed, they do not teach the physics of the process as well as an actual demonstration.

7.14
Paid Plaintiff's Experts

With or without high school teachers, you will often have expensive experts. When the defense asks them how much they are being paid, the sole purpose is to impeach them by attacking their motive for testifying. Some judges—not all—will agree that this opens the door to you showing their real motives.

On redirect, this means you should be able to question the expert about his real motives—such as the fact that "With 650 people a day dying in hospitals from negligence, those of us doctors who care about good medicine more than protecting careless doctors participate in trials like his when we are certain that medical negligence caused the harm." Or, "I know how they build cars in Detroit; I worked there 25 years. Too much of it is careless and purely profit driven, and that kills too many people. So when I see a case like this, where someone was killed because of that kind of thing, I want to help a jury set things right."

Such motivation can also explain why this expert testifies so often for plaintiffs: "The companies don't need me. They already know what they're doing wrong."

7.15
Purpose of the Expert

The real purpose of an expert is not to give conclusions, but to teach jurors come to their own conclusions. The best weapon against opposition experts is not your experts' credentials (though field work beyond the theoretical is helpful). The best weapon is for you to structure the expert's testimony as follows:

1. Have him explain his methodology for analyzing cases like this *in general*. Make no reference to this particular case. This anchors his expertise and methodology. It must be clear enough for the average juror to take home and explain to his average 14-year-old kid.

2. Show the jury how to use his methodology on the facts of the case—and how that leads, step by step, to his conclusion. This too must be clear enough for the average juror to take home and explain to his average 14-year-old kid.

This simple one-two combination carries more persuasive weight than all the credentials and authoritative pronouncements in the world. Add to it some textual references that back up both numbers 1 and 2, and the defense will have a frustrating time trying to dislodge your expert's testimony.

If an expert is not good at both numbers 1 and 2, don't use that expert again and warn your colleagues. Useful experts are good methodology teachers.

CHAPTER EIGHT
CROSS-EXAMINATION

Most often the defense case pushes your harms case out of the spotlight. Don't let it. Keep the jurors thinking about harm at every opportunity.

8.1
Hitchhiking: Using Defense Liability Experts for Damages

Defense experts are not going to break down during your cross and say, "Oh my, I have been making a terrible mistake. Your client is really severely depressed after all, and I just missed it. He'll never work again. No way. All from that brain damage. Wow. How could I have been so wrong? Sorry."

So since you can't get far taking him head on when it comes to liability, try first to make use of him. Give him something new to talk about: harm. And quote him in closing.

"Hitchhiking" is the subversion of defense liability experts into plaintiff's damages experts. Rather than (or in addition to) fighting them on negligence or causation, embrace them to help you with damages:

Q: Doctor, John's brain damage is minor?

A: Very minor.

Q: Not enough to cause severe depression?

A: Not at all.

Q: You have the experience to know?

A: I do.

Q: You have patients with depression?

A: Of course.

Q: Severe?

A: Yes.

Q: So severe nothing can help?

A: I have patients like that.

Q: Permanently?

A: Yes.

Q: They can never hold a job again?

A: Yes.

Q: You understand why their severe depression keeps them from working?

A: Obviously.

Q: Such as _________?

A: Yes.

Q: And _________?

A: Yes.

Q: And _________?

A: Yes.

Q: And _________?

A: Yes.

Q: And _________?

A: Yes.

And so forth. You have just added a damages expert, and it's on the defense tab.

This works in many situations. A defense expert testifies your client's back problem is from a previous condition. Before or instead of battling that, explain through him what makes a back problem so painful, disabling, and permanent.

When hitchhiking, be friendly. The witness is on your side for this sequence, and you want that to be apparent to the jurors.

When a defense expert claims the defendant did not cause your client's bad back, that expert will probably still agree that that kind of bad back incapacitates and hurts. Hitchhike; he's got to pick you up. And it can be a great ride.

Do the same thing concerning patients whose brain damage does not show on imaging. By gently challenging the expert's qualifications to know about such things, you can probably get her to tell the jury how there can be brain damage that does not image, and how she can be sure that some of her own patients have brain damage even though it does not image.

This method is extremely valuable with maladies some jurors have trouble believing in. For example, some jurors have great difficulty believing that depression is involuntary and powerful. This can be worse for your case than what the defense standard-of-care defense expert says about liability. But that standard of care expert has to admit that depression is real, that his own patients who complain of depression really have it, that it is involuntary, that it can be incapacitating, that many patients cannot ever be cured, that you cannot look at a person and see it, etc. So use this defense witness to help you with those jurors. Let him turn depression and its consequences real for your jurors.

Defense will object. "This is not what he's here to testify about!" But this is cross-examination. You're trying to see if this expert knows anything about this kind of problem. So this is fair game.

The only thing he will not admit is that this kind of problem did not happen to your client—but the witness wasn't going to admit that anyway.

Use this method before attacking the defense expert's liability opinions. You do not want to undermine credibility before he talks about your harms.

Starting cross with harms questions can also have the benefit of relaxing the expert and taking him off guard: he does not start cross-examination in conflict with you. You might even develop some rapport with him. That leaves him vulnerable to later impeachment.

Here are other effective cross-examination measures for defense liability experts:

> You've had patients with ________, yes?
>
> Sometimes there was nothing you could do to make it any better, right?
>
> Some of those patients had to stop working at their jobs, right?
>
> And some never got back to work?
>
> Why not?

> Doctor, have you ever changed the diaper on a 20-year old?
>
> Know anyone who has?
>
> Why does she have to?

> Doctor, depression can be real, yes?
>
> You've treated it?
>
> Patients cannot get rid of it just by wishing, can they?
>
> Doctor, you treat patients with depression?

Some of them dozens of times?

Over a period of years?

How much does it cost per visit?

Why don't they get better?

Why don't they just 'go home and cheer up'?

A blade that flies off the shaft could hurt someone, right?

Could hit the user in the face?

The blade could be going fast enough to cut to the bone?

It could blind a person?

An electrical explosion can hurt someone?

Burn through the skin?

All three layers of skin?

When seeking future lost income for permanent incapacity to work, ask the defense standard of care expert, "Doctor, what makes you a good doctor?" The doctor may give you some indispensable qualities or abilities. If not, ask, "Doctor, in a job like yours, do you also need to be able to ____?" "Yes." "And ________?" Fill in the blank with indispensable qualities or abilities. Then ask, "Doctor, if something happened to you so that you no longer had those qualities or abilities [name them], you wouldn't still be able to do your job, right? You'd be out of work?"

In closing, connect that with your client's situation.

The president of the defendant manufacturing company will deny there was a design defect. But:

—"Mr. Barber, your saw can cut through a leather jacket?"

—"Through human skin?"

—"Bone?"

—"Even the largest bone in someone's arm?"

In such ways, the defense can be your best damages ally.

Here is a mental exercise to help you make the most extensive use of defense witnesses. Ask yourself how you would present your entire case if you were to have no case-in-chief, but only cross-exam of defense witnesses. See how much you can get in. In some cases, you will be able to show that every fact and assertion in your case is corroborated by one or another of the defense witnesses.

In trial, do your case-in-chief in the normal way—but in closing, point out that you could have done without your own witnesses because the defense did it all for you. Then take the jurors through every link of your case citing "*only* the defense witnesses, ladies and gentlemen."

Hitchhiking can get you a long way. But like hitchhiking on the highway, it can be dangerous unless you carefully prepare. A well-armed highway hitchhiker will safely get where he's going. The same is true in trial.

Hitchhiking gathers evidence in a powerful and interesting way. It keeps the jurors' minds on harm and damages during the defense's liability case. Like highway hitchhiking, it's free. Unlike highway hitchhiking, you don't even have to say thank you.

8.2

Undermining Defense Life-Expectancy Estimates

Life-expectancy estimates from the defense are often based on junk science or no science at all. They are partisan-based, not scientific. When a defense expert says your client will live until, say, 35 instead of 82, ask the expert if he will pay for her care for each additional year she lives.

> When she calls you at age 36, will you send her the money you're trying to keep her from getting now?
>
> You don't want that gamble?

This question has a good-faith impeachment basis; it establishes he is not positive his conclusion is correct. Nonetheless, be prepared for an objection, though the defense will not quite know any grounds. The judge may sustain it anyway. But you've already made your point.

In closing, point out that if anyone should be forced to gamble, it's the defendant who put your client in this position.

No one can predict when anyone will die. Doctors can be somewhat accurate with an acute situation where death is days, weeks, or months away. But when it is a matter of years, all doctors can do is guess. So object to the defense guess coming in. It is junk-science based, using and calling for speculation, and rests on insufficient statistical data. Disease-process does not reliably predict mortality; it is often wrong by decades.

If the defense guess does get in, have your expert make those same points with the jury. In trial, position the defense expert as arrogant—playing God—by predicting what no mortal in history has ever been able to guess. And in closing remind the jury that the defense expert has no confidence in his own prediction because he will not put his money where his mouth is.

In jury voir dire, ask jurors who they have known or heard of who outlived what the doctors predicted. Ask the juror why he thinks that happened.

8.3

Undermining Malingering and Exaggeration of Symptoms

No physician has a scientific way to say to a reasonable degree of medical certainty that someone is faking or exaggerating. So on cross, probe the "science" behind what he is saying. There is none. A patient can be in dire pain with no possible objective verification or measurement. So calling her a malingerer or exaggerator is nothing but guesswork.

If your client is not very credible, try to have such junk-science testimony barred. Virginia attorney Roger Creager has had some success having such testimony barred. See Appendix F.

If it is not barred, invite the defense witness propounding malingering or exaggeration to explain the science backing up his claims. Have your own experts give you the information in advance to help you show on cross that the defense claims derive from partisan guessing, not science.

If your client is credible, do not try to bar defense testimony on malingering, exaggeration, or any other topic that makes your client out to be lying. When you have a credible client, such testimony can be a gift. See 9.23.

8.4
"Litigation Syndrome" and Other Bogusaria[1]

The defense may claim your client has "litigation syndrome" or some such malady. Only unicorns really get it. The defense expert will explain that it is an unconscious (and thus not dishonest) syndrome in which your client is under the delusion that her problems still exist when they do not.

It is called "litigation syndrome" or whatever (the nomenclature of Bogusaria has not yet been regularized) because it will end when the case ends. When suffering from "litigation syndrome," the litigant becomes so focused on her injuries over the course of litigation that they have lasted this long only because there's a case going on. "Otherwise she'd be cured, yes indeed!"

Maybe it's possible. So is the Loch Ness monster. Yet it's enormously prejudicial. (I guess the Loch Ness monster is prejudicial, too.) A responsible judge will ask for its scientific basis and find there

1. "Bogusaria" /bo-gus-ar-i-a/ —abbreviated "BS"—is any of a category of medical maladies that exist only for purposes of defense testimony. It is apparently admissible.

is none. "Litigation syndrome" is an invented malady no one has ever had. It is a diagnosis used nowhere in medicine except for purposes of litigation. No treating physician tells a patient, "Oh, your signs and symptoms are just *litigation syndrome*; you'll be fine when the case ends."

That would violate a physician's duty to do a differential diagnosis.

If a defense expert claims "litigation syndrome," ask how he would deal with such a patient in his clinic. Would he do a differential diagnosis as required and medically rule out every other reasonable possibility before sending her home with a pat on her "litigation-syndromed" head? Or would he leap to a diagnosis of litigation syndrome and ignore every other reasonable possibility? (I.e., Would he do the required differential diagnosis—or would he commit malpractice?)

Then ask what he has done to rule out the other possibilities in this case.

The key point: If this expert provided the conclusion in his clinic that he is providing on the witness stand, he would be guilty of malpractice. Prepare the jury for this by having your own medical expert explain what a differential diagnosis is, what "rule out" means, and thus why such a "diagnosis" would be malpractice in a clinic. (See Appendix C.)

Trace carefully other trial testimony by this defense expert. How often has he testified identically? How often has he followed up to see if any plaintiffs got better after the case ended?

In these days of tort "reform," some physicians feel justified in offering these scientifically and medically bogus opinions. These physicians feel under siege by trial attorneys, so to them, "All's fair in love and war." This is why they so easily lie on the stand: to keep the lid on plaintiff's cases. And along the way they make a fortune doing it. That is why you need to track down what they have said in other trials, and check out its validity in retrospect.

When you have unmasked one of them, do not keep it a secret. Make sure every other plaintiff's attorney learns about it so that doctor can never lie about another plaintiff.[2]

Go behind the scenes. It's not enough to attack an opinion. Show how this doctor makes his living. Show how often he gives the same testimony. Show how his testimony does not square with the truth—as with plaintiffs who did not suddenly lose their symptoms when the trial ended, or children who did not die in the four years he predicted.

When the defense expert uses tests to support his opinions, have your experts dissect and debunk how he ran them and analyzed or scored them. Show how the defense expert routinely and intentionally tilts the results to favor the defense.

Do not treat this kind of dishonest testimony as if it is just a difference of opinion. It is lying. The defense expert finds this a good way to make a great living. Sufficient research into how he gets to his opinions often unearths dishonest methods. In trial, be polite to these snakes (let the facts you unearth speak for themselves), but conduct your behind-the-scenes work with all the aggressiveness of looking for information with which to impeach a jailhouse snitch. You are dealing with criminals in white coats.

99.9% of physicians are honest and would never stoop to such testimony. That's why those who do stoop make such good money. Being rare they are in demand—or they are new at it and would like to become in demand.

2. Florida attorney Dorothy Clay Sims has taken the time to learn how some lying brain-damage "experts" falsify testing and test results. She is now a specialist in unmasking them in trial.

CHAPTER NINE
CLOSING

> After all, if that much money is too much for one person, so is that much harm.
>
> "Verdict" means "to speak the truth." The truth your compensation verdict must speak is the amount of money it will take to equalize—compensate, balance—the harm. Nothing else gets thrown in the scales. Nothing else is the truth.

9.1
Purpose of Closing

At the beginning of closings, the vast majority of jurors believe they have made up their minds. And years of research by JuryWatch and other jury research firms show that only rarely does a juror change his mind during closing. Jurors rarely even move from undecided to one side or the other. In almost all cases, the vast majority of mind changing takes place not during closings but during deliberations.

If the jurors could vote at the start of closings, the result would usually be the same or nearly the same as a vote after closings. This means the real purpose of closing is not to change minds, because you are just not likely to be able to change any. In fact, vehement arguments are just as likely to harden some jurors against you.

Yes, that is about as anti-intuitive as you can get. But it has been thoroughly researched and it is true. So if closing is not to change minds, what is it for? The goal that will actually do you some good, and that you can achieve, is to arm and motivate your favorable jurors—your deliberations advocates—to argue on your behalf in deliberations. Your advocate jurors are far more able to change minds in deliberations than are you in closing. But for your advocate jurors to do this, you have to arm them with the tools they need to change minds.

How well you arm your advocate jurors controls the outcome of the case, including verdict size.

But before you start trying to arm your advocate jurors, you have to get them listening.

9.2
Make Them Listen

Unfortunately, jurors usually listen to little that is said in closings. You think they are listening because they look like they are. But their minds are elsewhere. We all mastered that useful deception by second grade. It fooled our teachers then and it fools you now.

Most jurors do not listen to closing because they think they have made up their minds. Even the few still trying to make up their minds stop listening as soon as they realize that the closing is just rehashing what they have already heard. Few jurors listen to rehashing. So no matter what else you do or do not do in closing, do not rehash.

But do make the jurors listen. So start closing by saying: "Folks, in a little while you'll go into the deliberation room and you'll have two jobs." That surprises them into listening for a moment, because they think they have only one job. You probably think that too.

Continue: "One of your jobs is to answer the questions the judge gives you. Your other job will be to explain to the other jurors why you feel the way you do about each question. So for the next ___ minutes, I'd like to give you some ways to do that."

This taps into a common juror fear: their insecurity about speaking in front of this group they hardly know. So now your favorable jurors will listen because they want all the help they can get. Jurors leaning against you will listen to hear what you are going to say that they will have to contend with in deliberations. And the undecided jurors will listen, but they would have anyway.

If you close first and last, use this strategy at the start of your second closing so it does not make jurors listen closely to the defense closing as well as yours. Then save all your important stuff for your second closing (unless second closing is strictly for rebuttal).

9.3
Arm Your Jurors

Because few jurors are persuaded in closing, your efforts will be more fruitful (and just as persuasive) if you use closing to arm jurors already on your side to go into deliberations and persuade the others for you.

Your advocate jurors have a far greater chance of persuading hostile jurors than you do. This is because jurors have more credibility with each other than they do with you, the attorney the hostile jurors oppose and have probably opposed for some time.

You never win a case. No lawyer has ever won any case. All you can do is arm your advocate jurors to go win it for you. Like a basketball coach, you can only train your players to go win for you.

Fortunately, arming your advocate jurors as described below is the most effective and least risky way to make a last attempt to persuade hostile or undecided jurors.

Your juror advocates. Good things happen when you arm your advocate jurors and they speak on your behalf in deliberations. First, they get right to work persuading unfavorable jurors.

Second, once a juror speaks on your behalf, she is less likely to back down later. A juror who does not speak can back down more easily because she has not taken a public stand, so has no social price to pay for backing down.

Third, when a favorable juror speaks in the terms you provide, other favorable jurors are more likely to quickly and strongly voice agreement. When favorable jurors hear each other say things they agree with, their unity and resolve reinforce each other, creating a powerful force in the group. This is a primary dynamic of group decision making.

One-liners. To arm your favorable jurors, the National Jury Project's Susan Macpherson advises that you boil down each of your important arguments to a brief, plain-English sentence. Under ten words. Five or six is better. "Dr. Fischer cut without looking." These one-liners are the best way to arm your jurors.

Do not re-explain the whole point. The jurors already know it. They do not need to hear: "On September 17, 1998, at 4:20 P.M. in the afternoon in the operating room in Granville Memorial Hospital in Oxford, North Carolina, Western Hemisphere, Dr. Ulysses Moses Giordano operated without seeing the liver artery on 38-year-old John Lawrence Smith, so when the doctor cut into the tissue surrounding the area, he cut through the artery." When you repeat details the jurors already know, they stop listening. No one listens to what they already know. And once they stop listening, it is hard to get them back. Just say, "Dr. Fischer cut without looking." Give them an easily remembered one-liner—a boil-down of the more involved point—that they will be comfortable saying in deliberations.

Use one-liners this way: "In deliberations, if anyone asks what Dr. Fisher did wrong, remind them 'Dr. Fisher cut without looking.' " Jurors will remember this. They will say those very words in deliberations. Especially if you say the one-liner twice and give the jurors time to write it down. If someone says X, tell them Y. "If someone in deliberations says there is no sense giving all that money for pain, answer, '*Pain is the worst harm in the case.*' As bad as all the other harms are, 'pain is the worst harm in the case.' Its dollar value is more than the losses for medical expenses and future care. Why? Because *it's the worst harm in the case,* and the only allowed measure of money is the amount of harm."

Reduce every major issue to a one-liner as simple as, "It's the worst harm in the case."

No juror will sit in deliberations and say: "The maximum proportionality of the compensable damages is the physical pain deriving from the defendant driver's negligent operation of a motor vehicle at approximately 8:30 P.M. on the evening of January 21, 2000." No one will listen to you talk like that in closing (or any other time, either). No juror will use those words in deliberations. But they'll use "*Pain is the worst harm in the case.*" It is a good tool.

You need a one-liner like it for every important issue.

If the jury is allowed to take notes, go slowly enough for jurors to be able to write your one-liners down. You can even say: "You may want to write this down. If someone in deliberations asks why you should give all that money for pain, remind them that '*Pain is the worst harm in the case.*' "

One-liners are memory-jogging reviews. Jurors will say them. One-liners are the next best thing to being in deliberations yourself —and often better.

9.4
Help Jurors Respond to Friends

A similar technique can help with a little-recognized but common problem. Some jurors can be reluctant to give much money if they anticipate criticism afterwards by people they know or people in the community. This can be particularly true when a case is likely to get publicity or to be talked about afterwards. But it has some effect in any case where the damages figure might be high.

To help offset this problem, in closing say, "When this case is over, if someone asks you, 'Why in the world did you decide to give all that money to that lady?' just tell them, '____________________.' "

Fill in the blank with your one-liner for that issue. "She'll hurt for the rest of her life."

You should do this for every issue, but it's especially important on money issues. Jurors worry about being criticized for giving a lot of money. They don't worry about being criticized for giving too little, so they often do.

9.5
Structure

The following structure is designed for a single closing following the defense closing. You will need to make adjustments if you close first and last. In such situations, be careful not to find yourself prevented from talking about important topics if you are allowed only to rebut the defense closing. You will need to move the parts of the structure around to conform with what you expect the defense to bring up.

Closing structure derives from opening.

Part One. Why We're Suing

This will focus juror attention where you want it.

"Please remember we're suing ______ for # reasons."

A. The first reason we're suing is because she __________ ______________.

B. *Briefly* summarize what was wrong with doing that and how it caused harm.

C. *Briefly* summarize what the defendant should have done instead.

D. *Briefly* summarize what good that would have done.

Provide a one-liner for each reason you're suing.

Part Two. Undermining (Except for Damages)

You've heard the defense claim that __________________ __________________. If someone brings that up in deliberations remind them that . . . .

For example,

You've heard the defense claim that Dr. Akroyd was justified in believing it was a urinary tract infection. If someone brings that up in deliberations, remind them that no matter what Dr. Akroyd was justified in thinking, he was still *required to consider cancer and required to try to rule it out.* Dr. X, Y, and Z, as well as the defense's Dr. A, all agree that cancer should have been on Dr. Akroyd's differential list. And every doctor on both sides of this case—including Dr.

Akroyd himself—told you that once something is on the differential list, the doctor is not allowed to ignore it until he has ruled it out. So if anyone in deliberations thinks Dr. Akroyd was justified in thinking infection, remind them Dr. Akroyd was still *required to consider cancer and try to rule it out.* If he had, he would quickly have discovered that cancer could not be ruled out, so he would have had treatment started in plenty of time. That's why no matter what, he was required to consider cancer. That's the standard of care.

At the end of the explanation, provide a one-liner:

He was required to rule cancer out.

Do not rehash, do not "marshal the evidence," do not consider this your last chance to persuade. The troops are in the armory getting their weapons for battle. The intricacies of the case are not weapons. The troops need brief explanations and a one-liner for each major point.

Do this for each liability point—including causation—you need to undermine. Cover everything, but be concise and be *brief.* Closing is a bad time to be wordy. (So is every other time.) Be especially careful to undermine each defense theme ("doctors can't see the future") and each defense one-liner ("accidents happen"). Don't let defense themes and one-liners get into deliberations without you giving your favorable jurors the words to undermine them.

Part Three. Massage Liability Instructions (See 9.7 below)

Show each jury instruction, one at a time. Explain in plain English —not a hint of a legal term—what the instruction means, even if you think it is clear. Take no chances. Deal with every possible way the instruction can possibly be misunderstood.

For example, when the defense has three experts to your one, make sure the jurors understand that "greater weight of the evidence" does not mean counting witnesses. Otherwise jurors will count witnesses. Count on it.

Once you have explained what the instruction does and does not mean, explain briefly—without much repetition from what you have said above—how the evidence fits that instruction.

Remind the jurors that if there is any disagreement or uncertainty about meaning, they need to reread the instruction sheet—if there is one—and if there is still any uncertainty or disagreement, they need to send out a request for the judge to come talk to them.

Be sure to include the preponderance instruction (9.10 below). This can be pivotal for both liability and money.

Part Four. Harms

If your client has previous harms or other harms the defendant did not cause, distinguish them from the harms for which you are seeking compensation. Provide a two-column chart with the unrelated harms on the left and the harms the defendant caused on the right.

UNRELATED HARMS	HARMS CAUSED BY DEFENDANT

- Review the results of that damage: physical, mental, emotional; and the consequences.
- Deal with causation and degree-of-harm issues in dispute.
- Review the helps and fixes: treatments, surgeries, care items, etc.

Story. The best form of review is to incorporate the harms into a story about your client contending day-to-day with the harms. You might consider telling such a story in the first person, as long as you can do it without making him seem like a whiner.

Part Five. Economic Damages

Cover medical and care bills, lost income, etc. This is where the minimum life-care plan goes (9.6).

Part Six. Money

(See arguments below in this chapter)

Be sure to include the "Impure thoughts" and "Scales" arguments (5.8., 9.14, below.)

Part Seven. Massage Damages Instructions

(See 9.9 below)

Part Eight. Review Your One-Liners

(See 9.4 above)

Part Nine. Motivating Arguments

(e.g. "Two Futures," 9.21 below)

Part Ten. Massage Verdict Issues

(9.7 below)

Show each question the judge will give them to answer. Use a facsimile or at least a close visual approximation of how the questions will look on the verdict sheet—especially including the answer spaces.

Then tell and show what answers they should write.

Part 11. Stop

Say "thank you" and sit down. Every additional word you say will detract from your effectiveness. Please, shh!

9.6
Minimum Life-Care Plan in Closing

If your minimum life-care plan (or your informal list of needs) has been properly presented in testimony (see 7.7), show in closing what reducing the amount by even a little will really do. Otherwise some jurors will think of the plan as intangible and easily lower its value. Since minimum life-care money is usually a major component of your economic damages total, and since your economic damages total is often the benchmark upon which jurors will base their non-economics decision, you must protect your minimum life-care figure.

To do that, prepare a line-item chart of every important life-care item or group of items. List each by name (no explanation; the jurors already heard that). Show the cost of each. Enlarge the chart so every juror can see the smallest print. This may take several charts.

Hand out copies as well, so each juror has one in their hands while you are talking about it.

Suppose, for example, the list begins as follows:

Speech therapy	Six years	$13,500
Leg braces	Lifetime	24,567
Pain medication	Lifetime	57,400
Etc.		
Etc.		
Etc.		
	TOTAL	$3,527,450

Display the list. Say: "The amount on the bottom is what we need to take care of John. But I can't tell you what amount to give. It's up to you. So here's what you do. In deliberations, if there's something on the life-care plan that you all agree John should not have, cross it off. It's entirely up to you. Cross off any item you all agree he should not get. And reduce the total down here at the bottom by the cost of that item. That way John gets what you think he should get and he does not get anything you think he should not get."

If you have removed from the life-care plan every item that can seem unnecessary or luxurious, and if you have made sure every price has been justified, this method will keep you from losing any life-care money. Your favorable jurors will use this method in deliberations.

Without this tool, an unfavorable juror who wants to lower the minimum life-care figure usually succeeds saying, "Boy, three and a half million is a lot, but I'd go with half." Your favorable jurors don't know how to argue with him, so they are likely to fold.

But when you have used the method suggested above, your favorable jurors will say to the low-ball juror: "Oh yeah? Show us what you want to take out of that life-care plan and if we all agree, we'll see how low it takes us." Your favorable jurors will not easily back down, because you showed the practical consequences of taking money out of the life-care plan. They will find little, if anything, in the life-care plan they think John should to do without. And the low-ball juror will seem unreasonable for trying to omit items.

The use of this method usually means the jurors will hardly discuss the life-care plan before deciding to fully fund it. And all you have done is shown the true cost of omitting any part of it.[1]

Life expectancy. Point out in closing that your client has the right to be taken care of without worrying about running out of money. She is not likely to die right on schedule according to life expectancy. She has the right and good grounds to hope for a longer life, just like everyone else. And she has the right to the money she needs to take care of her injuries no matter how long she lives.

1. When this technique works for you, thank Georgia's Don Keenan, Esq.

Point out that we all worry about running out of money, but your client—unlike everyone else—can no longer do anything about it.

She is worried right now about running out of money if she outlives her statutory life expectancy. She knows if she gets only enough money to take care of her until she reaches her average life expectancy, there is a 50% chance she will outlive the money. Find out and show the spread beyond that age—such as, "57% live longer than the average, 40% live more than ten years longer, 30% live 15 years longer, 15% live 25 years longer, and 5% live longer than that." Argue that she has the right not to have to lie awake at night worrying what she will do for money if she lives longer than the chart or the defense says—especially because if that happens, she'll be old enough to have the most desperate need of the money. She did not ask to be put in this position.

When appropriate, have an expert explain that your client will probably live longer than the chart or the defendant says.

Early death. One of the most outrageous defense tactics is to tell jurors to provide *less* money for the minimum life-care plan on the grounds that the plaintiff will soon die due to the condition she's in. Of course, she's in that condition because of the defendant's negligence. So for each year the defendant has taken away, she is entitled to money for shortened life expectancy. Point out that if Sally does die 20 years sooner, it will be because of the defendant's negligence. Ask, "Should the defendant pay less if it turns out they killed her?" And,

> The defendant wants you to provide enough money to care for Sally for only a few years. At least they admit she should get something. But they seem to want to force Sally and her family to hope she dies at the defendant's convenience, because that's when the defendants want the money to run out.
>
> Sally is in terror and anguish over the possibility she heard in this courtroom that she might lose 20 years of life because of the defendant's negligence. The defense created that terror and anguish to try to get out of their responsibilities to her. Her own doctors never told her she would die 20 years sooner because it's not true. But obviously it is scaring her badly, and causing her a lot of pain. It would anyone.

> The pain of that level of fear and anguish is more serious than the mere cost of care for those same 20 years. So by arguing an early death for Sally, the defense is actually asking you for a much higher verdict for shortening her life.
>
> How much higher? It's easy to figure out.
>
> You can figure out the *minimum* value of Sally's anguish over each year the defendant says they've taken away from her. Look at the cost of the minimum life-care plan for that 20 years. It's $4 million. 20 years of Sally's life is obviously worth many times the cost of care for those years.
>
> So let's figure it out: If Sally does die at 52 instead of 72, the verdict should be the $4 million the minimum life-care calls for, times three or four—because loss of life is many times worse than the cost of any minimum life-care plan. So it's at least $12 million for those 20 years, or as much as $16 million or more.

The approach helps turn your full minimum life-care amount into a floor instead of a ceiling, and gives you a chance at a lot more if the jury has reason to be angry at the defendant.

If you have caps on non-economic damages, add:

> But what is important is for you to simply fund the minimum life-care plan including for those 20 years, so Sally will be cared for when it turns out she lives those 20 years after all.

Sally did not sign on to gamble. The defendant gambled her well-being when he was negligent. Now he is gambling with her well-being again by saying maybe she'll die fast so she won't need much care money. What if she does? And why should that worry be hers instead of the defendant's? Sally has already suffered the consequences of the defendant's gambling. She should not have to do it a second time. It's the defendant's turn.

Senior citizens and life expectancy. Another problem with life expectancy is that many older jurors have noticed various life expectancy estimates pertaining to themselves and their contemporaries. Thus, their own experience may have led them to think that life expectancy is less than the average on the charts, since most of the exceptions they have seen—their own contemporaries—died early. Judicial notice of the chart does not persuade them. Instead, have an expert explain the step-by-step empirical process by which the chart arrives at its averages. This will give your favorable jurors a way in deliberations to deal with the recalcitrant juror on this topic.

9.7
Massaging the Jury Instructions and Questions

Jurors do not know the law. Jury instructions do not help. In general, jurors know no more about the law after they hear the instructions than they did before. The judge almost always reads too much of it for anyone to absorb, and the language of the instructions is usually impenetrable. The writers want to be accurate but do not seem to want to communicate.

Even when the language of the instructions is crystal clear, do not assume the jurors will listen, understand, and remember. They do not. In fact, due to the confusing barrage of instructions, many jurors actually understand less law after the instructions than before.

In a recent case, in the overwhelming barrage of new concepts and information, a few jurors remembered one particular word: "malice." The judge had used it in connection with gross negligence. But most gross negligence instructions are confusing and buried in the middle of the litany of instructions. So a few jurors remembered the word "malice" but not its context. They remembered only that the judge had said the word, and not what it related to.

Because counsel had not massaged the instructions, something catastrophic was brewing. As it turned out (not just by coincidence), the jurors who heard the word "malice" were defense-prone. Insofar as they were paying attention to the instructions, it would have been to find whatever they could to defeat the plaintiff. That's why they remembered "malice."

During deliberations, these jurors reminded the others that the judge had said "malice"—and why would she have said it unless it meant that the jury had to find malice to decide there had been negligence?

So a relatively easy negligence case returned a no-cause verdict. Why? Plaintiff's counsel had not massaged the instructions, or at least not done it clearly enough. How does one explain that to one's client? "Um, well, I . . . ."

Most juror misunderstandings of the law endanger the party with the burden. When the law is not clear in jurors' minds, defense-prone jurors can cite it—incorrectly—to support their point of view. The Devil cites Scriptures and defense-prone jurors cite instructions. Those on the other side of both need to be armed to respond.

So you have to do two things: First, explain the law and the verdict issues in closing.

Second, make the jurors comfortable in calling on the judge for clarification during deliberations when there is even a small disagreement or uncertainty about what the law is or what a verdict question means. If they have the instructions, tell them to refer to them—and if the disagreement or uncertainty remains, call the judge.

As soon as your charge conference ends, write out each instruction that is important to your case on a separate projection slide or piece of butcher paper. One instruction per page or slide—and only the part of the instruction you need to explain. For example:

> Negligence is the failure to exercise reasonable care.

Do this for each important instruction and for each verdict question. In the verdict questions include the response blanks:

> Was the negligence of the truck driver a cause of harm to the plaintiff?
>
> _____Yes   _____No

Go through each instruction and each question, one at a time. As you come to each one, first explain in plain English what it means. Practice this in advance or you will not do it clearly. Then explain how the evidence applies to that instruction or question.

For example: "Negligence is the failure to exercise reasonable care." Explain that "failure" means either doing the wrong thing, or not doing something the defendant should have done to prevent harm.

When it comes to vocabulary, take nothing for granted. "Reasonable," for example, does not mean "moderate," as in "a moderately priced dinner." But that is always what jurors—and most attorneys — think it means. In fact, it means "based on reason"—*reasonable care means the amount of care called for by reason.* "What did reason—logic—dictate that the defendant should have done?" This is a much higher and more sensible standard than mere "moderate" care.

Explain this meaning of "reasonable" in every context the word appears.

Explain the plain-English meaning of every instruction and verdict issue you show to the jury. Be sure to see section 9.10 on how to explain preponderance in a way that will get jurors to make their decisions on that basis. Otherwise they do not, especially when it comes to money.

Jurors have particular trouble with the concepts of cause and compensation (see 9.9 below). Thorough and clear explanations are necessary.

If you wish, you can structure your entire closing around the technique of massaging the instructions and verdict questions.

9.8
Massaging Language

When massaging the instructions, it is important to relate the language you have been using to the language in the instructions. So if you have used the word "harms" as I have used it in this book, you would need to go through the instruction carrying the damages elements and explain that each one is a harm: the physical damage, the costs of treatment, the non-economic damage, etc.

9.9

Massaging "To Compensate"

One of your more important tasks in massaging the instructions is to explain "compensate." The meaning is not apparent to most jurors. Rarely will anything the judge say clarify it. As with most misunderstandings of the law, this one will hurt you, not the defense.

Start by explaining that—as my JuryWatch partner Debra Miller puts it—the instruction to compensate is the jurors' *call to action.*

The action is to equalize the money and harm. Nothing else can be part of the equation.

Then explain that "compensate" means to *balance.* The word "compensate" derives from "to weigh the same as," which derives from "to hang at the same level" in a balance scale. ("Com" meaning "with"; "pend" meaning "hang" = to hang with.) In trial the requirement to compensate means that the weight of the harm must be equaled (balanced) by the weight of money. *Nothing else is allowed in the scale*—just harm on one side and money on the other. No *outside reasons.* Explain as shown below—and take your time. Be clear. Try not to elaborate on the following argument and not to abridge it, except for the parts that are not relevant to your particular case. It's one of your most important arguments.

> The law says to *'compensate'* John. What does 'compensate' mean?
>
> And what does 'compensate' *not* mean?
>
> 'Compensate' is an old word meaning 'balance the scales.' [Use your hands.] 'Make two things weigh the same,' or 'hang at the same level.' [Hands.] One side heavier, the scales do not balance. [Hands.] Uncompensated. Each side equal, it's compensated. [Hands.]
>
> Equalized. [Hands.]
>
> Your most important task is to know what counts as part of the weight. And what does not count. If this scale [hand] holds the harms and losses, what are you allowed to put in

this other scale [hand] to balance them? Outside reasons are not allowed.

A person has a job. Her work goes into the scale on this side [hands]. The longer she works, the heavier the scale and the lower it goes. [Hands.]

Now the boss must pay the worker—*compensate* her. The boss must *balance* the work with money. *Equalize.*

The more money the boss puts in the other scale [hands], the closer he comes to *compensating—balancing* the work with an equalizing amount of pay. If the boss pays too little, the worker is *under*-compensated [hands], or underpaid. If the boss pays too much, the worker is *over*-compensated [hands], or overpaid.

Compensation means balance. [Show.] Equalized.

The boss is not allowed to lower the compensation by putting any *outside reasons* into either scale.

So the boss must not say, 'I think I'll give her less money than it takes to balance her work, because her living expenses are low so more money won't do any good.' That's an outside reason. Not allowed. Makes no difference how low the worker's living expenses are. The boss has to pay based on the amount of work. No deduction for any outside reason.

The boss cannot say, 'Paying enough money to balance her work will force us to raise the prices of our products, so we'll pay her half,' or 'It's more money than anyone needs,' or 'This worker is used to living on very little money so she doesn't need more,' or 'It might seem like a windfall,' or 'Her husband also works, so she doesn't need much,' or 'Her family chops its own wood and grows its own crops; they get along fine without the full amount it would take to compensate her.'

The boss is not even allowed to lower her pay because 'She's got some other source of money.' And the boss certainly cannot lower the compensation because he feels sorry for the owner of the company having to pay the right amount, or because he's worried it might hurt the company. The worker did the work. No lowering the compensation for any outside reason.

Same thing in a trial. Just substitute losses and harms for work. The law in every courthouse in America says nothing goes in the scale [hand] but the losses and harms caused by the defendant. No outside reasons. Your most important job is to make sure everyone follows that law.

So in this scale [hand] goes the amount of money that balances the losses and harms caused by the defendant. No outside reasons can lower it.

The judge will explain compensation. It's important to pay close attention to what she says. It is also important to pay close attention to what she does not say. She'll tell you to provide the amount of money that compensates for—balances—matches—equals—the losses and harms caused by the defendant. She will not tell you to take anything else into account, because you are not allowed to. No outside reasons.

The judge will not tell you to lower the verdict on the grounds that the full amount might not do any good, or might seem like a windfall, or might be too much money for one person, or might drive up the prices of things people have to buy. Those are *outside reasons.* Not allowed.

Or whether the money will make the pain go away, or be more money that John ever would have had or more than he could ever spend.

One *outside reason* is whether the right amount of money might change John's lifestyle. But it was the defendant's negligence that changed John's lifestyle [or ' . . . the family's lifestyle']. But even if the equalizing amount of money does change John's lifestyle, it just makes up for the lifestyle the defendant took away. So you will not hear the judge telling you to lower the verdict to avoid changing John's lifestyle—because that would be an *outside reason.* The law does not allow it.

> Other *outside reasons* include whether you like or dislike John or the defendant, or whether you feel sorry for the defendant.
>
> Outside reasons have nothing to do with compensation.[2]
>
> Jurors must not let other jurors take any of those *outside reasons* into account.
>
> Jurors must not let other jurors take any of those *outside reasons* into account.

[That's not a typo. Say it twice.]

> Of course we all want to use our own beliefs and concerns. But judges and jurors need the strength and wisdom to keep *outside reasons* outside. The law allows no outside *opinions,* outside *politics,* or any other *outside reasons.* We have to obey the law that is the law right now, not what we might prefer the law to be. Jurors have no more important job than to adhere to the law as it is right now.[3]
>
> So in deliberations, if any *outside reasons* come up, remember: *Only the losses and harms.*
>
> *Outside reasons* undermine the purpose of the law. So in deliberations, if a juror wants to use an outside reason, remind him: *Only* losses and harms.
>
> If that juror still wants to use an *outside reason,* ask your foreperson to knock on the door and tell the bailiff you need the judge to come tell you the law again. [If the judge sends written jury instructions into deliberations, say, 'If that juror still wants to use an *outside reason,* ask your foreperson to read aloud instruction # ___.' If that does not take care of

---

2. If "outside reaons" have come into evidence for purposes other than deciding damages, explain to jurors the limited purpose they came in for, and that they cannot be used to decide money. You might even get the judge to give an instruction to that effect—especially if you moved earlier to keep an "outside reason" out.

3. These two sentences may not fly in Maryland, Georgia, Oregon, and Indiana, where jurors are allowed to ignore the law. So reword: "The judge wants you to follow the law as the law is right now, not the way some jurors might want it to be." If the judge wants no such thing, say, "All I'm asking you to do is follow the law as the law is right now, not the way some jurors might want it to be."

the problem, ask your foreperson to knock on the door and tell the bailiff you need the judge.]

[This threat of bringing in the judge to correct a wayward juror is an extremely effective way to arm your favorable jurors.]

If a jury lowers the verdict for any *outside reasons,* the law's purpose will be undermined.

As a juror, you are the boss. You have to keep out the outside reasons. That's the law, and your oath as jurors is to follow the law.

Here's an outside reason that's especially important to keep out: A juror might think that maybe John might have some other way to pay his bills, such as a rich uncle or some other source. John has no such thing, but even if he did, it would be an *outside reason.* So the law does not allow it in the scales. *Nothing goes in the scales but the value of the losses and harms* caused by the defendant.

Anything else undermines the purpose of the law.

So what is the purpose of the law?

The purpose of the law is that it is society's only way of making a negligent truck driver [or whatever] meet his responsibility—by fully balancing, compensating, making up for the losses and harms he caused.

If your verdict is for less than the full and fair amount that equalizes the harm—if your verdict is a symbolic amount, or a token amount, or anything else less than the full measure of the losses and harms *as John feels them,* if you take any *outside reasons* into account even a little, then the defendant walks away without having been made to meet his responsibility.

If possible, this argument should come after the various arguments below about figuring out the right amount to give in damages. I put it here so you can see where you're eventually going as you use those arguments below. Ideally, if you have an opening-closing and closing-closing this argument should come late in the second closing. But if your second closing can only rebut the defense closing, don't gamble. These days you really need this argument. So get it in when you know you can.

9.10
Massaging Preponderance

This is the culmination of the preponderance technique that begins in jury voir dire or opening (see 5.45 and 6.15). In closing, when massaging the juror instructions and verdict questions (see 9.7 above), as you come to the first instruction that includes burden, explain what it means: "more likely than not." Use your hands to show how little the balance needs to tilt. As in voir dire, do not use the words "preponderance" or "burden." They confuse no matter how carefully you explain. And be careful to say nothing that can create the impression that the defense has any kind of burden.

When you come to the first verdict issue, put your finger on the space for the answer and say:

> You answer this 'yes' if you decide it is more likely 'yes' than 'no.' You can have doubts either way—all the doubts you want.
>
> If you come down to thinking the answer is more likely yes, even by just a little bit, then the only legal answer is 'yes.' We've shown you much more than just more-likely-than-not [raise one hand high, the other low] but 'more likely than not' is all it takes. That's how everyone here expects you to make all your decisions. Mr. Defense Attorney agrees, and in a little while the judge will tell you it's the law.
>
> So during deliberations, if anyone says they're just not sure, or they're not convinced beyond a reasonable doubt, remind them that all we have to do is persuade you that the answer is more likely yes than no. If they are still uncomfortable with that, ask your foreperson to tell the bailiff that you need the judge to come give you the instruction again on 'preponderance,' which means more likely than not. [Or if the judge sends the instructions into deliberations: '. . . ask your foreperson to pick up the instructions and read number nine aloud to everyone. If that does not help, ask your

foreperson to tell the bailiff you need the judge to come talk to the jury.']

As you massage each succeeding verdict question, mention "more likely than not." "If you believe that $100,000 is more likely than not the fair amount, then that's your answer even if there are doubts."

9.11
The Law

Jurors often minimize verdicts or give no liability because "the defendant may have been negligent but he broke no laws." Explain that negligence *is* breaking the law because *the law requires care.*

> The negligence law is in place to cover carelessness when more specific laws or rules have not been written. This is because the legislature knows it cannot cover every single specific kind of carelessness. And no one wants to live in a country where there is a law for every single thing. But the lack of a specific law does not give anyone license to be careless. The law of negligence requires care. Carelessness breaks that law.

9.12
Intangibles Argument: Ratio To Tangible Losses

Near the end of closing, show a line-item chart for every element of damages the instructions mention. Please see the example on the next page.

Past medical expenses	**$____________________**
Past care	**$____________________**
Future care	**$____________________**
Past lost income	**$____________________**
Future lost income	**$____________________**

Past loss of use of leg	**$____________________**
Future loss of use of leg	**$____________________**
Past physical pain	**$____________________**
Future physical pain	**$____________________**
Past emotional suffering	**$____________________**
Future emotional suffering	**$____________________**
Past loss of life's pleasures	**$____________________**
Future loss of life's pleasures	**$____________________**
[Any other loss the jury finds[4]]	**$____________________**

Separate economic from non-economic losses, as shown (but do not label them as such). This results in a chart that graphically, not merely textually, shows the many areas of damages the jury is supposed to compensate for. Often the result is that the non-economic visually outweigh the economic damages, which is a good proportion for the jurors to see.

Do not itemize to the point of trivialization. Each line should be for a significant, substantial harm. If a hand has been harmed, do not make each finger a line-item. In preparing the lists before trial, leave the amounts blank so in closing you can fill in figures as you talk through them—at least for those items you are allowed to fill in.

4. "Any other loss the jury finds" sometimes appears in the statute but not in the pattern instruction. If so, even if you cannot get the judge to add it (some judges are instruction cowards), use it here. Give an example of that kind of loss if you can think of one. If not, use it anyway. You never know what the jury will think of.

Uncover each line only as you get to it. This keeps jurors with you as you work down the chart. Otherwise, they read ahead without paying attention to what you are saying.

To use the list, start at the top, briefly justify the amount for each item, and write the figure in. Take your time writing each digit, and write neatly and large. No scrawling. If you are normally a scrawler, practice writing numbers clearly. Scrawling means sloppiness or tentativeness, and you want these figures to look strong and emphatic.

When you finish with the economic damages items, write in their subtotal. (In many jurisdictions this is as far as you can go with figures, because you cannot specify amounts for non-economics. In such circumstances, this method is even more important.)

Once you give the economic damages subtotal, say this:

> This $__________ all goes to other people for John's care and to making John even with where he would have been if none of this had ever happened. But not one cent goes to John for the greatest harm in this case: what this did to John's life. His human losses. To do justice, to balance the scales, you fill in the blanks on these next lines.

If you are permitted to fill in those lines, do so. If not, tell the jurors to look at how much greater these human losses are than the medical bills and lost wages. "It's many times worse to lose your leg than your job, so the amount that goes on this line [loss of use of leg] should be many times the amount on this line up here [future lost income]."

If you cannot talk about proportionality, use your hands: Left hand palm at waist level as you say the medical figure. Right hand palm up shoulder high or more for non-economics when you say, "This needs a substantial amount of money to balance the harm."

If the jury can take notes, watch the jurors who have been taking the most notes during trial to be sure they have time to write each figure down. Your look, if not too obvious, might even impel some to write it down. (If none of the busy note-takers is writing down any of this, you might consider making a last-ditch effort to settle the case.)

Itemization. If you covered this in jury selection, remind them here (or tell them for the first time) that in order to play by the rules every juror must evaluate the degree of each loss on the list and determine how much money it will take to balance that loss. The law does not allow them to ignore a damages element just because they do not personally agree it is something the law should allow to be compensated.

> So if during deliberations someone says they don't think emotional suffering should be compensated for, remind them that the laws they took an oath to uphold disagree with him, and everyone has to go along with the law. If you have to bring the judge in to re-read him that part of the instructions, do it.

9.13
Holistic Damages

If jurors are asked to decide on just one total figure for damages instead of a line-item list, and if the amount you are seeking for non-economic damages is vastly greater than the economic damages, itemization of economic damages in closing may not be the most effective approach. If, say, the total economic damages is $250,000 but the non-economic harms justify a $10 million to $20 million verdict, focusing on the relatively minor economic damages can drag your verdict down. Jurors tend to use the economic damage amount as a comparative benchmark on which to figure non-economic damage.

So instead of emphasizing your low economic damages by itemizing them, just mention them early in trial, and then leave them alone. Let them fade into the background while the foreground is the multiplicity and enormity of the non-economic harms. Then use the scales argument (9.14) and others to bolster your request for a total verdict. Keep the focus off what your client will do with the money, since that justifies only a small part of the fair verdict. Instead, focus on why the defendant has the responsibility to pay it.

In some cases, an expert can explain why medical and care costs are so low. It's usually because medical science has been able to do very little to help. Beyond this explanation, place your main focus on the overwhelming awfulness of the harms. Ask for a verdict that equalizes.

9.14

Scales: Calculating the Intangible Amounts

Either in voir dire or opening, you should have promised to teach jurors how to determine the amounts for non-economic damages. (See 5.25) The method you will now teach helps jurors arrive at a figure, and arms your favorable jurors with a concrete way to fight for the amount they want to give.

Start by explaining that the value of each non-economic harm[5] is determined by three factors:

How bad is the harm? (E.g., How much does it hurt?) Where on the scale does the intensity of each harm lie? Pain, for example, can be minor, medium, or extremely bad.

How long does it last? Where on the scale of time does each harm lie? Pain can last from a few moments all the way up through permanent.

How interfering is it? (How much does it prevent the plaintiff from doing?) Where on the scale of disability does each harm lie? A disability can interfere with functioning anywhere from just a little all the way up to total incapacity.

Sometimes a jury instruction will help you reinforce this approach: ". . . compensation for pain and suffering in accordance with severity and duration." But even with no such instruction, this strategy works.

Once you explain the basic principle, give an example. If physical pain is one of the harms, explain that the amount of money for pain is determined by how bad, how long, and how interfering the pain is:

> For example, if someone's negligence hurts someone's arm and the pain is not too bad, there should be money to make

---

5. Just a reminder never to use the terms "economic damages" or "non-economic damages."

up for that pain, but not much. That's low on the scale. That would be the kind of case in which I'd have to ask you for a verdict of a few thousand dollars over and above the medical costs and lost income. [The figures I use here are just for illustration. Choose your own.]

Now let's move up the scale: if the pain is worse, the kind of hurting a person can't forget about, maybe bad enough to keep him from doing some things, keeps him awake nights even when he takes all the drugs they give him, then it takes more money to make up for the pain. That would be the kind of case in which I'd have to ask you for a verdict into the tens of thousands of dollars beyond medical costs and lost income, maybe even a hundred thousand if the pain was bad enough.

Now let's go up the scale another step. What if the pain is so bad it takes over everything? Nothing makes it go away, the person can't do anything—the kind of agony that makes a person understand why pain is called the window into Hell. That high up the scale, a few thousand or even a hundred thousand or two cannot make up for the pain. In a case like that, I would have to ask you for a verdict of more like five or six hundred thousand dollars, closer to a million, over and above medical and lost income costs.

Now, you know that the pain in John's arm is well into that third scale.

The pain in his leg is not that bad, thank God, so it goes on the second scale. Add the second-scale amount for his leg to the first-scale amount for his arm, and that is your figure for the pain itself. [If permitted, do the math—on a chart.] Now let's look at how long that pain lasts.

Pain that lasts for a short time—a few weeks, maybe a month or two—would be lowest on the scale. It would not take much money to make up for it. That would be the kind of case in which I'd have to ask for maybe a thousand or two beyond medical and income costs, 10 or 20 or 30 thousand if it was high on the pain scale, too. But what if it lasts not for weeks but for two or three years? Then that thirty thousand is not enough, because the pain has intruded on a big part of the person's life. I'd have to ask for a few hundred thousand dollars, maybe even a million, depending where it fell on the scale of how much it hurt.

But at the top of the scale? If it's going to hurt not just for a few weeks or a few years, but for the rest of the person's life? And if that person has a life expectancy of 30 more years? All of it living every day, every hour, with this pain. And if the pain will get worse with time, as arthritis and other problems set in to make it hurt more, then we go even higher on the scale. We're beyond making up for it with just a few hundred thousand or even a million dollars. Now the person can't even lie there at night and take comfort in hope, the one thing we cling to when nothing else is left—hope that 'Someday this pain will be gone.' John cannot have that hope, because he knows it will never be gone. It will only get worse. That's the top of the scale.

So with this case at the top of this scale, it's the kind of case in which I have to ask for at least two million dollars beyond medical and income costs. And add that to the amount for where it is on the scale of how much it hurts.

Finally, how much does the pain interfere with the things a person normally does? What does it keep a person from doing? Low on the scale, just a little interference, if the person can do all but a few things he used to do, then it does not take much to make up for it. If it's just a limp but he can still walk and run, it might be a few thousand, ten, maybe twenty thousand.

But if there are many things the pain keeps him from doing, things that had been an important part of his normal life, things that made his life worth living and now they're taken away, it takes more money. If it's too painful to work around the house or in the yard, if he can't walk without assistance or ride in a car more than a few minutes because of the pain, that's a major intrusion on a person's life. That's the middle of the scale, which puts it in the range of a half million dollars, maybe more.

> At the top of the scale is the kind of case in which the pain is so bad that the person can do almost nothing. Everything his body used to be able to do, now someone else has to do for him. So we're back at the top where it takes a million or more dollars to make up for what he can't do anymore. Add that to the amount for how bad it hurts, and add that to the amount for how long it lasts. [And do the math.]

Use this method for each important non-economic harm: pain, emotional or cognitive problems, disability for other reasons, etc.

The method also works for wrongful death, because the ultimate permanence is death. Being deprived of a father's guidance for a few years is a mid-scale loss; permanently, and it's the top of the scale.

With this technique, you will never again be reduced to using the lamest assertion attorneys ever say to juries: "No one can give you a way to figure out how much money to give for pain or suffering. I cannot do that. Not even the judge can give you a way. You have to figure it out yourself." This translates into, "It's illegitimate."

Instead, in voir dire (or opening, if necessary) you can promise to give them a way at the end of the trial. Then in closing, give them this way.

Lesser harm. When the harm is only middlingly painful, or is not permanent, or interferes with only a moderate amount of activity, this technique works just as well.

> A small amount of harm is a small amount of money, a medium amount of harm is a medium amount of money, and a large amount of harm is a large amount of money. This case is in the middle. So it's the kind of case in which I have to ask you for more than the ten or 15 thousand a small amount of harm would require. But it's not one of those cases you hear about where the pain is so bad that I'd have to ask for many hundreds of thousands or even into the millions. This is in between, somewhere in the range of two or three hundred thousand dollars.

Jurors do not necessarily rush into deliberations and begin using the scales. They might not use them at all. But when a low-balling juror says—and he will—"I think $10,000 is enough," the scales explanation has armed your favorable jurors to say, "No, not $10,000; they told us that was for cases where the pain was much less. This is one of the hundred-thousand-dollar cases." Remember, your primary goal in closing is to arm your favorable jurors so they can win the case for you in deliberations. The scales argument does that.

9.15
Admit Some Fault

With a persuasive comparative negligence argument against you, it can be best when massaging the verdict questions to acknowledge that some jurors may think it fair to assign some blame to your client. Give a suggested range: "Someone might reasonably think that some of the fault was John's. You show how much of the fault you think was John's by giving it a percentage. You might think 5 or 10%, or some of you might even think as high as 15%. Whichever you all agree on, write it on this line here." Jurors appreciate the honesty.

This tells your favorable jurors the range to argue for, if need be. And it provides a benchmark that helps anchor the percentage jurors are likely to consider.

Often, you can proportionalize the amount of fault as being in the same ratio as the proportion of *what your client knew* versus *what the defendant knew* about the potential for danger. "The doctor knew all about the possible consequences. Mary did not even know 10% as much—so the limit of her responsibility is no more than 10%."

In jurisdictions where you lose if the jury assigns the plaintiff 50% or more negligence, and when there is a good possibility that the jury might decide 50% or more, be sure the jury understands the cut-off point. Otherwise your favorable jurors might think they are getting some money for your client even though they decide he is 51% at fault. Do not rely on the judge's instruction on this (or any) point. Often, jurors do not understand or even listen to the instructions. (So when massaging the comparative instruction, say, "If you write 51% or higher here, you are finished with deliberations." And if allowed, say, "John will get no money.")

9.16

Comparative Fault: Double-Dipping

In some cases, jurors are asked to apportion fault and then give an absolute figure for the total value of the damages. The judge then decreases the jury's dollar figure by the percentage they assign for comparative fault.

To prevent double-dipping against you, explain in closing that the judge will reduce their damages figure by their percentage of comparative negligence. Show how it works when you are massaging that verdict question. If you don't, they likely will double-dip against you. First they will assign, say, 25% comparative fault. Then they will lower their total damages figure by 25%. Then the judge will lower it by 25% again.

Write out an example as you explain.

> If you decide, say, that John was 5% to blame, then write 5% on this line. The judge will use that 5% to reduce the dollar amount(s) you write later. So if you decide that the total value of the harm, no matter who did it, is $100,000, write $100,000 on this line. Again, that's the amount no matter who did it; the value of the total harm. The judge will reduce it later by your 5% from this line, so John would get $95,000.

Beware of jury instructions or verdict issues that imply that all the money will come from the defendant when in fact it will not—such as because of comparative fault proportioning or a joint-and-several settlement. If a remedy is within the judge's discretion, argue to the judge that letting jurors be misled is a fraud on the jury, and it hurts your client by fooling jurors into putting less money on the total damages line than they believe the value of the losses to be.

9.17
The Circle

Draw a pie chart on butcher paper.

Segment a pie slice to represent medical expenses. Cut another pie slice for lost wages. Cut a pie slice for each economic loss. Write the figure for each tangible loss in its pie slice.

Your total pie cuts for economic losses should take up much less than half the circle.

Explain that the whole circle represents all the money needed to fix what can be fixed, help what can be helped, and make up for whatever cannot be fixed or helped. The circle represents the total amount to achieve justice.

The circle is particularly useful where you cannot suggest specific figures for intangible losses. It visually proportionalizes the dollar amount of the intangibles to the dollar amount of the tangibles. Most important, the jurors can draw this circle for themselves in deliberations. Suggest that they do so.

9.18
How Do You Decide on Appropriate Amounts?

Attorneys are often afraid to ask too little, and almost as afraid to ask too much.

Some attorneys try to gauge the "worth" of a case by comparing it to other cases. But no two cases are alike even if all the issues and evidence are similar. If nothing else, the parties are different. The nature and situations of the parties are weighty factors in juror decision making about money. Differences among attorneys also factor in.

So how do you know how much you can ask for without making the jurors think you are out of line, and without asking for far less than they would have at least considered?

The only good way is with focus groups. You should be doing focus groups anyway, even for small cases, because there is no better way to learn how to present (and not to present) your case in court. For larger cases, use a trial consultant. For smaller cases, you can do your own focus groups for very little money—under a thousand dollars. But you have to do focus groups properly or you will mislead yourself. My favorite trial advocacy author has an excellent book on how to do your own focus groups.[6]

A focus group cannot reliably predict how much you are likely to get. But it will help you determine a range of money that real jurors will likely consider reasonable. You cannot count on getting around one hundred thousand dollars just because your focus jurors found that amount reasonable. But if a number of focus jurors individually decide that one hundred thousand is within a reasonable range, then jurors will probably not find you out of line for asking that much—even if they eventually decide on a different figure.

You should ask the real jury for the highest amount the focus jurors found to be within a reasonable range. And be sure to tell them it is only a suggested amount—they can give more if they wish. Otherwise, they often believe they are allowed to give no more than you asked for.

Catastrophic cases. If your client's life has been lost or devastated by, say, permanent disability or severe pain, the amount you ask for should be very high. In a wrongful death case, do not ask for $500,000 because that's what those cases get in your area. That's what they get because usually barely more is requested. If you are successful in showing all the harm the death did, if you use the Scales (9.14), if you show that the measure of harm has to be gauged from your client's point of view, if you show that nothing belongs in the scales but the amount of harm, then you can ask for a verdict in the tens of millions of dollars. "Compensation means that enormous harm requires enormous money."

6. *How To Do Your Own Focus Groups* by David Ball (NITA, 2001).

9.19

Jurors' Weekends and Other Treasures

Be on the lookout for things the jurors themselves treasure that parallel what your client has lost. You can find these things in voir dire, as well as by what you know about people in the region. What do your jurors find valuable and how do those things relate to what your client lost?

For example, in areas where many people work at difficult, dangerous, extremely unpleasant jobs, such as in the West Virginia and eastern Kentucky coal mines, working folks live for their weekends. Knowing this, you can argue that, "John has lost all his weekends. And he's lost that long weekend called retirement, because his pain won't let him travel, work in the garden, play with his grandkids, or relax on the porch. John's pain won't give him a day off, ever."

This is not merely an analogy. It is personal to your jurors, so it gets them to personally understand and identify with John's situation.

Jurors tend to shield themselves emotionally from your client's catastrophic losses. By putting the harm in terms the jurors identify with, you keep them from walling themselves off.

If you have jurors with young children—jurors who showed themselves in voir dire to be enthusiastic family-centered folks—then emphasize your client's harms as they apply to his involvement with his kids and their welfare. Do not just show your client's feelings about being cut off from family involvements. Show how his kids feel about losing quality time and activities with dad. This represents a strong loss to dad, because he knows how his kids feel.

Know your audience. Without being cute, clever, or condescending, tailor some of your damages arguments to the things *they* treasure. They'll feel your client's harms more directly, and be more likely to attach tangible significance to intangible losses. Nothing turns an intangible to a tangible as effectively as making it personal.

9.20

The First Thing You Think of

> When the phone call we all dread comes in the middle of a night and it's about a loved one, that she's been hurt (or worse)—the first thing you think is not 'Oh my, I wonder how much her medical expenses are going to be,' or 'I wonder how much salary she'll lose.' Our first thoughts, our only thoughts, are about the important things: 'Is she alive? Is she okay? Is she in pain? Will she get better?'
>
> Those concerns are the real measures of harm. And when someone's not okay, when they're going to be in pain forever, those are the real measures of what the verdict should be.

9.21

Two Futures

The more you can show that money will make a difference, the more likely you are to get the money. Georgia's Don Keenan asks the jurors to come to the top of the mountain with him, and look down the next 50 (or whatever) years.

> Look this way—the way with no money—and you see a bleak future for Shawna: cold institutional care, separated from her loved ones, given whatever care an overworked orderly can spare the time to give her. But look the other way—the way built on the verdict you can provide—and you see Shawna surrounded by her family, loved, cherished, given the best care money can buy. . . .

In every case involving future harm—including most wrongful death cases where the family's pain will not easily heal—you can draw the picture of the two futures.

In punitive damages cases, show the list of past victims alongside a list of blank lines. In the future without a proper verdict, the blank lines will be filled in with the names of more victims. In the other future—created by a sufficient punitive damages figure—the blanks stay blank. No more victims.

Whether for compensation or punitive damages, the two futures argument gives jurors what they need most to provide a significant verdict: a feeling of worthwhileness for the money you are asking for. When jurors believe the money can accomplish something, they are far more willing to provide it.

9.22
Safety

Jurors tend to provide money for worthwhile purposes. One of the most worthwhile is to help keep your client safe. And jurors can get angry when you point out that the defendant's refusal to meet his responsibility has meant that your client has had to live at risk since the injury. (No money for night care, so he's vulnerable to intruders; no money for emergency egress, so he's in danger if there's a fire; etc.)

Bring in a safety expert to point out dangers to your disabled client that life-care planners and doctors may miss. For example, planners for paraplegics include fire exits from every room in the house—but sometimes pay no attention to the landscaping outside to make sure the paraplegic can quickly get his wheelchair far enough away from the house to be well out of danger. This is the kind of thing experienced safety experts are likely to see. That can add considerably to the money you can ask for and that jurors are likely to provide.

9.23
Judo Law and The "Gift Of Malingering"

The great Kentucky attorney Gary C. Johnson is an expert at what he calls "Judo Law." He explains, that "when the defense has something bad against your case, don't go on the defensive. Sit down and think. Think about it for as long as it takes to figure out how to turn it around and use it against them—so that it hits them harder than they can throw it at you."

Florida criminal defense attorney Roy Black teaches that in criminal cases you have to look at the worst things against you and figure out how to make them work for you. If you can do that, you win. If you can't you lose. Johnson calls this Judo Law because it operates on the principle of judo: taking what your opponent thrusts at you and turning its full force back against him.

For example, by employing Judo Law, you will find yourself grateful for defense accusations of malingering, pain exaggeration, and anything else that says your client is dishonest. If your client will likely be credible to the jury,[7] defense implications that she is being dishonest—along with her spouse and her physicians when they corroborate what she says about the level of her harm—give you the opportunity to use an extremely powerful damages argument.

> It was not enough for the defendants to cause so much physical harm, mental harm, and emotional harm. Now they have taken away the one thing they'd left intact: Sally's good name. Everything that has happened in this trial is now a permanent public record. And on that permanent public record, the defense has now called Sally a liar: Sally Robb is lying about her pain; Sally Robb is lying that she had to give up the job she loved; Sally Robb is lying that she cannot walk across a room without help. The defense has put this on the permanent public record that Sally's kids will one day come see—and they will, because as they get older they'll want to know about mom's trial. The media can put it on the news, and it is now part of the community: the accusation that Sally came in here, put her hand on the Bible, looked you in the eye, and lied to get money.
>
> In other words, they have wrecked the good name of Sally Robb. At this moment, the person with that name has been branded a liar. People who have not been at this trial, who have not heard all the proof, will forever have some suspicion that Sally might have lied. The defense has taken away Sally's own community's ability to trust her.
>
> Unlike some of the harms in this case, you can *fix* this one. At the instant your verdict is read aloud, Sally can have her good name back. The name 'Sally Robb' can mean what it

7. If your client is not likely to be credible, please see Appendix F for ways to prevent the defense from claiming that your client is malingering or exaggerating. Such claims are based on junk science because there is no way to prove malingering or symptom magnification.

> used to—*if* your verdict is for the full and fair amount—the five million dollars we talked about. If that is the verdict read out loud in this court, from that moment the community will know that the neutral jurors who sat and heard everything saw that Sally was telling the truth.
>
> But by whatever amount the verdict is lower, that's the amount of mistrust that will forever be attached to Sally's name. People who were not here will be justified in thinking that you did not believe her—or her husband, or children, or doctors—when she told you how badly she was hurt.
>
> But if your foreperson [or clerk] reads aloud your verdict for the full and fair amount, at that moment Sally's name is completely restored. The world will know that the neutral jury that heard everything knew she was telling the truth.

Don't ask for money for damage to her name. The point is that her name will be restored if the jury provides the full amount for the harms resulting from the defendant's negligence. This is a restorative argument: pay for the harms and her name is restored.

The argument is extraordinarily powerful partly because it gives a worthwhile and immediate purpose to non-economic damages. Jurors who are uncomfortable providing much money for lost quality of life (because money does no good) will be more comfortable providing that money to accomplish an important task: restoring Sally's name. And once you have firmly established the total dollar figure you are seeking, it becomes the amount required to restore it.

Often the defense uses mini-versions of malingering claims. "Her pharmacy records show that half the time she did not take her pain medications." Here, too, apply a little Judo Law. Instead of getting defensive, offer it up yourself in opening to support your case, not defend it:

> The only way she could keep her job was to quit taking half her pain pills so her head would be clear enough to do her work. Her pain pills make her woozy and unable to think clearly. That would get her fired. So to earn a living to support her children, she has to be in bad pain all day, five days a week. Only at home can she take her pain pills—by which time she's so exhausted from contending with the pain all

day at work that all she can do is rest to recover enough to start all over the next morning.

This turns her into a fighter who won't quit—as opposed to the liar the defense claimed.

9.24

Surveillance Videoing Causes Harm

The defense does love their spy cameras. They say, "Aha! Look what she did that afternoon! She went s*wimming*! Look at that! She's faking. Look at this video of her swimming around with her kids. Obviously she's better than she claims."

Apply a little Judo Law. The video proves *she has refused to give in to the damage*—even though she knew her extra efforts to make sure her kids could have a normal day every so often swimming with mom would have her flat on her back in pain for the next two days. Show a video of her lying down exhausted and in pain after one of those days.

Judo Law response: Show that the price she paid for weeding that garden or washing the car or swimming with her kids was agonizing pain and exhaustion the whole next day. But does she get up and do it again the day after that? You bet. "She won't quit but she needs your help to keep going."

There is a dark side to what the defense does when it sends out its creeps with video gear to sit in mystery vans and under bushes stalking your client. It's even creepier when the client is a child. Don't take this lying down. Stalking your client with cameras, secretly invading their privacy, peering at the house and the school and the car for hours at a time does no harm while it's happening—but when your client finds out, the feelings it creates can be awful—having nothing to do with the creeps catching her at anything that can impeach her.

So don't say it's merely a nasty thing to do. Explain how it actually causes harm: intense feelings of violation and intrusion; fears that the stalking creeps could have been dangerous. The insecurity of knowing you are that vulnerable.

First the defendant drags your client into this nightmare by injuring her in the first place. Then they make matters worse by refusing to be responsible for what they did. Now they expose her to more fear and danger by hiring some unknown creeps to stalk her with cameras.

Your client had no control over the honesty or decency of the creeps, and now your client will never know how far they really went. If they hid in bushes to video her in the park with her children, if they hid in vans to take videos of her coming out of her Ob-Gyn's office, how does she know they did not aim their camera in the bathroom window to see if she could really toilet herself or shower unassisted? And who knows who has those videos? Surely the creeps who do this kind of work are not so trustworthy that they heed the court's instruction to turn everything over.

These "silly" thoughts need not be proven to be true. The obvious truth is that a normal person would have them, and they cut deep. Such possibilities are very real and deeply disturbing to a client who is already struggling with the results of serious injuries.

Clients rarely tell you about these feelings because they feel silly —but they are not silly feelings at all. Ask your client how she felt when she first learned about the creeps stalking her. Anger sure—but then what? Fear? Shame? Humiliation? Ask the parents how they felt when they found out that some unnamed guys in cheap suits sat in dark vans following their child around—even to school and back. Is the kid still scared about it? And what do those pretty bushes across the street mean to the parents now that they know some goons with cameras concealed themselves there while videoing the house at night?

Ask your client if she worries about what personal things the creeps got to watch that they either did not video or did not turn over as the judge ordered.

If your client thinks she ever spotted the creeps, point out to the jury that the only way these professionals ever let themselves be seen is if they want to be seen. So "Did they let themselves be seen as a way to intimidate her into backing out of the lawsuit?" Being stalked in this way is threatening because you never know exactly who it is or when they will be there. And these stalkers and the people who hire them know that a little bit of threat against a person or against a person's child can result in them backing out of the case.

The best source for how creeps surveilling has caused harm is to talk in depth with the client who was surveilled. Have someone other than you do it, such as a good social worker or other expert skilled in drawing out problems that people can be reluctant to talk about. This extra research can provide a foundation for developing a strong anger case against the defense. And though it's a bit of a stretch, a proximate cause of this harm was the initial negligence—you might be able to seek compensation for it.

A few hefty verdicts like that around the country and maybe these creeps who crept into this line of work will creep back out.

9.25
Legalese

No legalese, not a word of it—especially not in closing, and especially not when you are talking about harm and damages. No technical terms either.

9.26
Vague Language

Avoid vague or confusing language. Be concrete. Pay special attention to the following:

Pronouns. No pronouns (his, hers, him, it, she, he, etc.) in closings. Pronouns wreak havoc with meaning: "Right after he lifted his leg against the hydrant, the policeman grabbed the dog's collar and suddenly he bit him on his butt."

Use proper nouns. They clarify. And the less you use pronouns, the more often you weld the defendant's name to the wrongdoing. Pronouns are ineffective when blaming. "He knew it was wrong" is less effective than "The defendant knew it was wrong."

Verbs. In closing (but not in opening) use strong, specific verbs. "Slam" is better than "hit" or "collide." (In opening be more moderate; you don't yet have the standing for strong language.)

Specifics. Use the most specific label possible: Not "vehicle" but "car." Not "car" but "Honda."

Put all three together and here is the difference language can make:

Vague:	"When he collided with him . . . ."
Better:	"When Jones hit Stan's car . . . ."
Concrete:	"When the defendant [point] slammed his dump truck into Stan's Honda . . . ."

9.27
Nominal Damages

In these times of tort "reform," strange things happen in the jury room. In some jurisdictions, judges routinely read a nominal damages charge even when there is no evidence supporting it. And while jurors don't listen closely to jury instructions, they often do hear the "one dollar" phrase in the nominal damages charge.

In more normal times, jurors would ignore it. But these days jurors seek out ways to shut plaintiffs down. They sometimes assume the judge is doing the same thing. ("I could tell; the judge didn't want them to get money"—even when the judge has been scrupulously neutral.) So when some jurors hear an instruction that says one dollar is a possible verdict (why else would the judge mention it?) they think it's the judge's way of saying that's all the verdict should be. Or they might think this is the judge's way of saying that insurance has taken care of this, so one dollar is all that's needed.

Result: One-dollar verdict. I am not making this up. It has happened.

The Moral: Get the judge to omit the nominal damages charge when it does not apply. It is almost always an impossible charge for the evidence to support. It is extremely prejudicial because that "one dollar" is the only figure the judge ever mentions.

9.28
"The Defendant Is Plenty Safe"

In many cases, you can show that the defendant has taken steps to make himself safe from the kind of negligence he did that harmed your client. For example, in a case where a fleet of mid-weight delivery trucks were never properly inspected, the company's owner drove a heavyweight Mercedes. So he was not likely to get hurt if one of his trucks with bad brakes ever hit him like one hit the plaintiff.

The purpose is to show that the defendant knows that what he's doing is dangerous—yet does it anyway because it's endangering only other people, not himself.

More generally, compare the care with which the defendant protects himself versus the lack of care he used with your client. For example, in a medical negligence case with bad medical records, compare those bad records to the neat, meticulous record-keeping used for billing. (And always scrutinize billing records for discrepancies with medical records.)

American railroads generally spend only a fraction of the money on public safety as they do on protecting their railroad yards. For example, railroad yards are usually monitored by expensive surveillance cameras and surveillance systems. But railroads have not provided inexpensive video cameras for engineers to see blind spots in front of their high-speed trains.

9.29
Closing: Miscellaneous Points

Proportion. Remember that a trial is about whatever it spends most of its time being about, not what it spends little time on. (See Chapter 1.4) This is particularly true in closing. It is monetary suicide to spend 90% of your closing on liability. Half and half—without padding—is the goal.

Do not omit any liability argument. But do not let liability overwhelm harm and money.

The judge's proportion of time. To support the legitimacy of money for non-economic damages, point out (when it is true) that the judge will spend more time instructing the jury on non-economic damages than on economic damages "because the law places so much importance on making up for those losses with money—and because these decisions require careful consideration of all the harms—*and nothing else*—in order to determine the proper amount."

Human losses experts. Georgia's Don C. Keenan has effectively argued something like this: "You saw experts on medicine, experts on rehabilitation, experts on life care, and an expert economist. But we showed you no experts on how much to give for Johnnie's human losses, because you are the experts on that. You know what it is to hold a child. You know the value of a child being able to walk. You know the value beyond wages of an adult being able to work, being able to sit up in a chair, being able to feed himself. That is why you are here, because you are the experts on this child's worst losses and what they will be as he gets older."

The judge sent them home. Tell the jurors that some people think that because it is hard to place a dollar figure on pain, there is no way to give money for it. Remind the jury that the judge sent home three people who had that opinion, because it made them unable to follow the law. "So if anyone in deliberations seems to be thinking that way, remind them."

Zero is a figure. Point out that "zero" is a dollar figure, so by giving nothing, the jury would be saying that the harm has no value.

"Reckon not the need!" To help overcome jurors' reluctance to provide money beyond necessities, point out that providing what your client "needs" does not by itself compensate. Anything to help make his life more pleasant or a little easier or any less limited is the part of the compensation required to make up for the harms money cannot fix.

Help her be helpful again. If your client had been a charitable and helping person before she was hurt and now can no longer be, one of her losses is the pleasure she took in helping others. If she can no longer carry meals to the elderly, or raise money for a charity, or visit the sick, or anything else she used to do to help, ask the jury to: "Help her help people again. She can't cook and carry those 20 meals a week anymore, but you can give back her inner satisfaction of knowing those folks are being well fed—if you include in your verdict the money for her to hire people and buy the food. That way her help can continue. It is the defendant's responsibility to replace what they took away."

Do not position this as a request for compensation for the receivers of the help. They aren't eligible. But your client is eligible to have every loss replaced. One of her big losses is the pleasure and satisfaction she gained from the help she used to give.

Law's purpose; jury's purpose.

> The purpose of the law is to balance the harm. The purpose of the jury is to figure out what it will take to balance the harm.

"Can't put a price on it." One reason jurors resist money for non-economic damages is because: "You can't put a price on a life" or suffering or whatever. In closing, say, "When anyone in deliberations says 'You can't put a price on it,' that means they are talking about something expensive. So you have to work together to decide how expensive."

Taking money from a good cause. If the defense argues that taking too much verdict money from the defendant will hurt a worthwhile organization such as a hospital, object. Ask for a curative instruction that the hospital is insured for more than you are asking. The defendant is not allowed to defraud the jury just because something is not in evidence.

If the judge does not agree (or if you decide your appeals court is too strict about insurance to want her to agree), you should still ask the judge to instruct the jury that they are not to take anything like that into account—because their verdict amount must be based only on harm caused by the defendant's negligence.

And in closing point out that "There is no evidence that the defendant will have to pay any of this verdict no matter how large it is."

Compact. Try to reduce your case to a brief compact between parties:

> When a driver puts his key in the ignition, he has a compact by law with his car's manufacturer: That the manufacturer has sold him a car that is safe for its intended purposes, and that the driver will do his best to drive safely. Ford violated that compact. So the law makes Ford responsible.
>
> When you drive down the road, you have a compact by law with every motorist: That *you* will do your best to avoid hurting them, and that they will do the same for you. Defendant Jones violated that compact. That makes Jones responsible.

Give more. When you give your dollar requests, explain to jurors that they are free to give more. Many jurors say after trials that the jury would have given more if they had known they were allowed to.

Juror questions. *Questions with no good answers.* Attorneys often tell the jurors to listen to see if the opposition will answer certain questions in closing. "Listen to hear if Mr. Defendum explains how the doctor's choice to stay home helped John." This can be a useful tactic. It is even more useful if you save it for your second closing when the defense can no longer answer your questions. Say:

> When you get into deliberations, if there are jurors who think Doctor Jones did not cause this harm, please ask those jurors these questions: ________________ . . . .

Go slowly, especially if they are taking notes. Give the unanswerable questions that make your point. Do the same for damages. Then explain how each unanswered question is case pivotal.

Defense *questions with good answers.* If you have ever talked to jurors after losing a case, you know how much you wish you'd been in the jury room so you could have answered some of the things they said in deliberations that led to your losing. You had the answers! That painful lesson teaches that you need to anticipate every question that defense-prone jurors are likely to bring up.

Provide those questions to your favorable jurors in closing when the defense no longer gets to say anything.

Then—and this may be the most important thing you do in closing—provide the answers in simple, concise language. Don't rehash anything; they know the evidence, they've heard the arguments. Just give the answers and explain why the answers are correct.

> During deliberations, if anyone asks, 'How can anyone know the flooring was installed wrong?' remind them *there were no brackets.*
>
> During deliberations, when someone asks. 'How can anyone know John could not work for those six weeks?' remind them *John kept trying but the boss kept sending him home.*

Focus groups are not only the best possible way to prepare for any trial, but they also tell what these defense questions from jurors are likely to be. Once you know them, you can pose them and answer them as effectively as if you were in deliberations.

9.30
Closing Quickies

> Foreseeablity creates responsibility. Responsibility means paying enough money to equal the level of the harm.
>
> Money cannot bring back the dead, but it helps the living get on with life.
>
> We are asking for money for Andrea's pain because there is no magic to make the pain go away. (Consultant Eric Oliver's suggestion.)
>
> We are not here seeking sympathy. We are here to collect a debt.

Your verdict amount should be the difference between what could have been and what is.

Debra Miller, my Jurywatch partner, suggests this useful idea: "The defense wants harm to be on sale."

CHAPTER TEN
PUNITIVE DAMAGES

Jurors have many reasons for not giving much in punitive damages. Thus, a punitive damages campaign is rarely effective unless you pursue it on a variety of fronts throughout trial.

10.1
Explain Intentionality

Just as they do with simple negligence, jurors looking at enhanced negligence tend to forgive anything inadvertent. "The company didn't kill the guy on purpose." If the instruction mentions intent, when massaging the instructions (see 9.7), show exactly what intent means. Explain that intent does *not* mean intending to hurt anyone. Willful or wanton behavior means knowingly allowing or creating danger, but *not intentionally hurting anyone*. Intentionally hurting someone is malice.

So, for example, a company saving money on how they build something is okay—but not when the company does it *knowing* it will create or allow a danger. That means intentionally creating or allowing a danger. It does not mean intentionally hurting anyone.

Violating any safety rule can be seen as willful because the safety rule states what to do to prevent danger.

Emphasize this understanding of intentionality from jury voir dire onwards. Ask questions regarding juror experiences and attitudes about it. (See 5.46) Weave it through testimony: "Mr. Expert, what would a driver with the defendant's experience have known about the danger of not checking his brakes before starting out?"

10.2
Show Foreseeability

Make sure jurors understand that it was not necessary for the defendant to have foreseen this particular outcome, or even one like it. All the defendant had to foresee was that any harm could be a reasonable outcome. Exactly what you say depends on your specific law, but make sure your jurors know enough to interpret the law correctly, and not in a narrower way that will hurt you. This is important with negligence, but jurors look at it much more closely when deciding whether the defendant has done something that merits punitives.

10.3
Show Pattern of Wrongdoing

No matter how intentional, or gross, malicious, or downright evil the wrongdoing was, jurors can remain reluctant to give punitives until they see the defendant has done this kind of wrong over and over, or is still doing it. (Don't refer to similar wrongdoing by the defendant outside the state. It exposes the defendant to being punished twice for the same act.[1])

By showing that the wrongdoing represents the normal way the defendant operates, you give jurors a worthwhile reason to provide a large amount. So your strongest tool can be charts showing each instance of the company's similar wrongdoing.

Jurors tend to give less in punitives for what the defendant did only to your client, because it serves no greater purpose. The wrongdoing is over, the jury has compensated your client, so why discourage the defendant from future wrongdoing? It's already over. So you want to show multiple wrongs—especially when they imply the inevitably or probability of similar future wrongdoing. As far as jurors are concerned, the wrongs need not be exactly the same; they need only represent the same low level of dealing with safety.

Can you show three roughly similar incidents? A dozen? A thousand? Do so, if allowed. Make them a centerpiece of trial. Refer to them in jury voir dire, describe them in opening, cover them emphatically in

1. *State Farm Mutual Automobile Insurance Co. v. Campbell et al*, 538 US 408 (2003).

your case-in-chief, subvert opposition witnesses into confirming them (see 8.1), focus on them in closing, and use visuals to show them.

Show what the defendants did and do, and show the harmful effects it has been having whenever they do it.

10.4
Pursue All Three Purposes of Punitive Damages

No matter how clearly the judge explains punitive damages, tell the jurors yourself that they should give enough in punitive damages to accomplish all three of its purposes: to punish, to make the defendant quit doing anything like it again, and to discourage others from doing anything like it. Argue that each of the three purposes is worthwhile all by itself, and that all three have to be accomplished.

Jurors understand how punitives punish, but unless they are angry at the defendant they are rarely moved to punish. It is easier to motivate jurors to use money to prevent future wrongdoing. Show how much it will take to make that happen. Argue that the company counts on jurors not being willing to make them pay enough to make them stop—so they keep doing it.

10.5
Prove that Punitives Work

Especially in this tort-"reform" era, many jurors do not believe that punitives prevent future wrongdoing. Such jurors (and many plaintiff's attorneys, too) believe that punitives merely make the company raise prices to cover the cost, so that the company goes on with business as usual. Thus, "we" pay the cost and nothing changes.

Jurors also worry that the company will make up for the loss by firing employees, whom jurors want to protect.

These common beliefs are fostered by a wide variety of media, corporate interests, and politicians. This means you have to treat the efficacy of punitives as a major issue in contention. Over the course of trial you must prove that punitives have an effect, and that the company cannot raise prices or fire employees to cover the loss. Just arguing it in closing is not enough.

Do that with an expert. An investment analyst knows how to determine what a particular company can do about significant losses. Have such an expert explain the workings of the company in a way that shows that money deprivation does in fact change its policies—that the company does not merely pass losses on in the form of higher prices, or fire its workers. Have the expert explain something like this:

> Historically, when an Acme product has lost a lot of money because not enough people bought it, Acme did not raise prices of other products to cover the loss, nor fire workers. They cannot raise prices without making their products uncompetitive. They cannot fire workers without leaving themselves unable to compete. Instead, Acme has always either redesigned the product so it will sell better, or taken it off the market. In 1993, the Acme power Blaxet-Cutter was not selling because it didn't cut blaxets very well, and no one bought it. Acme lost a lot of money on it. But they could not make up for the loss by raising other prices without losing sales, so instead Acme redesigned their Blaxet-Cutter to make it cut well enough for people to buy.
>
> In other words, large money losses lead them to change what they do. They redesign or discontinue. So if the safety problems of a product cost them a lot of money because of a verdict, Acme will redesign the product or get it off the market. They can't pass a huge loss on to the consumer and they can't fire workers to make up for it.

If allowed, your expert should give examples of other companies that have changed how they do business because of large punitive verdicts. Provide evidence of products redesigned, policies rewritten, and practices overhauled—and show that prices were not raised and workers were not fired.

10.6
Show What It Will Take To Teach a Lesson

While some jurors believe that punitives will not change anything, others think that just making a company pay compensation is enough to teach it a lesson. This is particularly true when compensatory damages are high.

If the facts support it and you can get it in, show that this company has paid verdicts before without reforming its behavior, so we need a large verdict to create change. *But do not kill the defendant:*

10.7
Do Not Kill the Defendant

Have an expert explain how much money the defendant could pay in punitive damages without closing the company or eliminating jobs. Position punitive damages as a constructive way of reforming behavior, not as a death sentence for the company or for workers' jobs.

There are rare exceptions to this, such as when jurors are convinced that a company does something so awful, so murderously wrong, that it must be driven out of business. The Florida jurors who decided the tobacco companies should pay $145 billion presumably thought that closing the tobacco companies was necessary to save lives. But few juries will see reason to close or seriously harm a company, because that hurts individuals who did nothing wrong.

Establish that your expert has studied the company's finances, and have the expert say: "Acme will not be able to afford to continue their dangerous practices if they are forced to pay $_______. And to stay competitive, they would not be able to fire employees—and they won't even if they have to pay punitive damages of up to $_____."

Argue this:

> The only way to make Acme reform is to make them pay so much in damages that they can never afford to pay that much again. That way they can't regard verdicts against them as just the cost of doing business—because next time they hurt someone this way, they'll know a jury can put them out of business.

10.8

Send a *Real* Message

Explain that the punitive verdict must be large enough for the people who run the company to hear it. Personalize the people in charge: the board of directors (give names) in a distant city (specify), or the stockholders who will see the stock fall if there is a large enough punitive verdict. If that happens the stockholders will force the company to reform in order to avoid another such drop in share value. In closing, create a little vignette of the meeting where the owners will decide to change the company's practices.

Show that the people who run the company have demonstrated that they do not care about the welfare of people "around here." They might have shown this by the kind of wrongdoing in this and other instances, by other wrongdoings, by the way they conducted the case, and even by their choice of the individual who is in court as the company representative. "If they were paying attention and if they cared, they'd have sent someone here who runs the company, who makes decisions—not someone who knows little about the case and has nothing to do with making decisions."

10.9

Seek Publicity

Explain that because an important purpose of punitives is to discourage others from similar wrongdoing, this verdict must be large enough to get enough publicity so that everyone across the country in the same business will hear about it. "It has to be a large enough verdict to be reported on the front page of newspapers everywhere. It has to be on network news. It has to be posted on Web sites. That is the only way others in this business will see they had better not do (or better stop doing) what Acme has been doing. A small verdict does not make the news. It will discourage others only if others and their stockholders read about it at breakfast or see it on the news. So a small verdict cannot fulfill the law's purposes of punitive damages, which include discouraging others from the same kind of wrongdoing."

10.10

Don't Make the Plaintiff Rich

Nationally, a third of the jurors know before being jurors that the plaintiff gets the punitive damages money. In deliberations, that third tells the other jurors.

This is a problem because some jurors who may be so angry at the company that they would gladly close it down and hang the bosses can still be reluctant to give much money to your client (and you). This is hard to overcome, especially with some kinds of plaintiffs, so try to seek this attitude out and get rid of it in jury selection. (See 5.31)

Some seated jurors will still feel that way, so you need an argument to deal with it.

Solve it or ignore it? It is a case-by-case judgment call whether to deal with this problem or leave it alone. By dealing with it, jurors who do not know that the money goes to your client find out. By not dealing with it, you potentially decrease a punitive verdict by a significant amount. If focus groups or other research shows you that jurors in the trial venue mostly know where the money goes, you should deal with the problem in voir dire and again in closing. If focus groups show otherwise, leave it alone. (If you are preparing for a significant punitive damages case without focus groups, you are . . . well, you know.)

How to deal with it. Consider admitting in closing that it might be somewhat wrong for your client to get as much money as is needed to accomplish the necessary purposes of punitive damages. But ask the jurors to compare any minor bad consequences of giving your client money to the widespread severe consequences the entire public will suffer if the jury allows the company to continue its wrongdoings.

Point out that the law specifies the criteria for jurors to consider when deciding how much to give in punitive damages—and that worrying about your client getting the money is not one of those criteria. (This is similar to the "impure thoughts" method; see 5.8.)

In jury voir dire, ask jurors how much they would be bothered by seeing your client get the enormous kind of verdict that punitive damages may require.

Emphasize and prove that the company can easily absorb the cost of a small verdict, so that only a large verdict will lead to change.

Explain that the law in general has two kinds of punishments: The first is punishment for breaking criminal laws, a task for which the law, the legislature, and society rely on cops and jails. The second is punishment for knowingly breaking civil laws that exist to keep people safe; the law, the legislature, and society entrust this task to juries. To do that, jurors are given the tool of assessing punitive damages large enough to have the intended effects regardless of where the money goes. The law and the legislature enable the jury to accomplish all three purposes of punitive damages (punish, deter defendant, deter others).

In some states, a percentage of each punitive verdict goes to the state. Some jurors know this. It's not legally material to the jurors' decision-making, but can make a lot of difference. So the communities in which you practice ought to know about it. Citizens have the right to know what the laws are. You have the right to help teach them. Just not always in trial.

Set the standards. Point out that you are not asking the jury to be vengeful or mean, but that the community relies on them to decide on a high enough punitive damages figure to accomplish the law's three purposes. "There is no other way to make this kind of wrongdoing stop, because the legislature and the law assume you will take care of it, and have designated you to do it. No one else can."

The legislature intends for citizen juries to set the standards for the consequences of intentionally making dangerous choices. The jury sets that standard by the size of their punitive verdict.

Point out that if wrongdoers can count on juries not wanting to impose serious consequences for intentionally making dangerous choices, then wrongdoers will know that the system cannot hurt them. That means they will continue their intentional wrongdoing forever, with only the occasional annoyance of having to write a check for so little money that it's worth their while to continue the wrongdoing.

A bank robber who gets $25,000 per heist is not going to quit because he gets fined $15,000.

10.11
Arm Favorable Jurors

See 9.3 about creating five- to ten-word simple and clear sentences that boil down the main issues of the case so your favorable jurors can argue for you in deliberations. Use such sentences as well for each main point of your punitives case—sentences that jurors will use in deliberations and that they know they will be able to comfortably use later with family and friends who will wonder why they gave such a large verdict.

For example, tell the jurors: "When someone asks, 'Why eight million dollars?' respond, 'Three hundred and sixteen kids.' That's how to respond. 'Because Acme did the same thing to three hundred and sixteen kids.' "

10.12
Validation of the Judge

> The judge has decided that in this case—as opposed to other cases—that you will be able to decide there was wanton negligence and that you can decide the defendant should pay punitive damages. The judge made this decision because there is evidence you can base it on.

10.13
Purpose

Argue that "The purpose of the law on punitive damages is to make the defendant give back every cent he earned by doing what he did—not just some of it but all of it—and on top of that to pay enough of a penalty to make it financially impossible for him to gamble on not getting caught if he does it again."

CHAPTER ELEVEN
YOU AND TORT "REFORM"

"I was 100% convinced that the doctor did what they said to that poor lady. She deserved what her lawyer was asking for. But I decided no. We can't let lawyers damage the medical profession any more. Sometimes we have to sacrifice the individual to the big picture."
—Juror comment, December 2004

11.1
Stepping out of the Stereotype

You need to take control of the way jurors think about you. Not you as part of a group, but you as an individual attorney.

I hate to say "Do what I say or die," but if you and your colleagues do not quickly start doing the kinds of things this chapter is about—without waiting for your organizations to do it for you—your profession will die, and with it a lot more. As of this writing your profession is in intensive care. Unfortunately no one is providing the care. You have to do it yourself.

The trial lawyer organizations have been using every resource, ounce of energy, and heroic effort to battle tort "reform" in the legislatures. (The civil defense bar has been oddly silent, given that their futures are just as much on the line.) But little has been done to effectively join the battle on the public-opinion level. In addition, the forces behind tort "reform" have had almost unlimited resources and have not allowed themselves to be disadvantaged by truth. So in spite of the trial lawyer's organizations having fought hard in the legislatures, tort "reform"—now ominously relabeled "legal reform"—is winning huge victories that were undreamt of when the movement started 25 years ago.

But the legislative arena is not the only killing ground. So is the courtroom. As much as a third of the jury pool is now poisoned. Of the 60 people in your next jury pool, JuryWatch's research shows that in most cases, 15 to 20 will likely "know" you are dishonest; predatory; pathologically greedy; responsible for driving doctors, businesses, and jobs out of the state; damaging to American businesses by placing them at a disadvantage with foreign competitors no one sues; responsible for the lack of flu shots in the winter of 2004/2005; and akin to a kind of domestic internal terrorist. This is the stereotype that applies to you.

And most of the population believes you and your client are likely to lie in order to win. (Many jurors also think the defense lies. But jurors forgive some lying by an accused. And even if they do not, you are the one with the burden. If jurors think you are lying, you lose even if your opponent is Pinocchio.)

So what can you do? No matter what your involvement with your trial lawyer association's legislative efforts, in order to serve your clients you face an additional requirement. You must let the public see that you are different from the indelible stereotype that many now have of your profession. This task starts long before the first day of trial.

This is not a call for you to fight against the larger forces of tort "reform," or to alter the public's stereotypical image of trial lawyers. It is, rather, a call for you to show that such a stereotype does not apply to you.

You can't do this simply by seeming credible. Even if you are one of the fortunate few who have the personal attribute of conveying absolute credibility from the moment jurors see you (think Gerry Spence), many jurors no longer believe in "credibility."

> Did you find Attorney Smith credible?
>
> Very. But *lawyers are taught to seem credible.* They go to seminars to learn how. Credibility is their job and anyone can learn it. That's why I didn't believe him.

And this:

> Why did you believe the plaintiff's experts and not the defense's?

> They both sounded okay so we were ignoring both sides. None of us had the experience to know which ones were right. But then one of us said that plaintiff lawyers pay legislators to vote for pain and suffering money, so obviously they also pay experts to say what they want.

I wish I were making this up.

You are the butt of Jay Leno jokes that get meaner and meaner every year. You are the focus of talk show vitriol, political attacks, and even pastoral warnings, not-for-profit status be damned. With good reason you are probably at least a little self-conscious when you introduce yourself to a layperson as a trial lawyer.

So you can't overcome it all just by seeming credible in trial.

Not all of this comes from tort "reformers." Some is from plaintiff's attorneys whose advertising would turn their own mother against them, and probably has. And mother is right. One lawyer in a large city —who I'm sure had a mother at one time or another—ran an ad campaign that aroused so much suspicion that entire rooms full of people groaned and laughed when they heard his name. And they assumed that every *attorney working on that kind of case had to be just as disgusting*—as well as attorneys working on other kinds of cases.

When Vioxx advertising started, most of the barrage of advertisements did not bother to mention that Merck might have done something wrong. In the haste to sign up as many clients as their "McLitigator" offices could handle, they left out the only thing that could have justified to the public that anyone would sue: that Merck might have done something wrong. The resulting public impression was that despite Merck being a decent company that voluntarily ran its own testing and yanked Vioxx as soon as its testing discovered a problem, nonetheless the usual trial lawyer vultures lined up to get rich off of this unpreventable misfortune.

In later interviews and newspaper advertising, Merck's president reinforced that public perception so blunderingly created by the McLitigators.

Apparently not yet satisfied with the damage they had done to the profession, some of these Vioxx lawyers next held a well-publicized organizational meeting in a large city. Guess which one.

Las Vegas.

Not even the Mafia does that anymore! They are sensitive to public opinion. But this group of trial lawyers either did not care about the public or never gave the public opinion thought. They just wanted to sign up clients.

In Colorado after a seminar, a lawyer approached and told me his name. It had a distressingly familiar ring. We all hear it all the time on TV ads, and it leaves a lousy taste in the mouth of every juror. "Are you him?" I asked, ready to say something as insulting as I could possibly think of. "No," he said. "I'm not 'him.' "

"Damn," I said to myself, because I had just thought of something really colorful and vile to call him.

"But I have the same name," the poor guy said. "Jurors think I'm him."

I asked, "Do they throw their chairs at you?" But then I told him how to handle the problem.

So let us not merely blame the forces of tort "reform." Many plaintiff's attorneys are digging graves for the rest of you. These characters don't care what they are doing to the jury pool. They probably have no intention of ever getting in front of a jury. They want a bunch of cases they can settle fast. They are every bit as harmful as tort "reformers" make them out to be.

Many of the Vioxx attorneys are decent folks who will serve their clients well. But they have all been tarred with the same brush by the bad ones. So has every other plaintiff's lawyer—because the bad ads and the bad acts are the ones that jurors see and remember.

So due to tort-"reform" efforts along with the creepiness of some of the McLitigators, jurors believe that you are a major crisis: You are, for example, driving physicians out of whatever state you live in. The fact that physicians are not leaving does not keep people from believing they are. "Heck, three of 'em passed me on the freeway; they couldn't get out fast enough."

Result? You, dear reader, are seen as the crisis. That is what many jurors think about you as you walk into court. And you can't fix it for yourself just by what you do in trial. You have to start earlier.

You may be the most decent human being on the planet, the most caring, the most honest—but you are stereotyped. Stereotyping is called "attributional bias," the mechanism of, for example, racism. You can't shake it off any more than a Black man could at the hands of a racist. It does not go away, not over the course of a trial and probably not over the course of a lifetime.

You cannot run from the stereotype. Some trial lawyers' organizations have desperately tried to run by changing their names from "trial lawyers" to "consumer attorneys." Of course the public takes this as an admission that something really is wrong with trial lawyers.

You cannot hide from the stereotype. Nor can you change it.

The only solution is to transcend it.

For many years, the National Jury Project's Susan Macpherson has worked closely with such social ills. She explains that you can rarely convince anyone that their stereotypical "understanding" of you or anyone else is wrong. It is too deeply ingrained. But, she teaches, there is something you can do about it—and this is what you must start doing long before you ever get to trial: You have to do things (not simply say things) that show you are an exception to the stereotype. You can't suddenly make jurors believe they are wrong about the stereotype they have come to believe after years of powerful conditioning. That will take years, if it can be done at all. But you have cases next week and next month and next year, and cannot wait.

So how do you show (not just say) that you are an exception to the bad stereotype? How do you get the message to the jury pool? Hopefully you are convinced that you must start doing this right away. Some of us who see trials and talk to jurors day in and day know that either you start doing something about it now, or start looking for another line of work while you can still afford the bus fare to job interviews.

In addition to showing the prospective jury pool that you are an exception to the stereotype (in ways such as those described below), you also have to start showing them what the crises really are. For example, between 400 and 600 people die every day in American hospitals from medical negligence. Of course that's a crisis, but so far hardly anyone knows about it.

Are product safety standards a crisis? Look at the statistics, and of course they are.

How about physicians who lie under oath to prevent recovery for a malpractice victim? Part of the crisis?

Accident reconstructionists who barely know physics but earn hundreds of dollars an hour to help insurance companies get out of paying? Part of a crisis?

Undrinkable ground water in the entire eastern end of a state, is that a crisis?

A civil justice system so poisoned that soon it will be useless to victims of the real crisis. Is that a crisis?

The public does not know about these crises or any of the others. And the credibility of trial lawyers has been so damaged that even if we spread the news, few would believe us.

But if the public knew, imagine how much easier your next med mal case would be.

So you have two tasks in this age of tort "reform's" dominance.

1. Show that you are an exception to the stereotype, and
2. Educate your *future* jurors about the real crises that can affect their decision making. In other words, start providing some antidotes to the poison.

Do not wait for the trial lawyer organizations to do this for you. Help them do it as much as you can, but you are your own grass roots. You need to get busy on your own.

Get busy doing what? Thank you for asking.

Exception to stereotype. West Virginia lawyer Jim Lees—one of the great trial advocacy teachers—said years ago that if lawyers want to change their image, they have to start doing things that help people besides themselves. This is not accomplished when you say that you are here to protect the public, because the public—already suspicious of you—knows you make your living by the things you do to "protect," and they believe that's your only motive.

Nor is it accomplished when you say you are there to protect the little people. Most of the American public that has allowed itself to be poisoned could not care less about the little people.

But what if you listen to Jim Lees and start doing things that *help people in ways that do not profit you?* And find ways to let your community know about them.

In airports, you may have seen a large poster ad that says, "Eat Healthy Food." It has a picture of a good, healthy dinner. On the bottom is says, "American College of Cardiology." It does not say, "*Heart attack? Come to us! You don't pay if we don't cure you! 800-555-5555.*" It is not a self-serving advertisement. It is a public service—exactly what you need to be.

What's the lawyer's equivalent of that ad? "Wear Your Seatbelt!" for example. With nothing but the name of your firm at the bottom.

What is the principle underlying such an ad that you can use in many effective ways? It takes the knowledge you have from your work as a lawyer—that people get hurt more seriously when they do not wear their seatbelts—and puts it to use to keep people from getting hurt.

I'm all for lawyer advertising—if it's the right kind. Texas political and trial consultant Richard Jenson advises that ads that carry a public service message are just as effective as the junk ads that help ruin the profession's reputation.

American trial lawyers as a group know more than anyone else in the world about the ways people get hurt. You have access to that information. Instead of just using it to sue people, use it to keep people from being hurt in the first place. You know lots of stuff the public does not, so why not tell them?

Teach consumers how to buy safe products, how to keep themselves safe in hospitals, how to tell when a motel or a car or a work site is safe. Don't wait for people to be hurt. *Prevent* them from being hurt. If doing that becomes part of your personal, individual reputation, when someone does get hurt then you will be the attorney they seek instead of those who run the sleazy ads.

Do this on your own. Don't wait for trial lawyer organizations to do it; there's no time. Start offering yourself for talks to community groups in which you explain how to help keep people safe. Develop a Web site that does the public some good, rather than one that touts your abilities and degrees and big verdicts. A good Web site should include:

Annotated links to various help groups that provide guidance and support for injured people.

Annotated lists of resources such as books that injured people have found helpful and inspiring. The great running back from the Pittsburgh Steeler's golden years, Rocky Bleier, was badly injured in Vietnam. He went back home to Wisconsin and worked endlessly in his old high school gym until he slowly, painfully, got back to being able to play again. His story—in the book *Running Back*—has inspired injured readers all over the country to wage the battles they have to wage to contend with their own injuries. Read the book, write a descriptive paragraph about it for your Web site, and tell people who visit your Web site how to get a copy of it. Find another dozen books like it.

Guidance—beyond just "get a lawyer"—for people who have been injured. What kind of doctors should they see? What kind of records should they keep? What kind of support groups and other resources are available?

Guidance for families on how to keep themselves safe in various situations. Show how to avoid the dangers involved in something—such as the measures to take when in the hospital, or the local roads that are most dangerous for younger kids on bikes.

A list of your favorite charities—and call it that: "Favorite Charities and Service Organizations." List each one, explain why you chose it, and describe how people can help. Part of this section should also explain why and how to be careful choosing charities and helping organizations to support.

Your Web site should carry the feel of an organization dedicated to helping people. And this is honest for you to do, because that is the impulse that led you to do plaintiff's work instead of any of the myriad of other fields of law, almost all easier and more lucrative. So go back and remember who you really are, and let that shape your Web site and the rest of what you do. Make sure your site shows that you are the kind of human being that does not match the stereotype of plaintiff's attorneys. Your Web site should show that you are there to help people—and not just those who might become your clients.

(No matter what's on your Web site, in jury selection ask if anyone has been to it. Make sure no one has been offended by anything in it.)

There are many other ways to set yourself outside the stereotype. Some of these ways also happen to be excellent and inexpensive methods of drawing in new clients.

Radio, TV. With a few other attorneys in or out of your firm, invest the time and a little money in running a local weekly public service call-in radio or TV show. Provide advice (short of "legal advice") about things people want to know about: the neighbor's tree hanging over my roof, things new immigrants should be concerned with, legal steps newlyweds or new parents or new divorcees should be concerned with, etc. And discuss trials of local and national interest. Audiences love this stuff and will listen regularly. You will never run out of material.

Towards the end of every show, tell a story-of-the-week: something that illustrates the value of what your profession—not just plaintiff's lawyers—does. A "Paul Harvey" kind of human interest story, or a quick tale of a trial and how it came out—and why.

Then run a one-minute weekly feature of something of service some local attorney has done recently: taken the reigns of a local charity, helped incorporate—pro bono—a new non-profit social service agency, taken on a cause—also pro bono—for legal services, coached a little league team, etc. This will accomplish two things: It will help show people that lawyers are decent contributors to their community, and it will encourage lawyers in the community to be just that.

Finish each show with a fact-of-the-week—a believe-it-or-not, and provide the source of the fact. The number of negligence deaths per day in American hospitals. Statistics showing that verdicts are going generally down, not up. The *increase* in the number of doctors in your state over the past year. The number of dangerous defects in a particular manufacturer's car over the past three years. How long a pharmaceutical company knew its medicine was causing harm. Facts that show the dishonesty on which tort "reform" is based. Don't argue. Just give facts.

You can accomplish this without all that much work. Rotate the show among three or four other attorneys. Step in for each other when someone has a last-minute conflict. (Trial consultants in your area may also be interested in helping.) The more you do the show, the sooner and the more your name and voice will start being recognizable. Since the show is a public service and not an infomercial to get clients, you will be seen as a person who is there to help, not to exploit. It takes only one or two jurors to bring this to the jury.

And of course in voir dire you will ask, "Who here has heard my radio [or TV] show on Monday afternoons, or listened to any of the reruns on my Web site?" Some might have. You need to know what they think.

You can do the same thing with a weekly newspaper column. Advice, answering queries, commenting on and helping people understand what's going on in trials of local and national interest, stories and facts of the week—the media can be used to help you get the story out about who you are and where the crises really are.

You will enjoy doing this. A little local celebrity is always fun, it brings in business, and will demonstrate that you are not part of the bad stereotype that stigmatizes your profession. And on behalf of your profession, you'll have more effect on the grass roots than any amount of paid advertising could ever have.

Public Service. There are many other things to do that will separate you from the stereotype. Adopt a highway—preferably the one outside my house. Actually, the ideal highway to adopt would be the main road to and from the courthouse. But any will do. And don't hire anyone to do the work; get you and your overweight partner out there once a month to do it yourself. Good public relations, good public service, good exercise. And it's free.

Volunteer to speak anyplace that will have you. Schools. Service clubs. Professional clubs. Talk to your local chamber of commerce; tell business owners how to make sure people don't get hurt in their stores and workplaces. Tell drivers the horror stories that happen when a driver does not have enough underinsured motorist coverage. Again, the topic is not how to avoid lawsuits but how to protect people.

Teach people how to protect themselves and their children from the kinds of harm that lawyers know so much about. In these talks (as well as in the radio/TV/newspaper projects), start by educating about the nature and extent of the dangers you are going to talk about (600 hospital deaths per day, etc.), or cite a recent serious case about those dangers. Then teach folks how to protect themselves from them.

When speaking to groups, allow time for their questions and comments. That's the best way for them to end up liking and trusting you. And you will learn a lot when you listen to them talk. Just like a good jury voir dire.

Don't sell your services; don't even talk about them. This is your chance to give something back in a useful way. And when your listeners need a lawyer or want to recommend a lawyer to someone, you'll be the one likely to get the nod. You don't need to ask them for it.

The ABA has a public dialogue series that provides topics for speaking and discussion with groups. Some state trial lawyer's associations also have useful materials.

Be creative in thinking up other ways to turn yourself into a public service. Print up tokens and arrange with a local taxi company to accept them, knowing you will pay the fare associated with them. Give a few dozen to local bars for their bartenders to give to people who have had too much to drink. Help keep those drivers off the road. You might even save a life or two.

These kinds of activities educate jurors about who you really are. Some educate jurors about the real crises in lieu of the fake crises people have been misled into thinking you are part of. Rural or city, small town or huge metropolis, you can start to set yourself apart from the stereotype.

Don C. Keenan's Atlanta law firm has had enormous impact for good on his city's children and the homeless. Keenan could close his firm tomorrow and still would have changed the lives of countless children forever. But his law firm will not close tomorrow, and because of all the public good it has done, people know about the firm. Partly for that reason, it is among the first that many people think of when they need an attorney.

So go do some good.

Caveat. As you start to set yourself apart from the stereotype, be careful not to do anything to reinforce the validity of the bad stereotype. Do not, for example, say or imply that you are an exception to the rule. Never say in trial that "this is not one of those frivolous or illegitimate cases like the McDonald's case." The public and the jurors will see through that, and your reinforcement of the stereotype will hurt you as much as everyone else. Don't build yourself up by ripping others down. It is wrong to do, and it does not work.

11.2
Being Yourself

This part is hard. It involves looking at yourself and doing something about what you see.

You are an integral part of how jurors regard your damages case.

The first rule is to be yourself. If jurors think you are putting up any kind of false front—even if it is only a seemingly harmless formality—it hurts. And it thrusts you right back into the stereotype.

Drop the formalism and "importance" of playing "lawyer-man" or "lawyer-woman" in trial. Formalism is the enemy of damages. So is an air of importance, because it makes jurors believe that you consider yourself more important than they are.

Any mask you adopt for trial—such as someone else's style or a demeanor that conveys formality or importance—is pretense, and jurors spot it as such. A mask conceals the real you and keeps jurors distanced from you. That makes it easier for jurors to disappoint you at verdict time.

There are a number of excellent trial advocates I got to know first by watching them in court. Only later did I get to see them in other settings: home, weekends, dinner, and so forth. Each of these attorneys acts the same way outside court as in. They have no special courtroom persona.

This is true of almost every great trial attorney.

You may think formality or an air of importance is "just who you are." And yes, if you have been doing it long enough, it probably is who you are—in court. But you are many different things, depending on where you are and what you are doing. You can choose any one of them to be bring to trial.

So don't make the bad choice of "who you are." Don't choose the wrong "you." Bring a normal human being to court: the self you are when being comfortable and informal with friends who are your equals.

When the "you" you bring to court is the formalizing character disguising his real self behind a mask of "lawyering," you seem like an inept kid trying to play grown-up. You may make yourself feel important or in control, but jurors wonder why you are strutting like a constipated chicken and talking like a bad actor. I know this does not apply to you, of course, but think about how many of your colleagues it does apply to, and don't let it creep up on you.

The fact that some mask or trait has become habitual does not make it less fake or less distancing. You have good and true "selves" to use in court. Get rid of ways of speaking and acting that show formality, arrogance, self-importance, "business-ish" attitudes, a display of always-in-control competence (which jurors find arrogant or fake), and anything else that makes you different in trial from the way you are among equal friends in pleasant, informal, real-life situations. This is essential to separating yourself from the negative stereotype.

And while you're at it, get rid of your uniforms. Blue suits and black suits are uniforms. Why dress in a way that nails you firmly to the stereotype?

11.3
Greed

Even the best case can be undermined if jurors think you have the wrong motives.

Jurors decide whether to trust you largely by what they come to believe your motives are. If the way you present, dress, and decorate yourself reflects the stereotype of the greedy plaintiff's attorney, your ability to persuade—especially about damages—will suffer.

When you reinforce the stereotype of being motivated by greed, many jurors will not trust your damages evidence and arguments.

Look long and hard to see yourself as jurors might see you. It is difficult, but possible, to spot and get rid of anything that fits the greed stereotype. This is not a deep psychological evaluation and overhaul. It just means leaving your Lexus home and driving to court in the Buick. And no Rolex, no Mont Blanc pen, no gold cuff links, no baby lamb briefcase. Send all that junk to me for safekeeping. No costly haircut. *Especially* no toupee (but don't send it to me). If you can't be honest enough to admit to losing your hair, jurors may conclude that you cannot be honest about anything as important as adding to your wealth. Besides, the only one who thinks your toupee is not obvious is you.

Your jewelry and clothing should reflect a successful career but not a greedy lifestyle.

Some jurors may admire your suit that costs a month of their income. Others will resent you for it and conclude that anyone who dresses that way is motivated only by money.

Once you confirm the greed stereotype, nothing you do or say in trial will make it go away.

Do not go too far. Wear good-quality clothing and drive a decent car. Jurors expect a decent lawyer to make a decent living. If you seem not to, they will think you are incompetent.

Exceptions. In some social or cultural communities, a show of wealth, usually but not always by a member of that same community, implies credibility and respectability, not greed. And in any setting, attorneys with special kinds of personalities can get away with dressing extravagantly. That is why you may know of some successful attorneys who deck themselves uniquely or expensively. But these are exceptions. In most of America, and with the vast majority of attorneys, showy wealth (by local standards) affirms the greedy lawyer stereotype.

Small communities. If you live in a smaller community where your personal reputation is likely to precede you to court, be careful what that reputation might be. For example, if you are trying cases in a community where most people know your house, do not live in a castle. Do not own highly visible assets (such as a string of rental apartments or a shopping center) that mark you as uncommonly wealthy. You can be as rich as you want, but why remind potential jurors on a daily basis? Your community reputation will affect how jurors hear your cases—and when it comes to damages, any greed-quotient that people attach to you will be a detracting factor.

Whatever a community knows about you can affect your trials. So drive politely and safely, never give anyone a one-fingered wave, treat shopkeepers and service people fairly and nicely, and be active in charitable and community affairs in ways that do not overtly help your business. Be seen at family events with your kids. If people believe you are caring and fair in real life, they will continue to believe it when they are on your juries.

You should even mow your own lawn and wash your own car. These humanizing activities enhance your reputation as a decent, honest, everyday kind of person. I know, you didn't go to law school to have to spend the rest of your life mowing your lawn, but times were different back then. And you need the exercise.

11.4
Advertising

If you advertise, be sure your ads project an image of caring. Take pains that they do not hint at greed.

Every good marketer pre-tests ads in focus groups. You would be foolish not to do the same—partly to see if the ad will attract cases, and partly to see if it will cause problems for you with future jurors.

Pre-test your prospective ads locally. An ad that is effective and tasteful in one locale can be ineffective and offensive in another.

Few jurors object to lawyer advertising. But when jurors think that ads are in bad taste or smell of greed or slime, they factor that into their decision making—sometimes so heavily that they will not trust you enough to let you win the case.

Well-created ads in good taste that reflect caring instead of greed can attract just as many cases as junk ads, and help with how jurors perceive you. And the best ads carry a message to help others, not you. "Wear your seatbelt." "Slow down in school zones."

In other words, evaluate your ads through the eyes of your future jurors.

11.5
Ethics of Advertising

Most firms that advertise are excellent. But the McLitigator firms accept many more cases (or cases that are more complex) than they can handle. Many prospective clients, knowing nothing about how to find a good attorney, select from firms that advertise. The more there are good firms that advertise, the less likely it is that a client will fall into a McLitigator's clutches.

That is why it is a public disservice for good firms not to advertise. Well-done, tasteful advertising by more firms will go a long way toward providing better legal services for the public.

11.6
The Positive Stance: Caring

Jurors give money because they care. They care more if you care.

The way to seem as if you care is really to care. Faking that you care is dangerous, because fakery is visible no matter how skilled an actor you are. Fake caring reinforces the plaintiff's attorney stereotype of greed. And fake caring is slime.

To make your care real, spend time with your client. In a wrongful death case, spend time with the client's family. Do not meet in your office; go to the home. Take part in the family's activities. Be there. Share in their lives beyond the time necessary to conduct business.

Raleigh attorney Donald H. Beskind tells about a successful plaintiff's attorney who brings his clients to spend a day at his home with his own family, then spends a day at the client's home. Not only does the attorney learn a lot, but the intimate at-home time creates compassion in the attorney, and connections between attorney and client. The compassion and the connections are obvious to jurors in trial.

Think about similarities between the plight of your client and the misfortunes you have been through yourself. Your own misfortunes can help you identify with your client. That identification will be apparent in court.

Look deep into the face of your client, or into the photograph of her face if she is dead. Look long and hard enough to contemplate who she is, what she feels, how she is like you, how she is like the people you love. Corny as it sounds, feel her pain and her loss. Get angry at the wrongdoing that hurt her. And decide in the center of your being that it is your personal mission to help her or her survivors as best as she or they can be helped.

Make that the foundation of everything you do in trial. It will give jurors a true picture of yourself that you want them to see. It will blow the greed stereotype out of the courthouse and replace it with caring. It will impel you to do your best work.

In a wrongful death case, go to the cemetery and contemplate who is lying under that stone. Go with the children or the widow. Ask them to tell you about the person lying there. On another day, go alone and talk to the deceased. Ask the deceased what he would like to tell the jury if he could. (Believe it or not, you will get answers!) Ask the deceased how he would like the case to come out. If you have never done anything like this, prepare yourself for a powerful experience.

It will help you get to the level of worrying not about your income or your ego but about your client—so that in trial the jurors will see that you have the right motivations. Those motivations will shine through.

APPENDIX A
SILENCE OF THE JURORS: A VOIR DIRE PRIMER

(This section assumes that you have reasonable leeway in voir dire. If you do not, there are many ways to seek improvements. See 5.1.)

A.1
The Law

"The voir dire examination of jurors . . . [is] to enable counsel to exercise intelligently the peremptory challenges allowed by law." [*State v. Brown,* 53 N.C. App. 82, 280 S.E.2d 31, cert denied, 304 N.C. 197, 285 S.E.2d 102 (1981).]

So the purpose is to gather information—for peremptories as well as for cause challenges.

A.2
The Conventional Error

You cannot select a jury based on demographics: race, age, nationality, occupation, or any other demographic grouping. Not all "Gen-Xers" think alike. Nor do all Jews or Blacks or middle-aged guys with beards or any other group. Stupidity of this sort runs rampant among racists and others who judge individuals on the basis of their demographic grouping. Don't bring it into jury selection. All teachers are not bad for your case. All middle-aged black women are not bad for your case. All young people are not bad for your case. This mentally lazy way out does not work.

I wish it did. It would make jury selection a cinch. Instead, you have to do some work.

Your job in jury selection is to find out how a prospective juror's deep-seated beliefs and attitudes will affect her decision making, and whether she is likely to tell herself the story of your case in a way that will help you.[1] For example, if your client signed an informed consent without understanding or reading it, you have to find out which jurors can regard this as reasonable, and which probably cannot. Will the story of the case that that juror tells herself embrace the failure to read before signing as normal or aberrant, as reasonable or unreasonable?

Economic and other social factors associated with certain demographic groups can sometimes give you a general idea, but without good questioning, you'll make a lot of wrong choices. Sometimes members of a particular demographic grouping share (or seem to share) certain attitudes, world views, or life experiences that can impact decision making. For example, inner-city resident will more likely understand why a young person might turn to crime, and thus be more lenient when he's charged. People brought up in the suburbs are far less likely to have that depth of understanding. But there will be many exceptions both ways. Some jurors will not have that understanding at all, but will think, "I grew up just like he did and I did not turn to crime, so throw the jerk in jail and lose the key." So it's dangerously wrong for you to try to short-circuit gathering information about individual jurors, and it is a disservice to the justice system when judges or rules force you to.

The first principle of jury selection: Every human being is an individual. You have to find out what kind of individual. In voir dire, that means getting them to talk to you.

A.3
Your Duty

Your duty is to apply some basic principles of two-way communication so the jurors in voir dire will give you more truth than silence. This primer explains how to apply those principles—especially the one that says you do better voir dire when you listen than when you talk.

1. See Eric Oliver's book *Facts Can't Speak for Themselves* (NITA 2005).

Unfortunately, listening is harder than talking. That's why—especially among attorneys—listening is rare.

A.4
Enjoyment Versus Control

The National Jury Project's Diane Wiley points out that it's hard to do jury voir dire well unless you enjoy it. When you do not enjoy it, jurors sense it. That makes them less likely to talk openly with you. It can also distance them from you throughout trial.

But how can anyone enjoy voir dire? It's unpredictable and uncontrollable; you get no discovery; no matter how much you prepare, there's no telling how things will go. You don't get to impeach prospective jurors. They can say anything and who knows what it will be and there's nothing you can—or should—do about it.

All this can make you so uncomfortable that you try to control prospective jurors like witnesses on cross-examination. Don't. You get useful information from jurors only when you altogether stop trying to control what they say. Of course, having chosen to go to law school, you are probably not the kind of person who enjoys giving up control. It may even give you a stomachache. So you may have some self-counseling to do to get yourself to enjoy giving up control. Your spouse and kids can probably help.

The guidelines below and in Chapter 5 will help you master the basic techniques to elicit the necessary uncontrolled outpouring of information from jurors. As you use these techniques and see how much they boost your chances of doing well with your case, you will begin to find jury voir dire enjoyable.

There is nothing more interesting and valuable than hearing what real people have to say. When you get yourself to listen well enough, you'll find it even more enjoyable than acting on your usually faulty assumption that the jurors want to (or think they need to) listen to you.

A waiter at my favorite restaurant says, when he brings my dinner, "Enjoy." From here on, as you read this section, as you prepare your jury voir dires, and as you conduct them, "Enjoy!" Otherwise it will be an ineffective voir dire and you don't get to send it back to the kitchen.

A.5

Voir Dire: To See Speaking

"Voir dire" means "to see speaking." Some people prefer to think it means "to speak the truth," which it does not. Either way, you don't get to see jurors do much speaking truth or anything else when you are talking. You learn nothing about them and they learn a terrible thing about you: that you talk too much, that you are trying to manipulate them, and that they should avoid being influenced by you as much as possible.

Your job is to drop a question into the jury box and then listen. So Rule 1 of voir dire is rather rude:

Rule One: Shut up and listen.

When you do more than 10% of the talking in voir dire, you are talking too much.

I know that you did all the listening you could stand while you were in law school, and intend never to do any listening again. I know "advocate" means "to speak." But please, not in jury voir dire.

In fact, listening in voir dire—even the required (by me) 90% of the time—is not enough. You have to listen with real interest. Your follow-up questions and the tone in which you ask them must show real interest in how the juror might answer.

A.6

Rapport

Human beings feel rapport with anyone who listens to them.

In the 1950s, high school girls were taught that the way to develop rapport with boys was to be a good listener, even when a boy blathered on about some topic of no interest whatever: his car's camshaft or how far the coach made him run at football practice. Those 1950s girls knew that the way to a boy's heart was listening to him with great interest. It worked on every one of us boys.

It works with jurors. When you listen with interest, they are yours from the start.

They talk to you more.

And the rapport you create by listening makes jurors more likely to want to see the evidence in a good light for your side.

Creating rapport does not mean ingratiation. Never be ingratiating; never do or say anything that can be seen as ingratiating. Ingratiation grates. In jury selection, you create rapport just by listening. Silence (yours, not the jurors') is golden.

A.7

Do Not Inform or Persuade

You cannot follow Rule 1 ("Shut up and listen") if you use voir dire to inform or persuade ("condition") jurors. This is one of the many times that ethics and good strategy go hand-in-hand. Informing and persuading should be your primary goal all the time in trial—except in jury voir dire. Jurors quickly figure out which way you want information to flow. If they think you want information to flow from you to them, they obediently talk less and pretend to listen. So make them feel that the total flow of information must be from them to you.

A.8

Have Your Cake and Eat It Too

There are, of course, some things you have to tell the jury in voir dire, such as, perhaps, your low burden of proof. But any question that *solely* informs will mar your information gathering and your credibility. So never ask a question like, "Does everybody know we only have to prove that what we say is more likely true than not true?" That question solely informs. It gathers no information except that some of the jurors can nod. It persuades no juror of anything. No one even remembers it. And since it is information thinly disguised as a question, jurors see that you are neither above chicanery nor good at it.

When you need to inform in voir dire, inform and gather information at the same time. To do this, ask double-purpose questions. The *primary* and most apparent purpose is to gather information; the secondary—and make sure it is only secondary—is giving information. For example, "Mr. Larson, we only have to prove that what we're saying is more likely than not. Some people feel that makes it too easy on us and too hard on the other side. What do you think about that?" and "What kinds of problems do you think that's caused with the justice system?" Such questions seem to jurors and the judge (and in fact are) primarily information-gathering. *Secondarily* they inform.

Resist the impulse to cajole jurors into favorable answers, such as by asking, "It would be unfair to be on this jury if you think more-likely-than-not is unfair, so tell me how you feel about it." That tells the jurors what they need to hide from you, and they will.

A.9
Ask Open-Ended Questions

Rule 1, "Shut up and listen," is simple and effective—and a real challenge. To help you meet that challenge, and for other reasons covered below, your jury voir dire questions should all be short, open-ended ("Please tell me about . . . " instead of "Do you . . . "), and designed to elicit a lot of talking ("What's your work-day like?" instead of "What kind of work do you do?" or the revealingly sexist "Do you work outside the home?") Simply ask short, open-ended questions. Then shut up and listen. In voir dire you'll get more information. And at home your family will start to like you.

Open-ended questions are questions that cannot be answered in only a word or phrase. Unlike closed-ended questions, open-ended questions contain no implicit limitation on the answer's length. The closed-ended "Do you know we only have to prove that what we say is more likely true than not true?" limits the response to one word, a grunt, or nothing. The open-ended "How do you feel about it being so easy on us?" does not. (Some judges take umbrage at hearing you say "feel." With such a judge, substitute the word "think": "What do you think about it being so easy on us?")

> ***Remember:*** You cannot make good jury selection decisions based on one-word answers. That is why closed-ended voir dire questions are amateurishly inept.

Why, what, how, tell me. Open-ended questions start one way, closed-ended another.

OPEN-ENDED questions start with:

Why[2]	Tell me why
What	Tell me what
How	Tell me how

Tell me about that

Closed-ended questions are not merely those that ask for a yes or no answer. They are questions that ask for a one-word or single-phrase answer.

CLOSED-ENDED questions start with:

When	Was
Where	Were
Is	Do
Are	Did

How many?

Starting with "when," "where," "is," "are," "was," "were," "do," "did," or "how many?" is the most common cause of violating rude Rule 1.

2. "Why" and "tell me why" are open-ended, but are somewhat confrontational and tend to make listeners defend what they are saying instead of elaborating on it. Use them sparingly. "Tell me about that" is usually more productive.

The only thing worse than a closed-ended question is the ghastly, "I take it by your silence that . . . ", a question that elicits no information of any kind whatsoever. You might as well ask it at nap-time.

Limited uses of closed-ended questions. There are only three legitimate uses of closed-ended questions in voir dire:

1. To introduce a new topic about which you will immediately ask open-ended follow-up questions: the closed-ended "How many of you have safety rules at work?" followed by open-ended questions such as, "Mr. Jones, tell me about the safety rules at your printing plant," and "How do you feel about having to follow those rules?" and "What happens when someone breaks those rules?" and so on.

2. The second use of closed-ended questions is to nudge quiet jurors into a response mode. Get them to raise their hands. ("Who here has ever been through jury selection?"[3]) This, as explained below, chips away at their reluctance to participate. It primes the pump.

3. The third use of closed-ended questions is in the final steps of a challenge for cause, as covered below.

Aside from those three uses, save your closed-ended questions for cross-examination and for housebreaking pets. (The answer to the closed-ended "And isn't it true, Fluffy, that you did this?" is "Woof." But think of all you'd learn if you instead asked the open-ended "Fluffy, tell me about this.")

A.10
The All-Purpose Follow-Up Questions

You learn little of any value in jury selection until the second or third follow-up question. Often, attorneys ask, "How many of you have ever been in a wreck?" Some hands go up. The attorney duly notes the names—and then moves on to a different topic! Yet having

3. I hate to keep invoking Eric Oliver, but the dog is smart and he points out that "Who here . . . " has an individual personal quality to it, while "How many of you . . . " has the opposite quality.

been in a wreck does not make anyone a good juror or a bad one. It's always a toss-up.

The only reason to ask a question on any new topic ("Who's ever been in a wreck?") is to follow up the answer. Here is the all-purpose follow-up question of choice:

> Please tell me about it.

After they tell you about it, say,

> Please tell me about *that*. (Or Eric Oliver again, "What else?")

And then,

> Thank you. And please tell me a little about that. (Or if Eric is watching, "Thank you. And what *else*?")

So:

> Q: Who here has been in a wreck?

Hands go up. Someone at your table notes the names because you have nothing to write with, since you know that taking notes during voir dire hinders communication. You call on a juror whose hand is up:

> Q: Please tell me about it.

You could have asked:

> Were you hurt? Or
>
> Whose fault was it? Or
>
> How did it happen?

But you were smart and instead said, "Please tell me about it."

This yields control to the juror. He can pick any sub-topic about the wreck he wants. His unprompted choice of sub-topic tells you something about his attitude towards the wreck. He might say, "This guy just slammed into me" (i.e., the wreck was *someone else's fault*).

He might say, "Worst thing I was ever involved in in my life." (i.e. the *seriousness* of the wreck is his most salient connection to it). It might be how badly he was injured. (So he'll *compare* that to the one in this case.) It might be what his injuries later kept him from doing. (Ditto.) It might be how he sued or got sued or decided not to sue or prayed he wouldn't be sued. It might be what happened to his insurance rates —or any of a number of other sub-topics. By your saying, "Tell me about it," you let him select his most salient sub-topic. For example:

> A: Well, they blamed me but it wasn't my fault. The jerk hit me.

So this juror knows the sting of being falsely accused. That means there's some chance he will identify with the defendant. Not necessarily, but follow up to find out:

> Q: Tell me about that.
>
> A: Well, people always got to blame someone else, and that's what he did. I was just driving along, and . . . .

"People always got to blame someone else." Not an attitude that is likely to help a plaintiff's cause. So this was important information to unearth. But you could not have unearthed it you'd chosen his subtopic by asking, say, "Did you get hurt?"

In response to "tell me about it," a juror might also say,

> A: Totaled my car. But I walked away without a scratch.

Not likely a good plaintiff's juror for a slow-speed rear-ender case. How likely is he to believe a low-speed impact leaving barely a dent could hurt anyone? But don't decide too soon. Keep going.

> Q: I'm glad you weren't hurt, but tell me about it.
>
> A: It was luck. I've seen plenty of wrecks with hardly any car damage where the driver got clobbered.

That's what a follow-up question does for you. And the only follow-up question you need is "Tell me about it." By giving up control over the choice of sub-topic and letting the juror control the direction of the conversation, you learn things you might not otherwise even suspect enough to ask about.

If, after a number of "tell me about its" and "what elses" you have not gotten to a sub-topic you need to hear about, go ahead and ask. "What kind of car were you in?"—if that's important to your case. But if you give the juror a chance to mention it *unprompted,* you'll know that it's something truly on his mind, rather than something he's talking about solely because you prompted it.

Here's another example of leaving the choice of sub-topic up to the juror:

> Q: Who here has—or knows anyone who has—ever been injured by using any kind of manufactured product?

Juror Jones raises her hand.

> Q: Please tell me about it.
>
> A: I cut my hand on a power screwdriver.[4]
>
> Q: Tell me about it.

Instead of "Tell me about it" you could have asked, "Tell me about what happened." But you don't know that *what happened* was the most important thing to this juror. It might be how badly she was injured, what a piece of junk the product was, how mad she was at Sears for selling it to her, how she should not have been using a power tool she knew nothing about, or . . . the possibilities are endless. In this instance, she said:

> A: The handle came loose.
>
> Q: Tell me about that.
>
> A: The metal underneath sliced into my hand. I wasn't looking, so I didn't see it until it cut me.
>
> Q: Tell me about that.
>
> A: I couldn't use my hand for a week.

4. Pay attention to the wording. Someone or other once said it's not what you say, it's how you say it. "I cut my hand on a power screwdriver" places blame differently than "A power screwdriver cut my hand."

Q: I'm sorry to hear that. Tell me about it.

A: Well, I couldn't do most of my job, and it was hard to get dressed in the morning.

By letting jurors choose their own sub-topics, you could have gotten very different responses showing very different things about how this juror is likely to relate to your case:

Q: Who here has—or knows anyone who has—ever been injured by using any kind of manufactured product?

Juror Jones raise her hand.

Q: Please tell me about it.

A: The handle came loose.

Q: Tell me about it.

A: It was an expensive piece of junk. First time I use it the handle comes loose. I brought it back and they said I used it wrong. But they gave me my money back. I told them not to put it back on the shelf. I bet they did.

Useful? And you'd never have gotten there if you had controlled the choice of sub-topic.

If you ask "Tell me about that" a few times and still do not learn some specific thing you want to know, such as whether she filed a claim, go into more leading but still open-ended follow-ups, such as "What did you do about it?" But don't start with those specifics.

A.11
Practice

Before trial, try asking someone ten questions in a row, all with some variation of "tell me about that." And you will want some wording variations: "Tell me about that." "What else about that?" "Say a little more on that, please?" "And . . . ?" Etc.

Then go into advanced practice: Ask someone 20 open-ended follow-ups in a row. Keep working at it until you can do it comfortably without backsliding into a closed-ended question such as "Did you . . . ?" I bet you will—until you practice.

Then gather a half-dozen people and practice on them as a group, as if they were a jury. Use one person's answer as the basis for follow-up questions, first to that person and then to the others. This is a basic method of good voir dire.

A.12
Lower the Barrier

Your tone, your body language, and your choice of words should tell the juror that any answer he gives will be as acceptable to you as any other answer. Do not ever disagree or argue. Do not make jurors feel that they taking a test or are in a contest in which they are expected to give right answers. Tell them over and over that there are no rules, no expectations, no right and no wrong responses. "The only right answer is what is right to you."

And don't be friendlier to jurors who answer in ways you like. Do not approve of their answers. Do not follow them up by leading them to say good things, in the hope that they will make other jurors see the light. That's a clever tactic that rarely has any effect and more often arouses juror suspicion.

With every response, "honor the answer," as Gerry Spence teaches. Don't listen to an answer and then just move on to someone or something else without reacting. Even a nod in acknowledgment tells the juror you thought enough of what he said to listen and absorb it.

During a recent jury selection, I heard the following "oh my" dialogue:

> Q: Mrs. Hicks, you know someone who was killed in a wreck?
>
> A: My husband.
>
> Q: Right, and Mr. Ehle, you had your hand up too?

This shows callousness and a low level of listening. It raises the barrier to prospective jurors telling you anything at all, much less anything bad.

You needn't go overboard with responses. A good response to Mrs. Hicks would have been, "I'm sorry to hear that." But you still need to know more about it, so ask, "Would you mind my asking a few questions about it?" But even if it's something you don't need to know more about, don't zip away from her when she says her husband was killed. Respond briefly, appropriately, and in an underplayed way. It makes this juror and others more willing to talk with you.

And it's decent thing to do—even when it's not about a death. Even if the answer was, "I live in Fairfield," acknowledge that she told you something.

Wording questions to lower the barrier. Good wording can lower the barrier to jurors telling you "bad" things. So instead of, "What <u>major</u> problems would you have including money in your verdict for pain and suffering?" ask, "What problems—<u>even small</u> ones—would you have including money in your verdict for pain and suffering?" Otherwise, a juror may truthfully say she has no *major* problems, and not mention the lesser problems you need to know about.

Another way to lower the barrier is to make the juror feel that having a "bad" response is acceptable. Obviously, "Will the fact that you were in a wreck make it impossible for you to be a fair juror in this case?" builds a barrier to any answer except "No." The question's wording makes the juror feel that "No" is the proper response. So many jurors will say "No" regardless of what they really think.

Instead, ask: "Anyone who'd been in a wreck like that one [hers] might have some problems being a juror in a case like this one. What do you think?" This justifies anything she might say, so she's more likely to admit something other than "no problem" if she thinks it might be a problem. Remember that during voir dire jurors are in an unfamiliar but very public and pressured situation. Most are extremely uncomfortable in saying anything anyone might disapprove of. So make them comfortable doing it or you'll often miss the most important information.

(When you ask questions about "this kind of case" or "this case," make sure the jurors know what the case is about.)

Some people. One of the most effective ways to lower the barrier to a bad answer is to ask, "Some people think X; other people think Y. Which group do you think you might be closer to, even a little?"

For example:

> Q: Mrs. Smith, some people don't put much confidence in the way the FDA checks the safety of drugs these days. Other people think the FDA does very well. Which do you think you might be closer to, even a little?

This gives the juror permission to give you the bad answer.

> Q: Ms. Jones, some people would never give money for pain and suffering because money can't make the pain go away. Other people think money for pain and suffering is fine.[5] Which group do you think you might be closer to, even a little?
>
> A: Maybe the first. A little.
>
> Q: Please tell me about that.

On carefully selected questions, you can go even farther in giving permission:

---

5. Do not say, "Some people think it's okay, and that they would listen to the judge when he says to later." That bullies the juror into giving you the good answer whether she means it or not, so you learn nothing and make the juror feel manipulated.

Q: Ms. Johnson, some people would never give money for pain and suffering because money can't make the pain go away. That's why my mother would never do it. Other people think money for pain and suffering is fine. (You might get an objection. Usually not. Try it. The objection won't hurt you.)

That makes it easy for jurors to reveal problems with money for pain and suffering, or whatever the question is about.

A.13
Poisoning The Jury

The old-school "wisdom" was that asking open-ended questions risks prospective jurors saying something bad for your case ("I hate money for pain and suffering"). While jurors can sometimes be poisoned by hearing another juror mention publicity about the case (because a juror might reveal bad facts that would not come into evidence), little else a juror says in voir dire can be poisonous enough to justify your leaving it hidden. Jurors in voir dire almost never have any effect on each other's thinking.

The concept of "poisoning the jury" relies on the naive belief that people change their minds easily. They don't. I recently helped an attorney select a death penalty jury. Counsel wanted an individually sequestered voir dire—but not out of fear that a shared knowledge of pretrial publicity might reveal to other jurors information that was not going to come into evidence. Nor because sometimes you can learn more when questioning a juror out of the others' hearing. Rather, the attorney feared that pro-death-penalty jurors discussing their opinions in front of other jurors would harden the hearts of jurors who did not initially feel as strongly about it.

But jurors don't think, "Thank God for Juror Number Seven! I always thought the death penalty should be used sparingly—but now I see the light! Hang 'em all!"

Jurors do not relinquish attitudes, biases, and opinions just because some other juror (or counsel) offers a contrasting one. In fact, when they hear attitudes they disagree with, jurors are more likely to cling to their own.

So do not worry about poisoning the jury. An opinion is not a death pill. An attitude is not a potion. Get the jurors talking. Get them to say things that show how bad they will be for you as jurors. And rest assured that it is almost impossible for them to poison the other jurors.

Even if something is potentially poisonous in voir dire, think how much worse it would be if it emerges for the first time in deliberations.

A.14
Making Jurors Comfortable Talking

Jurors are uncomfortable talking in front of strangers, particularly in a formal setting like court. Remember how bad and constricted you felt the first time you went to court as an attorney? During jury selection, many jurors feel worse.

Few attorneys are blessed with the kind of personality and presence that spontaneously make jurors eager to talk with them. To make matters worse, you are likely to be nervous at the start of trial. That nervousness makes jurors even less willing to talk with you, because no one is comfortable talking to a nervous person. Jurors are further discouraged from readily talking to you because your business clothes and your lawyerly demeanor make you seem, to jurors, to occupy a higher position than they do. Few people talk comfortably or frankly with those they perceive to be in a higher position. People are uncomfortable saying anything they fear that a higher-up might disagree with or find of little value.

Some jurors simply don't like being asked questions. Others are nervous and disguise their nervousness under a veil of sullenness.

Jurors are in an intimidating environment with a scary-looking person in a black robe looking down at them from on high who has told them to tell the truth or else. This crowd is not an easy one to get talking. To start with, make them comfortable.

DO:

- Be friendly.
- Be human.
- Respond with nods and approval to what they say.
- Be sensitive to their discomfort, including that of those who seem the most confident.

DO NOT:

- Do not wear power clothes. No dark blue or black suits; in fact, for voir dire, men should wear sport jacket, tie, and slacks. Women should avoid severely formal clothing.
- Do not be formal or "professional" or lawyerly in manner. Relax. Be human. Be yourself—the yourself from real life, not law.
- Do not write down what jurors say; let a colleague do it.
- Do not wear those silly half-reading spectacles that make you peer over the rims at people. It looks snooty. Jurors talk less when they think you are snooty.
- Do not act as if you are more important than the jurors.
- Do not try to impress jurors.

In short, the first task of getting people to talk to you is to get them comfortable.

Legalese. To make jurors comfortable, speak plain English. There is never a time—not in voir dire or any other time in trial or in your career—when you should speak or write legalese. Legalese means saying "*prior*" instead of "*before,*" "*subsequent*" instead of "*after,*" "*find*" instead of "*decide,*" "*action*" instead of "*lawsuit.*" It means using lawyer-like syntax ("The house was painted by Mr. Jones" instead of "Mr. Jones painted the house.").

As Raleigh attorney and law professor Donald Beskind points out, even when writing briefs or motions you do not have to use legal language. Clear motions are most easily digested, so write them clearly, not lawyerly.

As Jerry Lewis used to say, “Talk regular!”

Lawyerly language undermines your credibility, creates a barrier to rapport, and keeps jurors from understanding and wanting to please you. Jurors are distracted from the substance of what you are asking when they have to stop and think for a moment what “plaintiff” might mean. After all, at one time you had no idea what it meant, so how can you expect jurors to?

In the jury room and at lunch during recesses, jurors often mimic the silliness of lawyers who use legalese. These are often very funny imitations. So when you talk legalese to jurors, their looks of careful listening are quite possibly nothing but masks to cover up the their internal laughter at your amateurishness.

In voir dire, your talking like a lawyer inhibits jurors from talking to you. It intimidates, baffles, annoys, confuses, amuses, and hinders communication. Do not do it in voir dire, in opening, in testimony, or in closing.

Do not talk like a lawyer at home, either. Do not allow your job to condition your language so thoroughly that you go home and talk like a lawyer to your friends and family. Do you want your poor kids growing up talking like that? “Hit the ball outta here like you did your prior time at bat!” Instead, allow the normal language of your family’s everyday lives to condition and shape the way you talk in the office, in motions, and in trial—especially in voir dire.

This leads to a necessary expansion of Rule 1 of voir dire:

> Shut up and listen. When you do speak, be brief and *talk the way you talked before you went to law school.*

Good lawyers sound like people, not like lawyers. Good voir dire is conducted by lawyers who sound like people, because jurors more easily talk to people than to lawyers.

A.15

Get them Involved

Because the default state of many prospective jurors is silence, a good voir dire starts by getting them talking freely. That means getting them involved.

The worst way to get them involved is to start with a speech: "Hi, I'm David Ball and this is my only chance to get to talk with you, and I'm going to ask you some questions, I don't mean to be prying into your personal affairs but I have to because, well, you know, and there are no right answers only wrong answers, I mean there are no wrong answers only right answers and nothing I have to say will be evidence. My name is David Ball and I'm proud to represent my client here, Adrienne Westerly, who is my client, I practice in North Carolina here and I'm a little nervous having to ask you, a bunch of strangers, a bunch of personal questions that are really none of my business except that you know, they are my business because, well, you know, you have to be fair so you there I'll ask you first since you're, well, let me ask you, how do you feel about the burden of proof in a civil tort action?"[6]

Anything more than a brief sentence or two will often suppress how much they will talk to you.

So here's one way to start: say "Good morning." Then wait a moment for the jurors to say "good morning" back. That tiny bit of juror involvement is the first step. It announces by example what is going on here: you say something and they respond. It opens more doors of communication than even the best of little speeches.

The second step goes a little further. Virginia jury and trial consultant Jeffrey Frederick wisely teaches (among many other things) an easy and effective way to get jurors out of their passivity shells: ask a question that calls for jurors to raise their hands. Their physical act begins to bridge the passivity gap.

> How many of you have ever been through a jury selection process before?

6. I plugged my name in to protect the real perp, but otherwise that's almost verbatim. And you know who you are.

Some hands go up.

> How many of you have never done this?

Other hands go up. If someone responded to neither question, ask:

> Mr. Smith, I didn't see your hand. Have you ever been a juror?

This bridges the gap of silence and gently teaches even the most reluctant jurors that silence is out of order here.

A.16
Find the Talkative Juror

After getting the jurors to raise their hands, ask open-ended questions. Start with a talkative juror, who will be easier to get talking. That talkative pioneer will teach other jurors what they are expected to do when it is their turn, and make them more comfortable doing it.

"But," you say, "at the start of voir dire, how do you know who the most talkative juror might be?" Watch them as they congregate in the hall before jury call in the morning. Some will be talking, some listening. Remember who is talking, because one of them might be among the first group you will be questioning. If you cannot go observe them, send an assistant. If voir dire starts in the afternoon, eat lunch where the jurors eat, and observe who talks. I know you're busy with other things, but at this point nothing is more important than learning about the prospective jurors.

If you have no opportunity to observe them before voir dire, watch as they are ushered into the courtroom. Try to spot clues. Even a small remark or gesture as they file in can reveal a juror who is comfortable talking. The juror holding the door for others, or who seems outer-directed by looking around at other people, or who thanks whoever held the door for them, can prove to be a talkative one. It's worth the effort to find out, because your questioning a talkative juror eases the path for everyone else to talk comfortably.

Once prospective jurors are in the box, try to spot one who seems comfortable with being there or who seems interested in the process.

Jurors who seem intimidated, uncomfortable, or distanced are rarely talkative at first, so do not start with them. Talkative jurors might lean slightly forward as the judge introduces voir dire. Talkers might be among those who seem most comfortable during the judge's remarks, and may seem most aware of and interested in the other jurors. Talkers may even be among those who most comfortably and audibly respond to your "good morning."

Talkative jurors are more likely to be leaders in deliberations, so there is double benefit to spotting them. You cannot afford to have leaders on the jury who seem likely to be even mildly against your case, because leaders can sway an entire jury and tend not to be swayed themselves. (See "Identifying Leaders," below.)

If you mistakenly start with a juror who turns out not to be talkative, ask two or three questions, temporarily abandon that juror, and try someone else. Once you get a talkative juror, stay with him for a while. The questions suggested below will maximize that juror's talking. The more that juror talks freely, the easier it will be to get other jurors talking, because you will have established a conversational standard with that first talkative juror. You can reinforce it by going next to another talkative juror.

But it is hard to get most people talking if you're the one being talkative. This is an easy trap throughout voir dire, especially at the beginning. With every question you ask, remind yourself of Rule One: "Shut up and listen."

A.17
Questions To Get them Talking

To get jurors talking, first ask questions about the jurors and their own lives. Forget your case for a while. Jurors tend not to start talking easily if you begin with questions that can be difficult to answer. So ask about topics they are comfortable discussing: Most people are comfortable talking about their jobs, their families, their backgrounds, values they have learned from their parents and teach their children, and plans for the future. As long as you do not get too intrusive, most jurors are comfortable talking about such things. And hearing about those things will help you decide whether you want that juror.

For example:

> Tell me about your job; what is your work day like?

Do not ask, "What do you do for a living?" That closed-ended question gets one-word answers: "Astrophysicist." When you ask about their work day, jurors respond more fully. So you learn how they spend much of their time. This provides clues as to how they might respond to issues in the case. For example, if they work in a dangerous environment, they will have experience with safety rules and possibly with injuries and fault-finding. Use follow-up questions to get them talking about these things:

> What kind of safety rules are there at work?
>
> Tell me about them.
>
> What happens when someone breaks them?

Ask lots of follow-ups. For example, after asking about their work day, follow up with:

> What do you like about your work?
>
> What do you dislike about it?
>
> If you could choose, what kind of work would you like to do instead?
>
> Tell me about that.

You may worry that the judge will not let you ask so much. Find out in advance what your judge normally allows. You do not want to have to redesign your voir dire in the midst of actually doing it. If you learn the judge's limits ahead of time, you can plan for them and argue for improvements. If nothing else, you will know what to expect when you get to voir dire. (A well-researched memorandum of voir dire law can help you get more leeway in voir dire, and lets you see in advance what the judge will be willing to let you do.)

One of the best questions to get jurors talking is, "What makes [made] you good at your job?" or "What makes [made] you a good parent?" Even quieter folks are often eager to tell you why they are good at their jobs, even when they are bad at them. Folks like to brag, or at least validate themselves, especially in the dehumanizing environment of the courtroom. They appreciate ways to be recognized as the human beings they are instead of the lowly cogs the court system has turned them into.

After asking what makes them good at their jobs, follow up with "Tell me about that."

> Q: What makes you good at your job?
>
> A: I'm good with people.
>
> Q: Tell me about that.
>
> A: Have to wait on the public all day, and they can get pretty tiring. But I get along with them no matter what they're like.
>
> Q: Tell me how.

Then ask follow-ups that relate to case issues. For example:

> What would happen if you could no longer do those things you are good at?

So if a juror has said she is good at her job because she has a good memory for details, ask, "What if you lost your memory for details? How would that affect your job?"

A.18

When the Judge Stops You

With any question, the judge might say, "Hold on. What does that have to do with anything? Ask something else." This is often because the judge does not immediately see the information-seeking relevance of the question. When she says something is irrelevant, often she means that given her necessarily limited knowledge of the case and her few seconds of considering this particular question, she has not spotted its relevance. She is probably not a mean person who cackles in delight when she foils your plans. She is (usually) just trying to be a good judge. And as a good judge, she is willing to be informed—especially in advance of trial—about what makes things relevant to the case.

So if you anticipate that a judge might not see the information-seeking relevance of, say, "Tell me what makes you good at your job," it becomes your task to explain it. For example: "Judge, my client was hurt in ways that keep him from his job. We are claiming damages for it. I do not want jurors whose experiences make them think there are no special abilities necessary to doing a job. Such jurors would be candidates for me to challenge peremptorily, and this question helps me learn who they are."

Do not be afraid of arguing this. If you argue professionally and knowledgeably, the judge is not likely to hold a grudge over it even if she rules against you. And if nothing else, alerting the judge in this way to your jury selection concerns can make her more lenient next time you receive an objection to a voir dire question and she has to rule quickly. Thus, for every question you plan to ask in voir dire, be prepared to articulate your information-seeking reason to ask it. If you have reason to think in advance that there might be a problem, deal with it in advance.

Often, the judge needs a reminder (and maybe a memorandum of law) that voir dire is not solely for seeking information for cause challenges (as in, "Can you follow the law?"). Voir dire is also for gathering information on which to base an intelligent exercise of peremptory strikes. When a judge rejects your question and says, "Just ask them if they can follow the law," respectfully remind the judge that if a juror cannot follow or is even substantially impaired (*Wainwright v. Witt*, 496 U.S. 412 1985, Holding 1) from following the law, that goes not to peremptory but cause challenge. Thus, being limited to asking whether a juror can follow the law keeps you from being able to discharge your obligation of gathering information upon which to intelligently base peremptory challenges. It reduces you to making peremptory challenge choices mainly on the basis of demographics, which can easily run counter to *Batson* and its progeny.

The converse of the good-at-your-job question can elicit attitudes relevant to most malpractice cases:

> Mr. Jones, you're a plumber. Is it like other professions: are there good plumbers and some that are not so good?

That is your one closed-ended question on the topic. It is solely to open a new topic. When Mr. Jones says "Yes," open it up with "Tell me about it." The information-seeking purpose is to find out how disturbed this prospective juror is by carelessness, sloppiness, low standards, and so forth. You also want to know how he feels about those qualities in his own kind of work, because they are an important part of the life experience he is likely to draw upon when deciding how wrong the defendant's carelessness was.

And the question yields far more. Simply by the tone in which the juror answers it, you can learn how strongly he or she feels about incompetence and carelessness. With good follow-up questions you may even find out if this juror forgives negligent errors and omissions that are not intentional. This can uncover material for a challenge for cause.

The good-at-your-job question and its follow-ups are one of several good ways (others below) to get jurors talking. It helps you learn how each juror will respond to some key issues in your case. And it introduces case themes in the best possible way: by making those themes relevant to the jurors' own life experiences.

Well-designed and skillfully executed questions in this first "get 'em talking" part of voir dire can give you enough information for much of your decision making. Aside from job questions, you can ask:

> Tell me about the work your [husband/wife] does. What is a normal workday like for him/her?
>
> Tell me about your children.
>
> Where do you live?
>
> Tell me about that area; what's it like?
>
> How has the neighborhood changed over the years?

A.19

Do Not Argue

If you get an answer you disagree with, do not argue. Here is Rule 2 of voir dire:

Rule Two: You cannot change juror attitudes, beliefs, or opinions. It is damaging even to try.

Arguing with a juror makes an enemy of him (or at least makes him uncomfortable with you), and silences other jurors who might have harmful attitudes or opinions that they'd otherwise tell you. So you don't find out until you interview the jury after trial to find out why you lost.

Instead of arguing with jurors, encourage them to tell you all about those attitudes and opinions that are bad for your case:

> Lots of people—including my mother—think that if a car is not damaged much in a wreck, the passengers had to be okay. Others think a person can be badly hurt even if the car was barely dented. What have you seen or heard that would make you side one way or the other?

This is one of many ways to give jurors permission to tell you bad things. Other ways include constant repetition of, "There are no wrong answers; the only right answer is the answer that is right to you"; using body language and slow (not curt) nodding that encourage a juror to continue talking once he or she has embarked on a bad attitude; and giving genuine thanks to every juror for whatever they say. (Do not thank only the jurors who give harmful opinions and attitudes; thank everyone.)

Thus, when a juror says she does not think the loss of any particular qualities would make it hard for her to do her job because she would just find another way to do it, do not ask an argumentative question like, "But that would still hurt the quality of your work, wouldn't it?" That is arguing. Do not try to make her agree with you. Encourage her bad answers.

Argumentative questions also shut up and even alienate other jurors who might agree with the juror you are questioning, or who have opinions on other topics which they will hide later in order to avoid the uncomfortable prospect of your arguing with them.

If a juror says he would fall back on doing the job some other way, follow up by asking "Tell me about that." When he answers, compliment his flexibility. Do not argue. You have the entire trial to show that your client has no other ways to do his job. You only have voir dire to find out which jurors believe, for example, that there is always another way to do a job.

Arguing with a juror in voir dire can cost you the case. If the whole jury sees you lose an argument with a juror, your credibility and apparent competence may take a fatal hit.

A.20
After they Are Talking

Once you get the jurors talking frankly, the rest of voir dire is easier, even fun. Given the time you have for jury selection, decide on the topics most central to your case that can be affected by varying juror attitudes, life experiences, and opinions. Design closed-ended questions to introduce those topics ("Who here has ever been in a wreck?") and design open-ended questions that will get the information you want when a series of "Tell-me-about-its" do not. Such topics for a med mal case might include standards of care (which translates into a discussion in voir dire of the rules, regulations, and standards the jurors themselves have to follow at work and how they feel about them); experiences with, perceptions of, and opinions about the medical profession, and jurors' reactions to those experiences and perceptions; attitudes and opinions about the harms in the case and intangible damages in general; experiences in the jurors' own lives and in the lives of people they know well with respect to harms on a par with the those in this case—and how they feel about those experiences; burden of proof issues; and so forth.

It is usually better to cover a few topics thoroughly than to have too many topics to cover thoroughly in your allotted time.

A.21
Find the Question To Get the Information You Want

With many things, you cannot get a useful answer by asking head-on. "How do you feel about Black people?" or "How much confidence do you have in physicians?" You might get an informative answer or two, but no more. So instead, ask questions about life experiences that will reveal the answer you want without you having to overtly ask.

> Have you ever wanted to get a second opinion? [And "Tell me about that."]
>
> Have you ever suggested to anyone that they get a second opinion? [And "Tell me about that."]
>
> When you go to the doctor do you ask lots of questions? [And "Tell me about that."]

A.22
Identifying Leaders

Leaders are jurors who strongly influence other jurors during deliberations. A leader favorable to your side is obviously helpful. An unfavorable leader—even just one—can cost you the case or reduce damages by a factor of ten or more.

Thus, once you have spotted a leader, try to remove her unless she is very likely to be favorable. You can gamble on non-leaders, but not on leaders. Take no chances.

You decide whether a juror will be a leader in the following ways:

Look at occupation. A leader in the workplace is a likely jury leader. Managers, teachers, supervisors, administrators, bosses, and organizers are among those likely to be jury leaders. As you learn each juror's occupation, consider what human relationships are involved on the job. Is leadership part of the job? How many people are under him? How often is he in decision-making situations? What is his level of responsibility and decision making? How much coordinating does he do? How much is he involved in leading groups that are charged with making decisions? How much do other people listen to him? What does he say about himself as a leader?

Even if leadership is not part of the job, a juror's familiarity with a work-connected activity can unexpectedly make her a single-topic leader when that work-connected activity is related to the case. For example, a taxi driver may have no particular personal leadership qualities. But other jurors might take him as a reliable and thus persuasive authority on matters such as dangerous nighttime neighborhoods. An office clerk might be regarded as authoritative when it comes to business machines. Such authority gives an otherwise non-leader a leader's weight and status on that particular topic.

Articulate people, especially those who talk easily and effectively, are often leaders because deliberations are mainly a speaking event. To identify articulate and expressive people, ask open-ended voir dire questions. Jurors who answer fully and confidently are often leaders. (The converse is not true. Jurors who are relatively silent in jury selection can still be leaders.)

People with charisma are often jury leaders because other jurors voluntarily gravitate to their way of thinking.

People who are popular are often jury leaders even when they do not try to be. They are popular because they are well liked, so other jurors try to please them.

Celebrities, including local celebrities, tend to be leaders.

People in high-status professions, such as doctors, tend to be leaders.

People who easily offer opinions tend to be jury leaders, if they listen as readily as they speak. Jurors allow themselves to be led by fair coordinators who are good listeners. Jurors want to follow a respectful person who has the self-confidence not to bully and who will prevent others from bullying. Such a democratic leader can hold great power in deliberations because other jurors allow themselves to be coordinated by her, and many can eventually gravitate toward her opinions.

Problem solvers become jury leaders, as do take-charge people, as long as they can do so without stifling discussion.

Organizers are leaders but not necessarily opinion leaders. Because they are interested primarily in leading the progress of a group's activity (such as making a difficult decision), they are likely to be consensus makers and can lead the way to compromise verdicts.

If you have the principal burdens, be wary of prospective jurors who take stands in voir dire that seem intentionally different from other jurors' stands. This can indicate a common personality type that seeks stature by trying to confront people, challenge, or just resist the majority. This can be just for the pleasure of being seen as individual and different. Such ornery jurors can cause dissension and ill feelings, dividing the jury.

As with occupation, other life experiences can create single-topic leaders. With or without other personal qualities, some jurors are disproportionately influential on topics relating to their own life experiences—even if they do not seek to influence others. It is a matter of how other jurors regard them. A juror who has had extensive surgery can become influential on the medical issues in your case. A juror who cares for an invalid at home can be considered an authority on home care. Even a juror who was bonked in the head by a baseball 30 years ago might be regarded by his fellow jurors as an insightful expert on post-concussion behavior ("I got slammed and walked away just fine").

Ask jurors about spare-time activities, because volunteers and people with special training can also be single-topic leaders. For example, a library volunteer knows not only about books but about working with the public. So in case-related matters concerning working with the public, jurors may defer to that library volunteer's opinions. Even someone who has merely taken a Red Cross CPR course can be a strong influence on the jury's choice of which expert cardiologist to believe.

A juror with previous jury experience sometimes carries more weight than first-timers. She is also a more likely choice for foreperson. While the position of foreperson is not always influential, a foreperson with previous jury service may well be.

Come right out and ask prospective jurors to tell you the situations in which they are regarded as leaders, and which as followers. Their responses are not completely reliable, but will provide clues to be followed up.

Some leadership signs are subtle. When jurors are returning to the box after a recess, followers tend to sit down and look straight ahead. Leaders often look around to see if everyone is back in their seats.

During voir dire recesses, observe how jurors behave with each other. Those who talk most may be leaders. Also be on the lookout for people who take the initiative in such simple matters as seating arrangements, holding doors, even pushing the elevator button. Have an associate hang around the hallway to observe which jurors seem to be leading such decision-making processes as where to go for lunch.

Caveat. Someone can be a leader even if she does not seem likely to lead a person like you. A juror who is deferential to you might exert considerable control over other sorts of people. In a room of lieutenants, the general is boss. But a roomful of sergeants heeds the lieutenant. *Leadership is always a comparative quality.* So consider the makeup of the jury as a whole before concluding whether or not someone is a leader.

Also consider gender and race. For example, can the woman who is a potential leader on your behalf hold sway over the particular men who will be on the jury?

A.23
Other Areas of Inquiry

Introducing case weaknesses. You should also ask questions concerning your case weaknesses. Introducing your weaknesses yourself in voir dire makes them part of the background. That is better than allowing your opponent to hurl your weaknesses at you during his jury voir dire, and making it look like you were hiding them. Mr. Defense Attorney might ask:

> DEFENSE Q: One thing that Mr. Lucas did not tell you was that this case involves an abortion. So I have to ask you some questions about that.

So now jurors think you hid it.

If your client's heavy drinking or drug use will come into evidence, you should be the one to break the news to the jurors. You don't have to say he was a heavy drinker. But when you ask. "How many of you are close to people who drink heavily?" jurors will figure it out, so they will not think later that you were trying to hide anything. Responses to the question will provide information you need for jury selection. And by asking the question, you have presented the bad news when it will have the least bad effect: when juror attention is more on themselves as they respond to questions than it is on the case.

Depth of feeling. The fact that a juror says he believes something does not mean he believes it deeply. We all have attitudes and beliefs that run deep, but many opinions run shallow and barely influence what we do—such as deciding cases. This is why so much professional opinion polling is wrong. It is easy to mistake a deep-seated attitude for a shallow and passing opinion that can change by suppertime or next week, or that can easily be neutralized by other factors.

For example, many jurors say they favor damages caps. They may do so because they are mean and selfish people who care about no one but themselves. But more often it is because they believe that capping damages is fair and just. So the deep attitude is fairness and justice, and the desire for caps is just their current opinion as to how fairness and justice can be achieved. If they see a better way to achieve fairness and justice, they will seize it even if it contradicts their current opinion. Not everyone is like this, but enough people are that you have to take it into account when deselecting jurors. So consider the depth of a juror's opinion or attitude before deciding how high to place that juror on your strike list.

In a recent case, we were forced to use our three strikes to remove three jurors who would not only decide against us but follow us home later and beat us up. So we got stuck with a juror who identified herself as a *very* [italics hers] conservative *Republican* [italics hers] who firmly believed in damages caps because "Jesus would have *wanted* them [italics, well, who knows whose?] and she listened mostly to Rush Limbaugh even though she sometimes found him "slimy," but she also said "Yes, your Honor, of course I will follow the law as you give it to me." So His not-to-be-damned Honor smiled down at us over his concealed plastic replica of the Ten Commandments and overruled our motion to dismiss her for cause. She was seated.

Fortunately we were in a heaven of a jurisdiction where plaintiffs need only nine of twelve to win.

Surprisingly, the verdict was large, and even more surprisingly it was unanimous. In interviewing jurors afterwards we learned that the *Limbaugh/Jesus* lady pushed for a very different scale of damages than did the other jurors. Everyone else wanted a few million dollars of verdict. *Limbaugh/Jesus* wanted $20 million—because she could not stand the injustice that had been done to our client.

This is not all that rare. People who support tort "reform" are not necessarily mean and unjust. Many are simply misinformed. They want fairness and justice. On the basis of the misinformation, they "believe" in caps. But when they see the injustice done to your client, their same hunger for fairness and justice can occasionally drive a very substantial verdict.

So you cannot assume that a juror deeply believes anything he says he believes, and that it will shape his decision-making. Shallow beliefs are context-oriented—they shift as the context shifts. You need to probe beneath the surface: Why does the juror believe whatever he says he believes? Is it because that's what the media says to believe? Or does it touch his core values?

By the time you have asked, "Tell me about it" three or four times, you will usually see whether a belief is a fiercely held attitude or just a passing opinion.

Caveat: Promises. At no time in jury selection is it safe to elicit promises from jurors. Don't ask them to make deals with you ("Will you promise us to . . . ?"). Many jurors resent being asked to assure you of something when they still have heard none of the case. Besides, deals made with the jurors in jury selection aren't worth the breath it took to make them.

A.24
The Last Six Questions

At the end of every jury selection ask the following six questions. But first give the jurors a thumbnail sketch—no more than 50 words—of the case if they do not already know what it is. Then ask,

7. Inexplicably, some judges do not ask about hardship until after the attorneys have questioned everyone. This wastes everyone's time, and can make voir dire drag on endlessly while you start all over to fill slots you thought were long filled. Always petition to have the judge do hardship cause hearings first.

1. Given the kind of person you are, your attitudes, life experiences, opinions, everything about you, what is there about you that might help you, even a little, in being a juror on this kind of case? Other than your ability to be fair and listen to both sides?

Do not say ". . . in being a *good* juror . . . "; just "being a juror."

Because this is a positive kind of question, it often gets answers that negative questions ("what's wrong with you?") miss. "My background in engineering will help because I'll be able to tell why the ceiling fell down." Now you can decide if this self-proclaimed expert is dangerous for you. So ask, "Tell me about that," and so forth. From another juror you might hear, as I did, "I read a lot, and I probably know more than the professionals do about the problems with highway design." Or, "Our neighbors are physicians, and we've talked a lot about how hard it is to do that kind of work, so I'll be very qualified to gauge what the doctor did in this case."

The question is effective because often it does not occur to prospective jurors that there might be anything *wrong* with any of that. But depending which side you're on, it could be disastrous to let them on the jury.

Ask this question first of the most articulate and thoughtful juror you have. Ask follow-ups. This will get information you need, and simultaneously give other jurors some time to think about the question so they are more likely to have a useful answer when you get to them.

Be sure to include the last sentence of Number 1: "Other than your ability to be fair and listen to both sides." Otherwise everyone's answer will be "I can be fair and listen to both sides."

Then ask the other side of the coin:

2. Given the kind of person you are, your attitudes, life experiences, opinions, everything about you, what is there about you that you think might make it just a little bit *harder* for you to be a juror on this kind of case?

Don't say "make you a bad juror." And be sure to say "just a little bit."

Even if the judge has already filtered out prospective jurors for hardship,[7] some jurors will say they will find it hard to be a juror because they have a schedule conflict or some other reason they cannot serve. Sometimes it's the upcoming death of that same poor grandmother who died six times while the juror was in college. Other times you might hear about a real hardship problem. Either way, get out of it. Explain that you are not allowed to deal with that; the judge has to—unless, of course, this is a juror you want to get rid of. In that case, lead the juror into saying that she will not be able to concentrate on the evidence because she'll be worried about the problem.

Many jurors will have no useful responses to either final question numbers one or two. But they are still worth asking because from time to time you get information that even the most thorough of voir dires would have missed.

Then ask:

3. Responsibility means paying enough money compensation to fully equal the losses and the level of the harm—without putting anything into the scale except those losses and harms. That's the law. Who here thinks they might have trouble—even a little—keeping things off the scale that don't belong there?

Then go to the clean-up question:

4. What else is there—anything at all—that you would want to know about you, if you were me standing up here and trying to decide who will be on the jury? Anything? Even if you're not sure it makes any difference?

Again, this often gets nothing useful. But the occasional bombshell drops.

Jurors' rights questions. Dr. Sunwolf (her real and entire name), the brilliant attorney, trial consultant, and communications scholar, teaches that you should close every voir dire with these last two questions. You can ask these as group questions, but individually is better.

7. Inexplicably, some judges do not ask about hardship until after the attorneys have questioned everyone. This wastes everyone's time, and can make voir dire drag on endlessly while you start all over to fill slots you thought were long filled. Always petition to have the judge do hardship cause hearings first.

5. Mr. Jones, if you are a juror in this case, you will have some rights. It is extremely important that you understand these rights, and that you will exercise them as often as the need arises. First, you will have the right to hear all the testimony. So if a witness says something you don't hear, will you be comfortable raising your hand and telling the judge, 'Your honor, I did not hear what the witness said.' Will you do that?

This teaches jurors that you know the evidence is all on your side, because you are so concerned that they hear every word of it.

Then comes the kicker:

6. Mr. Jones, as a juror you will have a second right: the right to understand the law. Nothing can be more important. But every so often during deliberations, jurors disagree over what the law is. Sometimes a juror is just not sure. And sometimes a discussion will start about what the law really is. So if any of that happens, instead of trying to decide it among yourselves, will you be comfortable telling your foreperson to knock on the jury room door and ask the bailiff to tell the judge that there is something about the law you need to hear about again? [If the judge sends the instructions into deliberations, say, "Instead of trying to decide it among yourselves, will you be comfortable asking your foreperson to read out loud the written instructions the judge will give you about the law—and if that does not solve the problem, will you be comfortable telling the foreperson to knock on the jury room door and ask the bailiff to tell the judge that there is something about the law you need to hear about again? [Watch your wording on this question. Often, the judge cannot "explain" the law; she can only repeat the instruction on the law.]

This tells jurors that you believe that not only the facts but the law, too, are on your side. For establishing your credibility and good faith, that is exactly what you want them to think. These two jurors' rights questions also make the jurors feel that you, not your opponent, are empowering them to take over the case.

Most importantly, it keeps jurors from making up their own laws.

Dr. Sunwolf also advises that in closing, you remind jurors of these rights.

A.25
Challenging for Cause

Michigan Trial Consultant Eric Oliver says the primary purpose of jury selection is to pursue challenges for cause. Doing so is an easily acquired skill. Lawyers who have not mastered it often waste peremptories, and run out of them. So jurors are often seated who essentially decided the case before they ever got their jury summonses.

For any of a variety of reasons, when it is within their discretion, judges allow opposing counsel to rehabilitate. Some judges cursorily rehabilitate by asking, "Can you follow the law?" If you have skillfully laid the groundwork for your challenge, this cursory (or even a thorough) rehabilitation is less likely to succeed.

Good judges know that "Can you follow the law?" is coercive and thus gathers no reliable information. It borders on bullying. It intimidates even self-assured jurors into giving false answers. And "Yes, I can follow the law" is insufficient under the law, which hopefully the judge wants to follow. A prospective juror who would be merely "substantially impaired" from following the law should be excused for cause. [*Wainwright v. Witt,* 496 U.S. 412 1985.]

Whether or not your judge heeds *Wainwright,* you still need an effective way to pursue a challenge for cause. Here is one. Practice it before going to trial so that it becomes second nature. You will be surprised how many more cause dismissals you get over the course of your next few trials.

Start with open-ended questions. What do you do when you spot something that might support a challenge for cause? First, ask many open-ended questions about it:

> Tell me about that.

Tell me more about that.

Tell me more about *that.*

What have you read about it?

What have you heard about that?

How do you feel about it?

Why do you think _______ happens so much?

It is essential to start by eliciting ample responses to open-ended questions. This is because judges are supposed to rule on the totality (the "universe") of what a juror says, not merely on a single phrase that an attorney or the judge maneuvers the juror into saying, such as "I can follow the law." The more the juror says which shows his bias, the more of the totality leans towards dismissal for cause. Further, the more you get the juror to nail down his bias with certainty and emphasis, the more she will be reluctant to backtrack later when the judge or your opponent tries to rehabilitate her.[8]

The tone with which you conduct this entire process must not be hostile. You have to be friendly, understanding, and even admiring of the forcefulness with which the prospective juror firmly clings to his belief. Make the juror feel that it is a "badge of honor," as Texas trial consultant Robert Hirschhorn puts it, to be honest and forthright enough to be eligible to be removed for cause.

The transition to the next phase can be accomplished with:

You feel you have a right to hold onto your opinion, don't you?

Tell me why.

Shift to closed-ended questions. After eliciting all you can with open-ended questions, shift to closed-ended:

How long have you felt this way?

8. Check carefully to make sure that rehabilitation is allowed. Some judges allow rehabilitation and conduct it themselves even in venues where they lack the discretion to do so.

From all that you've said, it's safe for me to assume that you're not going to change your mind in the next few days [weeks], isn't it?

And you would not want to set your belief aside?

Setting it aside would be hard?

You seem to know your own mind, so I assume you're not going to set it aside just because someone comes along and tells you to set it aside?

Not even if it was me?

And if even the judge told you you'd have to set it aside to be a juror in this case, you still would find it very difficult to do that, right?

What you're doing is attempting to rehabilitate him while he's still under your control. If he backs off, you haven't lost anything since he would surely have backed off as soon as the judge or your opponent started rehabilitating. When you do it first, it gets a lot harder for the judge or your opponent to do it successfully. If they do, the juror has to contradict himself—which should be enough to make a judge suspicious of which answers are true. *Wainwright* also says that a prospective juror's substantial impairment with being able to follow the law does not have to be found with certainty; the mere suspicion of it is enough. The *Wainwright* conclusions and other applicable law should be in a memorandum of law for the judge.

You are trying to show the judge that this prospective juror is "substantially impaired" from following the law—not "unable" to follow the law. This means that following the law on a particular issue will be very difficult for her. Under *Wainwright*, that is enough for a cause dismissal. If your judge does not recognize the U.S. Supreme Court, you may need to go for a "cannot follow the law" threshold.

You certainly seem to know your own mind, so I assume you're not going to set it aside just because someone comes along and tells you to set it aside?

Not even if they told you that you'd have to set it aside in order to follow the law as a juror in this case?

And not even if even the judge told you you'd have to set it aside in order to follow the law?

You need to adapt your close-ended questions to the judge's particular standard. But with almost every judge, start out with open-ended questions that lead the juror to talk about how deeply he feels about this issue. That will make his words ring hollow if he later claims he can set his belief aside.

Research the judge. Different judges grant cause dismissals for different reasons and at different thresholds. You will improve your chances of getting cause dismissals if you find out in advance about your judge's practices. Ask attorneys who have appeared before that judge. Ask the judge. Ask the bailiff. Read transcripts. If nothing else, this research will tell you in advance what kinds of questions and strategies will be most likely to help you get problem jurors dismissed. It is hard to forge a good strategy on your feet in front of a jury. You want to plan it in advance, and you should rehearse it in advance, as suggested below.

A.26
Pretrial Practice

Even once mastered, the best trial techniques are useless unless you are fresh at doing them. That is why many of the best and most experienced lawyers do a practice voir dire before every trial.

Not more than three evenings before voir dire, preferably the night before, gather eight or ten strangers and spend a few hours voir diring them with the voir dire you will do in court. This helps you hit the ground running when you do it in court. It makes you more confident, secure, and relaxed—and that will make you more credible. It creates better rapport. And you will know what you are doing at the start of voir dire in court because you have just done it the night before in your office.

This is why actors rehearse and athletes scrimmage. They do not stop just because they are good and have lots of experience. In fact, it is the opposite: the better and more experienced they are, the more they practice and rehearse. If attorneys did the same it would raise the quality of trial practice in America to unrecognizable heights. But not everyone will do it—so you can gain an enormous advantage over them. Practice, practice, and practice. And then practice some more. Michael Jordan did not get good by reading about basketball in Chapel Hill. And he did not get better by skipping practice in Chicago. In fact even at the height of his career he came back to Chapel Hill to spend hours and days in the gym practicing the basics. He was a brilliant player, yes. But his greatest brilliance was realizing the necessity of endless practice from beginning to end of his playing career.

Your voir dire practice session will even make the judge like you more, because you will waste less time finding your feet as you get started with voir dire in court. You will seem more assured, comfortable, professional, and personable.

Do this kind of practice the night before every trial. The next day in actual voir dire you'll be as relaxed and competent as if it were the second day of real jury selection, not the first. Do not underestimate how valuable such a session is. Never go to trial without having done it. You will learn what kinds of questions are useful. You will develop a Pavlovian repulsion for asking questions such as:

> Does anyone feel they can't give my client a fair trial because he's Black?

Instead, you will develop the habit of seeking the same information by getting jurors to talk at length about it.

> Mr. Jackson, how do you think people in this community feel about what's been happening in race relations over the past few years?
>
> Please tell me more about that.
>
> Mr. Fabulous, how do you feel about what Mr. James said?

And,

> Tell me more.

Prospective jurors in deliberation. An advanced practice session will let you safely try new methods—such as the pinnacle of good jury voir dire: getting prospective jurors deliberating in front of you during voir dire.

Mr. Jones, what do you think about that? [I.e., what Mr. Smith just said.]

When Mr. Jones has answered, go back to Mr. Smith:

Mr. Smith, what about that? Then involve other jurors.

Miss Johnson, which way of thinking are you closer to?

And,

In what way?

Then just nod in the direction of another juror who seems ready to talk. Then another. Soon you won't have to nod; you'll just need to look. They'll talk spontaneously, arguing with each other—deliberating! As if they are auditioning for the part of juror. You'll not only hear what they feel about the topic and how strongly they feel it; you'll also see who can be articulate and persuasive, who is a leader, who folds, how well informed the various jurors are about the topic, and what kind of language they use when talking about the topic.

You'll also see how each juror interacts with the others—which is of the utmost importance in deliberations. Does she bully? Respect what others say? Does she listen—or does she just talk? Does she try to find common ground or does she emphasize where her opinion is different from someone else's? Does she pair up with others? Does she need to be right no matter what anyone says? Does she talk in moderate terms or extreme? Does she have leadership qualities? Etc.

When I tell you to practice the night before trial starts, you might say, "What?! Are you nuts? Do you realize how busy I am?" Yeah, I do. Do *you* realize how important good jury selection is?

If you don't have time to practice jury voir dire the night before trial, you lack the resources to do your job right; you are short-shrifting your client. Complaining that you have no time to practice something as crucial as jury voir dire is as bad as saying you don't have the staff to handle the complex case you have taken. If you don't have it or cannot get it (be it staff or voir dire practice time or anything else), you should not be doing the case. That's the *sine qua non* of being a responsible plaintiff's attorney.

A.27

Judge-Approved Questions, Judge-Conducted Voir Dire

In some jurisdictions, you have to submit jury voir dire questions for the judge to approve. Keep in mind that the judge rarely knows the case well, and never knows the case from your point of view. So help the judge see the appropriateness and need for each question you submit. Explain:

- How each submitted question will identify biases and attitudes necessary to intelligently exercise your challenges.
- How those biases and attitudes can affect juror decision making.
- How some such biases and attitudes might be appropriate for a cause dismissal, and others would be appropriate to consider for a peremptory dismissal.

Submit your questions this way:

Q: Who has ever had to use crutches? and

Who knows anyone who has ever had to use crutches?

(Follow up for details.)

Purpose. Plaintiff had hard time on crutches for six weeks. Prospective jurors who had easy time or know someone who did will likely undervalue Plaintiff's ordeal. So we must learn who used crutches and their difficulty with them.

Challenge Basis. In follow-up questioning, juror might say, "I had no trouble with crutches and can't see how anyone would." If further follow-up shows she would not compensate no matter the evidence, the Court should consider cause dismissal. If juror just seems reluctant, we would consider peremptory challenge.

This gives the judge justification for allowing the question. It also sensitizes the judge to your challenge concerns.

When submitting questions for the judge to ask, include the follow-up questions he should also ask. For example, if the initial question is, "Who here has ever missed more than a few weeks of work because of an injury?" follow up with:

> Please tell me about that.
>
> How long were you (or the person you know) out of work?
>
> Why?
>
> How much income did you (or the person you know) lose?
>
> How did you (or the person you know) feel about missing that much work?
>
> What difficulties were there when you (or the person you know) returned to work? Etc.

Some judges ask no follow-ups; others ask as many as you provide, and even more. Judges are more likely to ask when you provide the follow-up questions. They help judges better understand the purpose of the initial question, and can help the judge be a more useful information-gatherer for you.

APPENDIX B

STORY FOR OPENING STATEMENTS[1]

B.1

Storytelling[2]

Good storytelling is essential in Part Two of your opening ("Story of What The Defendant Did"). Anyone can tell the story well enough to make the jury listen. You need not be a gifted story teller. Simply apply the following principles:

One fact per sentence. Good storytelling is done simply: a simple narrative of what the defendant did. One fact per sentence. Do not say: "The truck driver drove through the red light, skidded across the center line, and hit an oncoming car head-on." That's three facts. Three facts requires three sentences: "The truck driver drove through the red light. He skidded across the center line. He hit an oncoming car head-on."

This simplicity creates emphasis and directness.

Present tense. Use the present tense. Past tense distances the listener. Present tense is more immediate. So instead of: "He drove through the red light," say "He drives through the red light."

Get into the present tense at the start of the story by saying:

> Please come back with me to June 12, 2003. We are in downtown Rochester. Acme Corporation's truck driver is headed West on . . . .

1. Be wary of using the techniques in this section outside the context of the structure described in Chapter 6.

2. See also 6.5.

B.2
Actions

A story has nothing to do with facts, descriptions, or explanations. If you want jurors to pay any attention, leave those things out of your opening story of what the defendant did—except for actions: things the defendant *did.* Not what he failed to do. Not what he should have done. Not what you need to explain. Just what he *did. Everything* else comes later when it can do you some good.

Actions the defendant did. This cannot be said too many times: your story in opening is nothing more than a narrative of *what the defendant did,* action by action. Each action is a separate thing the defendant did.

> An action is an active verb.
>
> An action is something someone does.

The grammatical subject of every sentence (the "noun") in the opening story should be the name of the defendant, and the predicate (the "verb") should be an action of the defendant's. Each new sentence should be the next thing the defendant does. Leave out anything in the story that you cannot express in exactly this way.

So don't say, "The car was a 2001 Chrysler." That is a fact, a description—but not an action. It's a state of being. Save it for later no matter how important it is. You can say "Joe Defendant starts his red Chrysler." "Starts" is an action.

People listen to actions. They listen less to descriptions, states of being, and explanations. This principle is at least 2,500 years old. It is the most basic principle of movies and plays. Well, maybe not French movies. But movies and plays that most Americans want to sit through.

Move forward in time. If each sentence is a successive action the defendant did, you will automatically follow the requirement that every sentence of the story move you forward in time—be it a split second or a century. If a sentence does not progress the story in time, leave it out of the story. You will get to that stuff soon enough when it will do you a lot more good than it will here, and where it will not turn down juror listening.

Short sentences. Grammatically speaking, use only simple sentences. Avoid compound or complex sentences. Simple sentences are easier to listen to. No semi-colons in your opening story, and very few commas. Remember that this early in opening jurors are nervous about whether they can possibly learn all they have to in order to do their job as jurors. They are looking for a guide who will make the case crystal clear. Show them from the first words in your story that you will be that guide.

Can your see it or hear it? The story is merely a report of what a video camera and microphone would have picked up if it had been following the defendant through the actions. Exclude anything the defendant failed to do. Exclude anything anyone thought or felt like. Save those things for later. If you want jurors to accept the story as true without wondering whether you are telling the truth, leave out the defendant's omissions.

Importance of each action. Do not hurry through one action to get to the next. Give each action time and importance. That does not mean to make every action seem to be of equal importance. But every action important enough to include in the story should be important enough not to rush through. Do not slide from one point into the next.

Read this next story aloud as though every separate point has importance:

> Come back with me to seven o'clock this morning.//
>
> My alarm rings.//
>
> I wake up.//
>
> I roll out of bed.//
>
> I open the curtains.//
>
> I look out.//
>
> I see snow falling.//
>
> I take a shower.//
>
> I go downstairs.//

I drink some coffee.//

I read the *Times.*//

I put on my coat.//

I go outside.//

I scrape the windshield.//

This looks stilted on the page, but spoken aloud in such a way as to give each event some importance, it will be listened to. Note the use of present tense. Note the simplicity. Note that every sentence contains a new action. Note the lack of description and explanation. Note the absence of anything that cannot be seen or heard.

You can fit in some descriptive material. But be sparing:

My electric alarm rings.//

I wake up slowly.//

I roll out of my messy bed.//

I open the red curtains.//

I look out.//

I see heavy snow falling.//

I take a hot shower.//

I go downstairs.//

I drink some cold coffee.//

I read the *Times.*//

I put on my winter coat.//

I go outside.//

I scrape heavy ice off the windshield.//

So you can get a good amount of information in, but don't overdo it. And tie each piece of information directly to the action.

Few tellers can effectively convey both the story (events) and the explanatory details (information) at once. Listeners tend to layer in only one new level at a time: first the actions (what *happened*), and later the explanations, omissions, thoughts, feelings, and so forth.

Practice this method of storytelling. If you have children, they will appreciate it. If you have no children, get a friend to listen.

B.3
Selectivity and Starting Point

Start your story with the first relevant thing the defendant did. This means you have to look for it in discovery. The truck wreck did not necessarily start when the truck came through the red light. It might have started even earlier, when the company hired this driver.

Remember that the earliest things a listener hears in a story can be what the listener goes on to think the whole story is about. This makes the listener hear everything that follows in that same light. Thus, starting with the wrong action can weaken your whole story.

Any story can be told a hundred ways. As you start your story in opening, emphasize the events the jury needs in order to understand what happened in the way you want them to understand it. This means you have to delay and subordinate events that hurt you. Do not conceal them; deal with them later in opening. Start the story with the events that help you.

This sounds easy, but you can fall into a trap by talking too early about the things your client did, no matter how proper or laudatory. Jurors tend to attach blame to the first actions they hear about. In this way, innocent actions can turn damning. This is a basic principle of dramatic storytelling. If I watch a character early in a play or movie while I am thinking there is some chance, however small, that he may be up to no good, I will tend to see even his most innocent actions as wrongful.

In trial, this happens when you tell jurors what your client did before they know all about what the other side did. This is because when jurors start hearing about what happened, the first thing they do is assign blame—and they can assign it only to the events they hear about. So jurors tend to assign blame to whomever you talk about first.

That's why your story needs to be solely about what the *defendant* did. Leave your client out of it except as the passive receiver of harm.

So if the doctor failed to diagnose your client's cancer, do not start by telling us what your client did ("Jane calls the doctor for an appointment . . . Goes to see him on January 8 . . . etc.") That makes jurors start by thinking about why Jane chose that doctor, why Jane did not ask for a second opinion, why she waited until January 8, etc. By the time you get to the first thing the doctor did, jurors have already nailed some blame on your client.

Instead, start by telling us what the doctor did: "Dr. Smith runs the test. He sends it to the lab. He looks at the result. He . . . ." That way jurors begin by thinking about what the doctor, not Jane, did wrong.

Even events that have nothing to do with your client can deflect blame from the defendant. For example, take a premises liability case: an assault in a motel room. Three vicious men beat an elderly couple in the couple's room. Do NOT start the story this way: "It's 3 A.M. January 12, 1998. Three Central Prison inmates shoot a prison guard through the head. The prisoners escape over the prison wall. They run. They get to a stoplight at an intersection. They surround a gray Buick. They pull the elderly driver out. She struggles against them. They shoot her in the chest. They drive off in her Buick. They lose their pursuers. They park in the dark behind the C'mon Inn Motel. They shove open the door to Room 123. John and Jane, my clients, wake in terror. The escapees demand money. One of them beats John while . . . ."

That is good storytelling. The jury will listen. They will get the full horror of what the escapees did to John and Jane. Jurors will get the point: these bad guys were really bad.

This would be fine, except that your case is not about escapees. It is about a motel owner who installed flimsy doors and who never told guests of any previous break-ins.

Starting the story with the escapees leads jurors to blame the escapees instead of the owner. Juror shock and anger will be directed at the prison escapees. By the time you finally get to the real story of your case—what the motel owner did—the jurors will be irrevocably blaming the escapees. You have created your own competition.

Here is a better beginning for the plaintiff:

> It's November 14, 1998. The owner of the C'mon Inn Motel goes to a hardware store. He looks at a selection of locks. He buys the three-dollar lock, the cheapest one. He goes back to his motel. He installs the three-dollar lock in the door to a guest room. Two months later, at nine in the evening, he's working the desk. An elderly couple comes in. They ask, 'We saw the sign that says it's safe; is it really?' 'Absolutely,' says the owner. That night in their room, the elderly couple is beaten and robbed.

Same case, different story. By shining your narrative light on the actions of the motel owner at the beginning of your story, you make jurors more likely to blame the owner instead of the escapees. The escapees are not in the story so they are not on the jurors' minds. So you do not deflect the blame from where you need it.

It is useful to test the beginning of your story by asking yourself what your beginning would lead jurors to think if it were all they were going to hear, and if they were looking to pin blame on whatever they hear first. Where are you making the jurors focus? Such testing is necessary because you know the whole story, so you already know what your focus is. But your focus is not your jurors' focus. You have to make your story create the focus you want.

"Would not happen to me." There is another reason to make sure you keep the initial focus off your client. When a juror hears that something bad has happened, she instinctively wants to believe that it would never happen to her. Thus, she seeks out comforting ways to separate herself from the plaintiff who was harmed.

For example, in the motel case, jurors say to themselves "Oh, that would not have happened to me because I would never have chosen to stay in a motel room that faced the back lot."

In a medical negligence case, jurors say, "Oh, that would not have happened to me because I would have gone for a second opinion."

(Jurors commonly say this even though they have never in their lives sought a second opinion!)

In a products liability case: "Oh, that would not have happened to me because I never would have bought that kind of car."

And in deliberations, they will tell other jurors: "The plaintiffs never should have stayed in that kind of room!" or "She should have gotten a second opinion!" or "It's his own fault for buying that kind of car!" And because this kind of thinking is common and unavoidable human nature—we all do it—these remarks will take their toll on the other jurors.

Due to this comforting psychological mechanism, jurors commonly rely on even the flimsiest of reasons to persuade themselves that this kind of harm would never have happened to them, because they would not have done what the plaintiff did.

That is why you should start with the defendant's actions ("The motel owner chooses a three-dollar lock"), so that jurors will focus on the defendant's actions, not the plaintiff's actions.

Please remember that the techniques described above are designed for use with the opening-statement structure described in Chapter 6. Most but not all the techniques will work with any kind of opening structure statement except for a "stream-of-consciousness" opening —with which hardly anything ever works unless you're trying to confuse and alienate jurors.

APPENDIX C
SAMPLE MEDICAL NEGLIGENCE OPENING

One of a trial consultant's most frequent tasks is helping attorneys put together their openings. The opening that follows is based on the opening from a 2005 Florida med mal case. I have reproduced the liability portion in detail, and outlined the damages portion.

In giving your opening, go slowly. Let jurors digest each phrase before you go on to the next. Use brief pauses to break up the thoughts into bite-sized pieces.

Good morning.

[RULE][1]

During this trial, you'll hear from two expert physicians:

Dr. Franklin Schneider, who runs the heart center at Central Medical University,

and Dr. Rebecca Aaron, an expert who teaches family medicine where she practices at Metropolitan Medical Pavilion.

[Note: During opening, use no qualitative adjectives, such as " . . . *outstanding* expert."]

They'll tell you about a basic rule of medicine:

that whenever a physician sees a patient

with any kinds of *abnormal signs* or *symptoms*

1. In most cases, the rule is just a sentence or two—such as, "A driver has to look where he's going. If he does not, and as a result hurts someone, then the driver is responsible for the harm."

the physician is required to use a method called Differential Diagnosis

to figure out the cause

of the patient's signs or symptoms.

Dr. Schneider will testify

that a physician is not allowed to make conclusions

without using a Differential Diagnosis.

Every doctor who testifies will agree.

Every patient who has ever been diagnosed by a physician has had a Differential Diagnosis.

Every doctor who testifies will agree

that a physician cannot assume or guess that the cause is one thing

as long as there's a reasonable possibility

that the cause could be something else *instead*

or something else *in addition.*

The experts will explain

that the physician is always required to *consider and deal* with *every* reasonable possibility.

No matter what the abnormal signs or symptoms are, no matter who the physician is,

the required diagnostic method is always the same.

It's called *Differential Diagnosis.*

The standard of care requires it. Every time.

[Continue taking small breaks after each important phrase.]

The experts will explain that the key phrase to remember about a Differential Diagnosis is "rule out." It means that the physician must rule out every reasonably possible cause of any abnormal signs or symptoms. Every doctor who testifies will tell you that a physician is not allowed to ignore any reasonably possible cause, or to assume the patient does not have this cause, until ruling it out with tests or other methods.

For example, if a patient has the symptom of a lump in her breast, the doctor is not allowed to ignore the possibility of cancer—not even if he's pretty sure it's something else. He is required to proceed as if the cause is cancer until he rules cancer out with tests or other methods.

The physician cannot say, "Well, it's probably just some fiber, so let's forget about cancer." The physician must consider and deal with every reasonable possibility until he rules it out.

Dr. Franklin and Dr. Aaron will show how Differential Diagnosis works and why it's always required. It's really simple.[2]

As you learn how a Differential Diagnosis works, you'll come to understand why doctors order tests. They are following the required rules of Differential Diagnosis.

You'll also learn why a doctor is often required to treat a patient for a particular problem even before the doctor knows whether or not it's the real problem. For example, when someone has chest pains, the doctor might have to give a pill for the heart even before being sure a heart problem is causing the chest pains. You'll hear why.

So how does a Differential Diagnosis work?

The standard of care requires several steps. No doctor is allowed to skip a step.

These steps are important to this case, so you may want to write them down:

STEP ONE: Gather information. The doctor must first gather all the information she can about the problem: all the signs and symptoms, any risk factors, the medical history. Gather all information.

2. Jurors worry about whether they'll be able to understand all they need to know. Assure them early on that they will. Then be their guide who makes that happen.

STEP TWO: The list. Based on all signs, symptoms, risk factors, and medical history, the doctor must list everything that could reasonably be causing the signs and symptoms.

There can be just a few causes or many.

Here's a Differential Diagnosis list:

[**SHOW:** the list of possible causes in this case.]

Two important things about a Differential Diagnosis list: First, the list has to be complete. If a doctor leaves something off that turns out to be the real cause, it goes undetected and untreated, so the patient can die.

Second, the doctor must put any *dangerous* possible causes at the top of the list. The more dangerous a possible cause is, the higher it goes on the list.

For example, chest pains can be caused by stomach gas or by heart attack.

Stomach gas is not dangerous, so the doctor would put it low on the list.

But heart attack as a cause of chest pain is dangerous, so the doctor must put heart attack high on the list.

The doctor is not allowed to ignore the possibility of heart attack even if he's sure the cause is gas.

Even if the doctor *proves* the cause is stomach gas, he still cannot ignore possible heart attack. This is because a patient can have stomach gas and heart attack at the same time.

In other words, one cause does not rule out any other cause. Tests and other methods are the only way to rule out causes. And that takes us to step three:

STEP THREE: Rule out. Experts Dr. Franklin and Dr. Aaron will explain that the doctor cannot ignore any cause on the list until he has ruled it out. That's the standard of care.

"*If there's any doubt, you cannot rule it out.*" That's the basic rule of Differential Diagnosis: "*If there's any doubt, you cannot rule it out.*" No guessing. No "almost sure." Every possible cause stays listed until it is ruled out. This is especially important with any *dangerous* causes.

This is how the medical profession makes sure doctors do not miss anything.

Expert Dr. Aaron tells her medical students that because doctors do not have a crystal ball to see the future, they always have to use a Differential Diagnosis to be sure they do not miss anything in the present. Every medical school teaches that doctors who take shortcuts—instead of doing the Differential Diagnosis properly—will kill patients.

Dr. Franklin will tell you that there is no requirement in medicine more important than using Differential Diagnosis properly. Clinics and hospitals all over the civilized world use Differential Diagnoses tens of thousands of times a day.

"*If there's any doubt, you cannot rule it out.*" How do doctors rule things out?

They use tests, or they treat the possible cause to see if it goes away, or they refer the patient to specialists.

As each possible cause is ruled out, the doctor crosses it off his list. When the doctor finds a cause that cannot be ruled out, she knows it can be the real cause, so she starts treatment.

When any possible cause on the list is dangerous, the doctor must test and take other steps *soon enough* to *save the patient* if that dangerous cause turns out to be the actual cause. Delay can endanger the patient's life.

Sometimes the problem turns out to be what the doctor would have guessed from the start. But very often it is something else. That's why the doctor must list every reasonably possible cause and leave it on the list until he rules it out.

STEP FOUR: Urgent danger. Often, a possible cause can be an urgent danger—something that can quickly cause serious harm or kill. When that's a possible cause—even if not very likely—the doctor must *immediately* rule it out or treat it.

So even if a doctor thinks a patient's chest pains almost certainly mean stomach gas, she still must test for heart trouble right away—because the patient can have both stomach gas and heart attack.

As long as an urgent danger remains possible, the doctor must immediately rule it out or treat it. No delay allowed.

Let me run you through an example. Let's say a man has a very bad headache.

> ***STEP ONE: Gather information.*** First, the doctor gathers information. She asks the man for every symptom. She does an exam to get more information. She learns, among other things, that he's groggy, the headache came on suddenly, and it's the worst headache he's ever had.
>
> ***STEP TWO: The list.*** Using that information, the doctor has to list every reasonably possible cause. She might list tension headache, migraine headache, brain bleed headache, and sinus headache.
>
> > [**SHOW:** list of those four possible causes. Brain bleed on top.]
>
> ***STEP THREE: Rule out.*** The doctor orders tests and takes other steps to see which possible causes she can rule out.
>
> ***STEP FOUR: Urgent danger.*** Three are not urgent dangers: tension, migraine, and sinus. But brain bleed can quickly kill. So the doctor cannot delay treating it or ruling it out. The doctor is not allowed to say later, "Well, I let him die of a brain bleed because I was sure it was a sinus headache." The standard of care requires the doctor to proceed as if the urgent danger is the real one. That means giving treatment even before the tests

come back—because by the time the tests come back, the patient can be dead.

The experts in this case will tell you that when a doctor chooses to ignore the requirements of a Differential Diagnosis and chooses to ignores an urgent danger, then if that danger comes to pass and harms the patient, the doctor is responsible for the harm.

The experts will also explain that when a doctor chooses not to *intervene* when *intervention* would save his patient, the doctor is responsible for the harm.

And when a doctor makes any choice that needlessly endangers a patient, if that danger harms the patient, the doctor is responsible for the harm.

[STORY OF WHAT THE DEFENDANT DID]

Now please let me tell you the story of what happened in this case.

April 14, 2000. Clinic of gynecologist Arlen Cortez.

> [**SHOW:** time line entry: "4/14—Cortez visit." Have nothing else visible yet.]

Dr. Cortez listens to a patient describe how her heart races when she lies down, and that she's had a test showing overactive thyroid—the gland here in the front of her neck.

> [Touch your neck where the gland is.]

Dr. Cortez learns the patient has had irregular menstrual cycles.

Dr. Cortez notes that the patient's eyes bulge.

Dr. Cortez concludes that the cause of these symptoms is approaching menopause. So Dr. Cortez prescribes Premphase, a hormone replacement drug. He also refers the patient to an internal medicine doctor, Dr. Brandon Maynard.

And Dr. Cortez orders a new thyroid test.

> [**Unveil next date.** Label says: "4/18—thyroid tests results."]

Four days later, April 18, Dr. Cortez gets the new thyroid test results. He sees the thyroid is overactive, producing too much thyroid hormone.

> [**Unveil next date.** Label says: "4/27—message to Cortez: new symptoms"]

Nine days later, April 27, Dr. Cortez's office takes a message to Dr. Cortez from the patient that she now has abdominal swelling and bloating, swollen feet, and is in need of help.

> [**Unveil next time line date:** "5/1—Maynard VISIT."]

May 1, three days later. Dr. Maynard sees the patient and her son.

Dr. Maynard learns about the overactive thyroid and that she's still on Premphase hormone. He sees her swollen legs and swollen abdomen. Dr. Maynard learns that when she lies down to sleep, her heart races, and she starts coughing. Dr. Maynard learns she has shortness of breath, extreme fatigue, and weakness all over. He sees the patient's son press her legs and ankles, and sees that they are so swollen that the son's fingers leave abnormal, deep indentations.

Dr. Maynard sees a vein pulsing in the patient's neck. He can see her blood moving through her veins.

Eight weeks later, Dr. Maynard will write into his records that the patient had no swelling of the abdomen, and that he could not see blood moving through her veins.

Dr. Maynard requests that a 24-hour portable heart-rate monitor test and an ultra-sound video of the inside of her abdomen be done.

> [**Unveil next time line date:** "Cortez stops premphase hormone."]

Next day, May 2. Dr. Cortez returns the patient's April 27th call and tells her to stop taking Premphase hormone.

> [**Unveil next time-line item:** "5/10—heart, abdomen tests"]

May 10. Dr. Maynard's 24-hour portable heart monitor test and the abdominal ultrasound are done.

> [**Unveil next item on same date:** "5/10—message to Cortez: more symptoms"]

Also May 10, Dr. Cortez gets a phone message from the patient that she now has swelling all over her body, her abdomen is so full of fluid that it is rock hard, and the patient asks if her abdomen should be drained.

> [**Unveil next date:** "5/11—Cortez's promises"]

Next day, May 11, Dr. Cortez calls back. Dr. Cortez learns the patient is still full of fluid, still extremely fatigued, still wants treatment. Dr. Cortez promises to get the portable 24-hour heart-rate test results and the abdominal ultrasound results.

Dr. Cortez also promises to confer with Dr. Maynard.

> [**Unveil:** "5/12—Maynard visit"]

Next day, May 12. Dr. Maynard sees the patient. He sees the abdominal ultrasound shows a lot of fluid and hard swelling.

Several weeks later, Dr. Maynard will write in his medical record that the patient's abdomen is not swollen, is *soft,* has *no* fluid—and her heart is no longer speeding.

Still on May 12, Dr. Maynard learns the patient is coughing, vomiting, weak, and cannot sleep. Dr. Maynard gives her a little thyroid medicine.

> [**Unveil:** "5/15. Death."]

Three days later. May 15. Early morning, The patient's daughter finds the patient in bed. No pulse. Calls 911. At hospital, the patient dies.

[**Unveil:** "5/19—Autopsy"]

The day after the patient dies, the family requests an autopsy. The autopsy report shows every organ in the patient's body is swollen, congested, full of fluid: her heart, liver, lungs, spleen, kidneys, abdomen and even her brain. Her feet, ankles, legs, abdomen, face: all badly swollen. Heart twice normal size. The patient died of preventable congestive heart failure.

[**Unveil:** "5/18—Maynard reads heart monitor." Pause for a moment so they see the date is later.]

Two days after the patient dies, Dr. Maynard reads the 24-hour portable heart monitor print-out from five days before that has been waiting in his office. He sees her heart was in bad shape and had needed immediate emergency intervention: For the whole 24-hour test, her heart was beating dangerously fast. Over 200.

Her name was Lillian Ambrose.

[WHO WE ARE SUING AND WHY]

Now let me explain who we are suing, and why.

We are suing Dr. Arlen Cortez.

We are suing Dr. Brandon Maynard.

We are suing Dr. Cortez for six reasons.[3]

[REASON ONE]

a. **[State the action or omission for which you are suing]:** The first reason we are suing Dr. Cortez is that at the April 14 appointment, he chose not to list on his Differential Diagnosis the urgent danger that

---

3. Here is the paradigm for each reason you are suing:

a. State the action or omission for which you are suing. Do not explain or elaborate.

b. Anchor what is wrong *in general*—not in this case—with that action or omission.

c. What harm did it do in this case?

d. What should the defendant have done instead?

e. What good would that have done?

Lillian's overactive thyroid could be the cause of her heart racing. Instead, Dr. Cortez just assumed Lillian's symptoms meant menopause.

b. **[Anchor what is wrong in general—not in this case—with that action or omission]** Dr. Aaron will explain that when a patient's heart is racing, it can be caused by an overactive thyroid. Since the heart is racing, it is an urgent danger, meaning that the patient can die at any moment.

So the doctor must list this possible cause and immediately treat it or rule it out, because the patient's life is at immediate stake.

Here's why it's an urgent danger:

[**SHOW:** diagram.]

An overactive thyroid creates too much thyroid hormone. The hormone speeds the heart too fast for the heart's valves to work properly. So the heart stops pumping out enough blood. That means too much blood stays in the heart and not enough goes to the body.

This is congestive heart disease. Untreated, it's fatal.

To try to pump more blood out, the heart strains so hard that it damages itself. It dangerously enlarges to hold the extra blood and to have more blood to pump out. The longer the heart speeds, the more the heart damages itself and dangerously enlarges.

Since the heart is full of blood that it cannot pump out, more blood coming back to the heart from the body cannot get into the heart. So blood and fluids back up throughout the body. This causes swelling arms, legs, feet, ankles, face, etcetera. It makes the eyes bulge. That's why swelling and bulging point to this urgent danger.

Because it's an urgent danger, the doctor must check the heart immediately because congestive heart failure can kill at any moment without further warning.

c. **[What harm did it do in this case?]** Because Dr. Cortez did not put overactive thyroid on his Differential list of possible causes of racing heart, he did not treat it or try to rule it out. Expert Dr. Franklin will explain that this violates the standard of care. Physicians are not allowed to conclude that the cause is one thing while it is reasonably possible that an urgent danger is the cause.

Result: Lillian died of congestive heart failure.

d. **[What should the defendant have done instead?]** Dr. Franklin and Dr. Aaron will testify that Dr. Cortez should have treated this as an urgent situation, as required, and immediately checked Lillian's heart.

e. **[What good would that have done?]** If Dr. Cortez had done that, he'd have seen the real problem and immediately put Lillian in the hospital. That would easily have saved Lillian's life. She'd have been in no further danger. Instead, Dr. Cortez gave Lillian Premphase hormone, making the problem even worse.

[REASON TWO]

a. The second reason we're suing Dr. Cortez is on April 14, he prescribed Premphase, a hormone drug used to treat menopause.

b. Dr. Franklin will testify that doctors must never give drugs known to worsen an urgently dangerous condition if there is any possibility that the patient has that urgently dangerous condition.

c. Dr. X will explain that Premphase hormone speeds up the heart just like excess thyroid hormone. This further damaged and enlarged Lillian's heart, made her feel much worse, and probably hastened her death.

d, e. If Dr. Cortez had not given Premphase but instead considered the urgent danger of congestive heart failure, Lillian would be alive today.

[REASON THREE]

a. The third reason we're suing Dr. Cortez is that he chose not to send Lillian to an internal medicine or heart doctor *immediately*. It was more than two weeks.

b. Dr. Aaron will explain that an urgent danger requires immediate action, not a two-week wait. *Every* urgent danger must quickly be ruled out or treated. Allowing two weeks to pass is a risky violation of the standard of care.

c. By allowing two weeks to pass before having a specialist look at Lillian's thyroid problem, and by not telling Lillian it was an emergency, Dr. Cortez allowed Lillian's congestive heart disease to go on damaging her heart.

d, e. Dr. Cortez should have had Lillian see a heart or internal medicine doctor *immediately*. Any heart or internal medicine doctor who followed the rules would quickly have cured her congestive heart disease.

[REASON FOUR]

a. The fourth reason we're suing Dr. Cortez is for leaving Lillian on Premphase hormone five days after a new test confirmed overactive thyroid.

b. Every doctor will testify that once a doctor knows a drug can be harmful, the doctor must get the patient off it immediately.

c. By keeping Lillian on Premphase despite confirmed overactive thyroid, Dr. Cortez allowed needless additional damage to Lillian's heart and moved her closer to death.

d, e. Dr. Cortez was required to stop Premphase hormone as soon as the new test confirmed overactive thyroid. That would have resulted in less heart damage.

[REASON FIVE]

a. The fifth reason we are suing Dr. Cortez is for choosing to ignore Lillian's bulging eyes.

b. Dr. Franklin will explain that doctors are not allowed to ignore signs of anything possibly dangerous. Bulging eyes are a sign of congestive heart disease, which is fatal.

c. By ignoring Lillian's bulging eyes, Dr. Cortez did nothing to rule out congested heart and allowed it to continue until it killed her.

d,e. If Dr. Cortez had taken Lillian's bulging eyes into account along with her other symptoms, the doctor would have listed congestive heart failure. Dr. Franklin explains that eyes bulge when a congested heart backs fluids up throughout the body. The backed-up fluid causes pressure inside the eyes so they bulge. If Dr. Cortez had taken this into account, as required, he'd have suspected possible congested heart, and taken the easy necessary steps to save Lillian's life.

We are suing Dr. Maynard for five reasons.

[REASON ONE]

a. The first reason we're suing Dr. Maynard is that the first time he saw Lillian, he chose to ignore seven urgent warning symptoms.

b. Dr. Franklin and Dr. Aaron will testify that when a doctor ignores warning symptoms, he won't know what to put on the Differential list. So the patient can die without the doctor ever thinking about why.

c. In this case, Dr. Maynard chose to ignore these six clear and important red-flag symptoms of urgent danger.

Red flag 1. *Shortness of breath.* In congestive heart failure, Dr. Franklin says, fluids from the congested heart back into the lungs, so the patient cannot take a full breath. This happens especially when the patient lies down to go to sleep, as with Lillian. So especially when a patient with Lillian's other symptoms lies down, any shortness of breath is a red flag for the urgent danger of congestive heart failure.

Red flag 2. *Hard, swollen abdomen.* Dr. Aaron will explain that congestive heart failure causes fluids and blood to back up into the abdomen, making it swell so much that it gets hard. Red flag for congestive heart failure.

Red flag 3. *Swelling in her neck.* Dr. Aaron will explain that fluids and blood back up throughout the body and cause swelling. Red flag for congestive heart failure.

Red flag 4. *Swollen legs.* Dr. Aaron will explain that the fluids and blood backing up from the congested heart swell the legs. Red flag for congestive heart failure.

Red flag 5. *Swollen ankles.* Dr. Aaron will explain this is for the same reason. Red flag for congestive heart failure.

Red flag 6. *Ankle and leg swelling so bad that pressing left pits and indentations.* Dr. Aaron will explain that when fluids and blood back up enough, they cause swelling. Red flag for congestive heart failure.

Dr. Aaron says that even two or three of these red flag warnings required Dr. Maynard to list congestive heart disease.

Dr. Aaron will also explain that this particular combination of symptoms could mean nothing else but congestive heart disease at the emergency stage where death could come at any moment.

Dr. Aaron says that by ignoring these red-flag symptoms, Dr. Maynard allowed congestive heart failure to kill Lillian.

d, e. According to Dr. Franklin, If Dr. Maynard had taken the red flags into account as required, he'd have been required to do an immediate chest X-ray and a heart test called an EKG, which would have shown Lillian's heart problems. That would have led to immediate treatment that always works.

[REASON TWO]

a. The second reason we're suing Dr. Maynard is that both times he saw Lillian, he chose not to list the urgent danger of congestive heart disease. The second time—48 hours before Lillian died—congestive heart disease was even more obvious, because by then her heart was already failing. And two days before her second visit, Dr. Maynard even saw the abdominal ultrasound report, which provided strong warning of congestive heart disease.

b. Dr. Franklin and Dr. Aaron will explain that physicians are required to list every reasonable possibility, because when they do not, by the time the physician starts suspecting the real cause it can be too late.

c. In this case, Dr. Maynard did not list or even think about congestive heart failure until too late, after Lillian had died.

d. Dr. Maynard should have listed congestive heart failure the first time he saw Lillian.

e. If he had, the required follow-up testing would have caught it and she'd still be alive.

[REASON THREE]

a. The third reason we're suing Dr. Maynard is that on Lillian's first visit to him, he chose not to treat her condition as an emergency. Instead, he requested a portable heart monitor test without saying it was urgent, so it was not done for ten days.

b. Dr. Franklin will explain that with an urgent danger, the standard of care does not allow the doctor to wait ten days. In that time, the patient can get much worse or die.

c. Dr. Franklin will explain that by allowing ten days to go by, Dr. Maynard let Lillian's condition get much worse. This put her into physical misery, and allowed her heart to get so much worse that death was near-certain.

d, e. If Dr. Maynard had ordered the heart monitor on an emergency basis, as required, Lillian's congested heart would have been discovered in plenty of time and she would have been saved.

[REASON FOUR]

a. The fourth reason we're suing Dr. Maynard is that despite the near-miracle of Lillian surviving ten more days—giving Dr. Maynard still another chance to do what was required—when the portable heart monitor results were ready, Dr. Maynard did not look at them. Dr. Aaron will tell you that Dr. Maynard dealt with Lillian as if she had been perfectly healthy.

b. Six different doctors will tell you during this trial that a doctor is required to look promptly at the results of tests he orders, not just after the patient dies.

c, d, e. The portable heart monitor showed that Lillian's pulse had been over 200 for the entire 24 hours. This warned that death was very near. Yet there was still time to save Lillian, so Dr. Maynard's ignoring the heart monitor print-outs let her die untreated.

The final reason we're suing Dr. Cortez and Dr. Maynard is that they refuse to admit their responsibility, so we have had to bring them to trial.

[UNDERMINING]

Before deciding to come to trial, several things had to be determined. For example, since neither Dr. Cortez nor Dr.

Maynard actually made Lillian's thyroid overactive, it had to be determined whether Lillian's death was the doctors' fault, even though congestive heart failure was what killed her. After all, if the doctors were not at fault for her death, we would have no reason to come to trial against them.

So we asked Dr. Franklin and Dr. Aaron. They explain that the standard of care requires physicians to *intervene* when death or harm can be prevented. It is a doctor's duty to intervene. In fact, the experts will explain, intervention is the only reason any doctor is ever there. Intervention is the entire purpose of the medical profession.

So it was determined that even though the defendants did not cause Lillian's overactive thyroid, they were required to intervene to prevent it from causing congestive heart failure and death. By not doing so, they violated the standard of care and are responsible for Lillian's death.

Another thing that had to be determined was this: Ten months before Lillian first saw Dr. Carter, a different doctor had told Lillian that her thyroid was overactive. So it had to be determined whether not seeing Dr. Cortez for ten months after learning about her thyroid reduces the defendant doctors' fault in any way.

We asked Dr. Franklin and Dr. Aaron about this. They will explain to you that the ten months made no difference, because Dr. Cortez or Dr. Maynard could easily have saved Lillian's life until the very last day. The length of time did no harm.

In fact, Dr. Cortez and Dr. Maynard themselves will admit that even if Lillian had come to them earlier, they'd have treated her in the same way.

Dr. Aaron points out that the defendants did nothing later on when Lillian's symptoms were very clear, so obviously they'd have done nothing ten months earlier when the symptoms were less clear.

So it was determined that no blame can be placed on Lillian, because the delay made it no harder for Dr. Cortez or

Dr. Maynard to save her. Until the day she died, Lillian was 100% curable.

Another thing that had to be determined has to do with the honesty of Lillian's son. He was at Dr. Maynard's examination of Lillian, and says that Dr. Maynard saw her seven symptoms. Dr. Maynard says she had no symptoms. So it had to be determined who was telling the truth.

We asked Dr. Aaron and Dr. Franklin about this. Could Lillian's son have made up those seven symptoms? Dr. Maynard charges that to make money in this lawsuit, Lillian's son looked on the internet to learn about symptoms of congestive heart failure, and then pretended that his mother had those symptoms in Dr. Maynard's office. But Dr. Franklin worked backwards from Lillian's death, and saw that she had to have had those seven symptoms the day Dr. Maynard saw her.

For example, Dr. Maynard says there was no swelling the day he saw her. But Dr. Franklin explains that some of the swelling seen in the autopsy had to have been there two weeks earlier, because it takes far more than two weeks to develop that much swelling.

And Dr. Maynard wrote in his record that Lillian's heart-rate was normal. But Dr. Franklin and Dr. Aaron will show you that on that day, a normal heart rate was impossible. Less than a day earlier, the 24-hour heart monitor had showed her heart rate at 200 for 24 hours—dangerously high. It would have been medically and physically impossible for her heart to slow down to normal that night and come back up in Dr. Maynard's office the next day. There's no way for that to happen.

Dr. Maynard also claims that Lillian's abdomen was not swollen the last time he saw her. But one day before, tests showed swelling. And when she died a day after Dr. Maynard saw her, it was swollen. Dr. Franklin will explain that no abdomen can unswell overnight and swell back up the next day when Dr. Maynard saw her. The swelling is from fluid that takes a long time to build up and does not go away unless a doctor drains it.

Dr. Aaron and Dr. Franklin will also explain that even without those symptoms, the other symptoms Dr. Maynard admits he saw were more than enough to know there was an urgent danger. So, the experts will testify, even if Dr. Maynard never saw any of the symptoms Lillian's son says he did, Dr. Maynard still caused Lillian's death by ignoring the symptoms he admits he saw.

The final way it was determined that Lillian's son is telling the truth is that just an hour before Dr. Maynard saw her, Lillian called Dr. Cortez and reported those very same symptoms that Dr. Maynard claims she did not have. Only one hour before. Those symptoms are in Dr. Cortez's records. And obviously Lillian had no motive to make them up, because at that point she did not know Dr. Maynard was going to let her die.

Why did Dr. Maynard falsify his records and call Lillian's son a liar? Dr. Aaron will explain that if Dr. Maynard admits the truth—that he saw even some of those seven symptoms —it would be an admission of medical negligence and of killing Lillian.

Another thing that had to be determined is that Dr. Maynard says he thought Lillian's abdominal swelling was from cancer, not from a heart problem. On that basis, he says, he did not order urgent care or send her to a heart doctor. Dr. Maynard says cancer is not an urgent danger, so there was no rush.

So it had to be determined whether the possibility of cancer allowed Dr. Maynard to ignore the possibility of congestive heart failure.

Again we asked the experts. Dr. Franklin and Dr. Aaron both say it made no difference whether Dr. Maynard thought it might be cancer. It made no difference even if it were cancer. Dr. Maynard was *still* required to consider congestive heart failure, because a patient can have both cancer and congestive heart failure at once. So cancer does not rule out congested heart. And as long as something is not ruled out, Dr. Maynard was not allowed to ignore it.

In fact, congestive heart failure should have been higher on Dr. Maynard's Differential list than cancer. This is because congestive heart failure is a very urgent danger; the patient can die that day. Cancer is serious, but nowhere near as urgent.

So even if Dr. Maynard thought it was cancer, he was still required to deal with congestive heart failure—and to do it without the slightest delay.

[DAMAGES]

We expect one of your most important tasks as jurors will be to figure out how much money it will cost to make up for the losses and harm Dr. Cortez and Dr. Maynard caused. The judge will tell you the only thing you are allowed to consider when deciding on money is the amount of losses and harm.

So over the course of trial we have to show you all the losses and harm. It's not to get sympathy. The time for sympathy is past. We're here only for you to determine the amount of losses and harm because that's the only basis you can use for deciding about money.

[CAUSATION]

So first you will hear experts explain exactly how the negligence killed Lillian. What happened to her heart and how did this cause her death?

Insert here a clear, step-by-step explanation of how overactive thyroid leads to a congested heart (use a good visual), and how a congested heart kills.

This incorporates causation and should also include undermining of defense contentions on causation. Cite experts for both. Do undermining the same was as you did above. For example, "It had to be determined that Lillian died of congestive heart failure, and not of an infection that was found during the autopsy. So we asked expert Dr. Branton about this. He will explain to you that . . . etc."

With each topic after causation, insert undermining as needed.

[PAIN (ETC.)]

> Then you will hear about how much Lillian hurt during her last weeks: what caused it, how bad it was, and how it got worse hour by hour until she died.

Insert here a clear, step-by-step explanation of what Lillian went through (if her pain is a damages element). Cite experts and lay witnesses to support what you say. Then undermine any defense claims.

Then go through the other damages elements one at a time. Remember that all the treatments are a basis for harms and losses: costs, discomfort, etc.

Remember that stories are more effective than a recitation of facts.

The damages section should be at least half the total time of your opening. It is followed by one sentence:

> By the end of this case, you will understand why the evidence is going to force me to ask you for a total verdict of ten million dollars.

If you cannot specify a total damages figure, say instead, "By the end of this case, you will understand why the evidence is going to force me to ask you for $________________ for Lillian's medical expenses and lost income—and many times more than that [if you can say that] for the worst harm in the case: what this did to her family."

> Thank you.

Now sit down! *Do not fall prey to the silly temptation to keep talking.*

APPENDIX D

HIGHWAY WRECK OPENING (NEGLIGENCE PORTION)

[RULE]

A driver has to look where he's going. [pause] If he does not, and as a result hurts someone, [pause] the driver is responsible for the harm. [pause]

An employer is responsible for harm done by an employee's on-the-job negligence. [pause]

Now let me tell you the story of what happened in this case.

[STORY OF WHAT THE DEFENDANT DID]

Let me take you back to March 28, 2004. Three in the afternoon. [pause]

Rain. Wet road. Light traffic. [pause]

John Carlin, an Acme driver, is driving a fully-loaded Acme 18-wheeler east on Main Street in Durham. [pause]

He passes Duke's east campus. [pause]

The Acme driver turns right onto Gregson Street. [pause]

He drives south on Gregson Street.

He speeds up to 45 miles per hour.

A block later the Acme driver drives under the railroad bridge. [pause]

Beyond the railroad bridge, the Acme driver approaches the red light at the intersection with Chapel Hill Street. [pause]

[**SHOW:** diagram of intersection and crosswalk.]

At the intersection, the Acme driver goes through the red light. [pause] On the far side of the intersection, the Acme driver runs down a 68-year-old pedestrian. [pause]

The Acme truck knocks the pedestrian 80 feet down Gregson Street, to here.

[**SHOW** on diagram.]

The Acme truck driver, John Carlin, slows and stops. He calls Acme on his cell phone to ask what to do. The supervisor at Acme tells him to wait in the van until the police get there. The Acme driver stays in the truck.

He watches the pedestrian crawl to the sidewalk to get away from oncoming traffic.

Passersby call 911.

When the police arrive, the Acme driver gets down out of his truck when they tell him to.

He tells them the pedestrian was crossing against the red light.

The emergency crew rushes the pedestrian to Duke hospital. The pedestrian's leg is broken in two places, and an arm bone is also broken.

The pedestrian was Allen Flowers. You met him during jury selection.

[WHO WE ARE SUING AND WHY]

Now let me tell you who we are suing and why.

We are suing the Acme driver, John Carlin, for four reasons

We are suing the Acme trucking company for two reasons.

[REASON ONE]

a. The first reason we're suing the Acme driver is that he chose not to look where he was going.

b. When a driver does not look, by the time he looks back at the road it can be too late to avoid hitting something.

c. In this case, because the driver was not looking he did not see the light until it was too late to stop for it, and he did not see Allen in the crosswalk until it was too late to stop or swerve away from Allen.

d. The Acme driver should have kept his eyes on the road.

e. If he'd done that, he'd have seen the red light in plenty of time to stop, because it is visible for 485 feet in advance. He'd also have seen Allen 20 feet further away in the crosswalk in plenty of time to stop or swerve.

[REASON TWO]

a. The second reason we're suing the Acme driver is that he drove through a red light. You will hear from four witnesses who saw him drive through the red light, including the driver of a car coming into the intersection from the truck's left who the truck nearly hit.

b. Driving through red lights is illegal and dangerous.

c. By driving through the red light he hit Allen Flowers, who was legally in the crosswalk.

d, e. If the Acme driver had stopped for the light he would not have hit Allen.

[REASON THREE]

a. The third reason we're suing the Acme driver is that he was driving 45 in a marked 35-miles-per-hour zone.

b. Speeding is always dangerous, especially when driving an 18-wheeler in the rain on local streets.

c. Because the Acme driver was speeding, he was going too fast to swerve when he finally looked back at the road and saw Allen in the crosswalk.

d, e. If the Acme driver had been going the speed limit, he'd have been able to swerve at the last minute and avoid hitting Allen.

We are suing Acme Trucking because employers are responsible for harm caused by their employees while on the job.

The final reason we are suing Acme Trucking and its driver is that they have refused to accept responsibility for what the Acme driver did to Allen Flowers—so we have had to bring them before a jury.

[UNDERMINING]

Before coming to trial it had to be determined whether Allen Flowers was in the crosswalk illegally. So we talked to witnesses at the scene. You will hear Ms. Peggy Drake tell you that she left the sidewalk and stepped into the street from the other side—at the same time that Allen left his side of the street. Mr. Drake says they both started after the walk sign was lit. You will also hear Edgar Littner, a driver who had stopped for the light that the Acme driver should have stopped for. He will tell you that Allen did not step into the crosswalk until after the walk sign went on, and that a couple of seconds later the Acme truck sped into the intersection against the light.

One more thing had to be determined: Was the red light not working? The Acme truck driver now says it was out. But Mr. Littner, who had stopped for it, says it was working and that it never went out. Three other witnesses saw it and they will testify tomorrow. And the Durham Roads and Signs department checked and reported there was never any trouble with that light.

[Then go into damages.]

APPENDIX E
TORT "REFORM" AND ITS EFFECT ON JURORS

TORT "REFORM" AND ITS EFFECT ON JURORS
February 2005
by Debra Miller[1]
JuryWatch, Inc.

A recent national poll conducted by USA Today/CNN/Gallup[2] asked the question, "Which of these statements do you think best describes the system that regulates the amount of money plaintiffs get when they win lawsuits—a state of crisis, a major problem, a minor problem or not a problem at all?" It's an awkwardly worded question for sure, but that's not the only problem. The good news is that only 12% of those polled identify "the system" in major crisis. The bad news is 45% identified a "major problem" while another 31% answered a "minor problem." Only 8% of those surveyed said that the current tort system is "not a problem at all."

That said, the effects of the war against trial lawyers cannot be effectively measured in quantitative surveys. Biases are measured in degrees, not multiple-choice opinions. We know through our extensive quantitative research that biases against trial lawyers and their clients have gathered strength, swiftly gained ground, and are having a very real effect on plaintiffs across the country. This "state of crisis" has been infused at every level of communication, including our national discussions on health care, insurance, employment, and community. The message is coming not only from doctors and politicians, but from media, news, commentary and corporate advertisements. Today's deliberating jurors go beyond weighing the effect of

1. ©Debra Miller 2005. Miller is a trial consultant in Wake Forest, North Carolina, and a partner in JuryWatch, Inc., a national trial consulting firm in Durham, North Carolina.

2. USA Today/CNN/Gallup poll based on telephone interviews with 1,008 adults nationally conducted January 7–9, 2005.

their decision making not only on the lawsuit's parties, but also on the entire community. Almost every dollar verdict is affected by these outside problems.

We've all heard that after 9/11, everything changed. In the search to distance ourselves from danger, preserving the family and the community status quo has become ever more important. It's "us" versus "them." The changes most damaging to trial lawyers and their clients are bound up with the way many jurors classify "us" versus "them." Their "us" includes the defendant hospital, the corporate retailer, even the out-of-state trucking company. But these jurors place you and your client squarely in the "them" camp. They see you as the one trying to upset the status quo, tip the responsibility apple cart away from the individual and onto society. Onto "us." Tort-"reform" forces have brought such jurors to believe that "This verdict will cost 'us.' "

As a result, most juror deliberations we see include debates about the cost—financial and otherwise—of the litigation to the community. The word "damages" itself has ominous associations: To many jurors, the "cost" of the litigation now includes the doctors, industry, and jobs such jurors think their region is losing; along with spiraling insurance rates, health care costs, retail prices, and costs of services. This cost of litigation takes into account the "harm" of allowing an individual plaintiff's lack of personal responsibility to be borne by society. The cost also includes rewarding "bad" behavior in plaintiffs who did not undertake what jurors consider due diligence, such as getting second opinions on negative medical tests. There is also growing resistance to "punishing" a defendant for close-enough-to-honest mistakes. When Bad Things Happen To Good People[3] is being replaced by When Bad Things Happen There Is A Good Reason. Many jurors hold plaintiffs to an incredibly high liability standard because many jurors seek to justify the harm, concluding that in some way, even if they can't quite figure out what it is, the plaintiff deserved it.

All this results in defense attorneys using and winning the deep pockets arguments. Starting in jury selection, defense attorneys at least implicitly and often explicitly position the greedy trial lawyer and his or her bag of tricks. Plaintiffs are seen as gold-diggers—why else would they go out and hire a lawyer? The largest corporation

3. Also the title of the book *When Bad Things Happen to Good People* by Harold S. Kushner (Avon Books, 1983).

among multiple defendants gets juror sympathy as a target of gold-digging—and "bad for business" becomes "bad for society." With such jurors, the damages debate in deliberations tips back and forth between "us" and "them," with the welfare of the plaintiff taking only third place in the considerations.

None of this is new. But it used to be a background problem. Now it is *the* problem, which as of this writing is becoming more and more significant in the size of verdicts and even in whether the plaintiff wins.

TRIAL LAWYER BIAS. My partner at JuryWatch, David Ball, likes to say that the first impression jurors have when they walk into trial is that there are obviously two (or more) sides—so by definition, one or the other has to be either badly mistaken or lying. Jurors see their job as deciding which of the two sides that is. In today's tort-"reform" context, you and your client are far behind in that battle before you even show up. Many jurors come into trial believing that plaintiff's lawyers are in it only for the money—so that your sole purpose is to mislead or trick six or twelve handpicked saps into unjustly giving you somebody else's hard-earned money.

Just as you cannot persuade racially or ethnically biased jurors to give up their biases for the length of trial, neither can you persuade jurors to give up whatever deeply held tort-"reform" biases they have. You cannot persuade jurors that trial lawyers in general are a kindly, justice-motivated lot. What you can do is show jurors that you are an exception to the trial-lawyer stereotype, in the courtroom and in your community.

IN THE COURTROOM. Think of all the stereotypes of trial lawyers, and be the opposite. Build and maintain your credibility by staying true to your nature and true to your client's nature. See the human being you represent, not just the legal complexities of his or her case. Keep your eye on what is central to your client's case: the wrong, the harm, and the help.

Start with your tone, your words and your body language. Many lawyers find jury selection their most unpleasant task. When done effectively enough to gather the information you need, jury voir dire forces you to take the risk of asking questions with no earthly idea of the answer. It invites the truly open-ended answer. It forces you to give up control.

How do you overcome your discomfort with the process and simultaneously begin to make jurors see that you are an exception to the tort-"reform"-induced stereotype?

Practice your jury voir dire in advance. Put as much effort into practicing jury selection as you do your openings and closings. Among other values, practicing this gets you comfortable—which is important because jurors' suspicions can be confirmed when they see you being uncomfortable in what should be your home arena.

Cultivate the noble art of listening. Be honest with yourself about whether or not you're any good at it. A lawyer who truly listens strikes jurors as more trustworthy than one who does not listen carefully. Thus, when you're not a good listener, you reinforce the very stereotype you have to set yourself apart from.

Careful listening has the obvious benefit that you hear more. Juror bias is measured in degrees, so when you listen carefully in voir dire, you learn more. Listen not just to what the prospective jurors say but also to the words and phrases they choose. Pay attention to what they choose to tell you as opposed to what they choose not to tell you. And "listen" to what's really going on in the prospective juror, not just to what he says.

Do not grill them. Keep jury selection conversational with open-ended questions.

Engage each juror without challenging his or her beliefs. If a juror says she hates lawyers, don't challenge it. You cannot change her bias. Ask her to tell you more about it. Her answers will not poison other jurors. Don't shy away because you don't like her answers. Do what is known as "honoring the answer"—express appreciation for her answer, and don't give even a slight verbal or physical hint of disagreement.

Listening carefully means listening to everyone. Ask each juror equally about family, work, hobbies, and the potential biases of the case. When you skip or slight a juror because you have no worries about him, he and others can start to think you don't like him. "Of course not," the juror or others can think. "He seems like a decent guy; why would one of these damned lawyers like him?"

Listening carefully allows you to differentiate between a bias strong enough to hurt you and the same bias too weak to hurt you. For example, many jurors believe, in theory, with caps on damages but only some of those jurors will act on that belief in deliberations. To differentiate, listen for a juror's points of hesitation versus her points of being very sure. With sufficient follow-ups, you will be able to tell a soft bias from a hard bias. Find their comfort line. Find their no-go zone.

Beyond being a good listener, you also want to be a good conveyer of truth. If you strike jurors as a good conveyer of truth, they regard you as an exception to the stereotype.

Unfortunately, most of a trial advocate's traditional arsenal makes him an ineffective conveyer of truth. Exaggeration, emotionalism, premature finger-pointing, and other hallmarks of plaintiff's attorneys approaches have been worked into the stereotype you must set yourself apart from. So throughout trial, lay out your facts the way a good reporter would. Give jurors the facts they need so that they, not you, can advocate for your client. We see far too much advocacy early in opening. Jurors want the *Dragnet* version of what happened—just the facts, Ma'am. They don't want to be told what to think about the facts, and they certainly don't want to be told what to think before they even know the facts.

So instead of showing your indignation by saying, "Dr. Defendant didn't even check her pulse," take out the attitude and just say, "Dr. Defendant chose not to check her pulse." Let the facts, not your advocacy or your emotions, start shaping the jurors' beliefs and emotions—at least until closing.

One of the biggest complaints we hear when interviewing jurors after trial is that the lawyer was condescending. This is not always a matter of tone. It is also due to over-repetition. "That lawyer thought we were stupid because he kept telling us the same thing all the time."

IN THE COURTROOM AND YOUR COMMUNITY. In brand advertising as well as politics, the well managed brand offers a consistent message with every point of human contact. Consistent values, consistent message at every point of contact. What are your values—and are they conveyed in your brand message? What image do you present at every point of human contact? Ask someone unfamiliar with you or your firm to look at your communications, including your brochures, your Web site, your advertising. Does your message feed the trial lawyer stereotype—or set you apart from it?

In all communications—in and out of trial—center your message on the wrong, the harm, and most importantly, the help. Every point of outside contact should be good public relations. After a recent trial, a plaintiff's lawyer was quoted in the press as saying, "My clients were thrilled with the verdict." Sounds like someone just won the lottery, not justice. This feeds the stereotype. There was no comment about what the verdict meant in terms of the wrong, the harm, or the help for this family still recovering from serious burns and trauma after the family car exploded.

Think about the help and expertise you and your firm can offer the community. What do you already offer your community? Maybe you or your firm sponsor a safe driving program, or offer advice on domestic violence, or on product safety. Wrong, harm, help. Communicate those stories on the front page of your Web site. If you don't think jurors check you out online, you're mistaken. Offer more than legal help. Provide resources, links to the American Heart Association, a children's charity, or a support group. Include a fact section with something that encompasses the wrong, the harm and the help:

> Did you know that over 100,000 Americans die each year from preventable medical mistakes? Learn what you can do to keep yourself and your family safe.

Go on a radio program to talk about the legal issues of the day or whatever topic is near and dear to your heart. Write a small column in your community paper. Make a difference about making a difference. The community will make a trial lawyer stereotype exception for you when you communicate honestly the wrong, the harm and the help *for the community.*

IN THE MEDIA:

—Newspapers

—CNN

—Allstate Ad

An example that typifies the extent of the problem is the Vioxx recall. Within hours, Merck was on the offensive, talking points written, public appearances booked. Merck CEO making the talk circuit rounds. Their story? On September 30, 2004, Merck pulled its pain reliever Vioxx from the market learning that taking the painkiller for 18 months or longer could increase the risk of a heart attack or stroke.

Merck Chairman Raymond Gilmartin's statement:

> We are taking this action because we believe it best serves the interests of patients. . . . Although we believe it would have been possible to continue to market Vioxx with labeling that would incorporate these new data, given the availability of alternative therapies, and the questions raised by the data, we concluded that a voluntary withdrawal is the responsible course to take.[4]

At a New York news conference,[5] Merck officials said that on the previous Friday they received the data and examined it over the weekend, consulting with various medical experts.

Chairman Raymond Gilmartin's to NBC:

> We acted responsibly at every step of the way here. . . . September 30 was the first time we had good evidence.

The message from too many trial lawyers? "Vioxx may have caused your heart attack or stroke. You may get cash."

The short story? Merck acts responsibly. Trial lawyers swarm in to pick up the cash. What the public heard stoked the tort-"reform" bias by reinforcing the perception that trial lawyers are hurting our health care, our employers, our stock market, our economy by seeking their own profits, and preying on the hurt, the injured, and the fearful.

What happened to the story the plaintiff's lawyers should have been telling right from the start—that Merck hid the dangers of Vioxx from its own customers, that long before recalling Vioxx, Merck's own research showed it could double or triple the risk of heart attack or

4. Merck news conference, September 30, 2004. Raymond V. Gilmartin, CEO, Merck & Company Inc. Peter S. Kim, Ph.D., president of Merck Research Laboratories.

5. NBC News, Chief Medical Correspondent Robert Bazell, interview with Merck CEO, Raymond Gilmartin.

stroke . . . and that anyone who took Vioxx and would like to learn more about its serious risks . . . ?

As plaintiff's lawyers you know that in trial your credibility and honesty and your clients' credibility and honesty are on trial. You also understand that the wrong and the harm and the help must be central to every communication. Part of your tort-"reform" challenge is to extend these principles to the public through the media. This is part of your job for your client, so that jurors are more likely to set you aside from the stereotype they bring in with them.

During the Vioxx recall, news stories about Vioxx were broken by ads for law firms. Not a pleasant juxtaposition or positioning for trial lawyers. If you or your firm advertise using the "we can get you money" pitch, stop it. Effective advertising enhances brand value rather than trading it off for the quick sale. You're hurting your profession. You are hurting your clients' chances at trial, and feeding the tort-"reform" beast. The "we can get you money" pitch is the tort "reformers'" best friend, so it's also the defense's best friend in trial.

Advertise with helping messages—beyond "we help get you a bunch of money." Sell help, not money. It's just as effective in getting you clients, and it leaves you and your profession in better shape when the jurors take their seats.

Get involved in shaping the public debate, outside the legal and legislative communities. It is not enough to talk about preserving the jury system or the rights of the people. Those are intangible and do nothing to reframe the crisis tort reformers are selling—that greedy trial lawyers are hurting America. Break the stereotype. Focus on what you can do to help your community. Be a part of the solution in whatever area is your specialty. When you become a part of the solution, making railroads or hospitals or highways safer, you add value to your brand. Remember, your brand goes with you each time you walk into a courtroom. Make it speak for you, your clients, and your profession.

APPENDIX F

WHAT IS A DEFENSE EXPERT REALLY ALLOWED TO SAY?

Defense experts commonly testify directly or by subtle innuendo beyond the limits of the facts and their expertise. For example, is there a medical or scientific way for an expert to know when someone is lying (as with malingering)? Or does that invade the province of the jury? Can an accident reconstructionist "diagnose" what is or what is not the cause of an injury? Or is diagnosis of physical injury invading the province of the medical doctor?

Because this is such a pervasive and under-attended problem, I asked one of the smartest attorneys I know (and my good friend) Virginia attorney Roger T. Creager to let me include one of his motions in this book. He graciously consented, so I now owe him a big dinner. So will you, once it helps your case.

I highly recommend what follows as necessary reading.

Roger T. Creager and the firm he belongs to, Marks & Harrison, P.C., in Richmond, Virginia, have used the arguments in the motion below in many traumatic brain injury cases (All names of the parties involved have been changed in the following motion, except those of the attorneys and law firms). They usually schedule a pretrial hearing on the evidentiary issues raised by the report or deposition testimony of the defense neuropsychologist. Many of these issues may need to be raised again during trial so the judge can rule more precisely.

Almost every time these arguments have been used, the judge has imposed numerous limitations on defense neuropsychologist testimony.

The admissibility of "malingering testimony" has not been fully addressed by the Virginia Supreme Court, and the handling of such testimony has not been uniform in the Virginia trial courts. In *Rose v. Jaques*, 268 Va. 137, 154-55, 597 S.E.2d 64 (2004), the Virginia Supreme Court upheld a trial court ruling excluding all of a defense neuropsychologist's proferred testimony regarding malingering. But the Supreme Court did not fully address the general admissibility of such testimony. The Court simply held that the record on appeal was insufficient to establish that the neuropsychologist had actually formed any opinion regarding malingering by the plaintiff. The Court noted that the expert's report stated that he was unable to offer a "formal diagnosis of malingering."

STATE OF VIRGINIA :
IN THE CIRCUIT COURT OF THE COUNTY
OF CHESTERFIELD

PAUL R. SMITH,[1]	)
Plaintiff.	)
v.	)
Law No.: CL02-1074	)
	)
TAE KWON KICK, INC.,	)
d/b/a TAE KWON KICK Classes	)
and/or	)
A.J. Lou's Tae Kwon City,	)
and	)
JENNIFER L. WEBB,	)
Defendants.	)

MEMORANDUM IN SUPPORT OF
MOTION TO LIMIT TESTIMONY OF JOHN O. THOMAS, PH.D.

Procedural Background and Facts

The Plaintiff, Paul R. Smith (Smith), has been diagnosed by both his treating medical doctors with a traumatic brain injury resulting from injuries sustained when he was kicked in the head during a Tae Kwon Do class on May 15, 2001 by Jennifer L. Webb (Webb), the instructor at a facility owned and operated by Tae Kwon Kick Classes, Inc. (Tae Kwon Kick). Webb is very experienced in Tae Kwon Do, which is similar to Karate, and holds a Black Belt in this form of martial arts. It is indisputable that a Tae Kwon Do kick from an experienced Black Belt can, if delivered to the head, cause serious injury or even death.

Webb was doing a "no-contact" demonstration of a kick during a Tae Kwan Do class in which Smith was a student. At Webb's direction, Smith was bent forward in a helpless position with his head towards Webb. Rather than stopping her kick short of Smith's head, however, Webb negligently caused or allowed her foot to violently strike Smith in the head. Because students involved in such demonstrations always would "play act" as though they are actually kicked, nothing seemed unusual when Smith fell backwards onto his buttocks. Smith felt something squish in the back of his neck, and felt funny, but he thought he would be all right.

1. All of the names in this motion, with the exception of the names of the attorneys and law firms, have been changed—ed.

In the following days, however, Smith had pain and stiffness in his neck, as well as difficulty concentrating and sleeping.

When his problems did not get better but instead worsened, Smith sought professional help from his primary care physician, Cole A. Jacobson, M.D., on May 17, 2001, just two days after the kick. On May 23, 2001, he returned with difficulties that included a "foggy" feeling, severe neck pain, and headaches. His scalp was tender, and he had pain and spasms in his neck. He was evaluated as having possibly sustained a concussion.

A subsequent computerized tomography (CT) scan ordered by Dr. Jacobson's office was normal as was a Magnetic Resonance Imaging (MRI) scan that was eventually also done, but this is often the case with mild brain injuries since CT and MRI scans cannot detect injuries and changes at the cellular level. On June 19, 2001, Dr. Jacobson saw Smith for continuing problems in mental functioning he had experienced since the kick to the head. Dr. Jacobson referred Smith to Elizabeth A. Acosta, M.D., a nationally-recognized neuropsychiatrist, who specializes in the evaluation, treatment, and care of persons suspected of having sustained a brain injury.

On June 20, 2001, Dr. Acosta performed a comprehensive evaluation of Smith. Dr. Acosta's medical diagnosis was that Smith had sustained a concussion on May 15, 2001. Dr. Jacobson had already previously arrived independently at the opinion that Smith had sustained a brain injury. Dr. Jacobson testified in his deposition that there is "[n]o question in my mind that he had a significant brain injury before I referred him to Dr. Acosta." October 21, 2003 Deposition of Cole A. Jacobson at 46. Dr. Acosta further diagnosed Smith with Post-Concussive Syndrome and Adjustment Disorder with anxiety, all caused by the original concussion from the Tae Kwon Do kick on May 15, 2001. Dr. Acosta and other specialists (occupational therapist, speech-language pathologist, physical therapist, message therapist) have treated Smith for these conditions with medications and therapies over the more than two years since June 20, 2001.

More than two years after Smith's injury, the Defendant hired a psychologist, John O. Thomas, Ph.D. (Thomas), to perform a neuropsychological evaluation of Smith. **Thomas is not a medical doctor.** Moreover, although he is referred to as a neuropsychologist, the license Thomas holds from the Commonwealth of Virginia is simply that of a psychologist. Virginia does not issue any special license or certification for neuropsychology. A neuropsychological evaluation consists of administering and scoring numerous tests, almost all of which are written tests, and a few of which are verbal. A neuropsychologist is not qualified to practice medicine or to perform any physical examination or medical evaluation of a person, and is not qualified or licensed to prescribe medications.

What a neuropsychologist is qualified to do is give certain tests of mental functioning and then score the results by comparing them to normative data, thereby indicating whether each set of test results falls within the High Average, Average, or Normal, Low Average, Borderline Impaired, or Impaired ranges. Thomas has in fact given tests to Smith, has scored them, and has determined the range for each set of test results. A copy of Thomas's report with all attachments is attached hereto as Exhibit A (hereinafter referred to as "Thomas's Report"). Page 15 of Thomas's Report summarizes the scoring of Smith's test results, and is attached hereto as Exhibit B. These results show that Smith's performance fell within the Impaired or Low Average ranges in numerous areas of functioning. This represents a change as compared with his pre-injury functioning, inasmuch as even Thomas admits that Smith's mental functioning prior to the Tae Kwon Do class on May 15, 2001 would have been at least in the Average range (Thomas's Report at 6).

Smith has no objection to Thomas testifying to the scored results of his testing, as set forth in Exhibit B. **The contents of Thomas's Report makes clear, however, that Thomas intends to use the scoring of his test results, which is the only proper subject of his testimony, as a mere "jumping off" point. Thomas's Report reveals that he intends to go beyond the proper subjects of his testimony, and use innuendo, implication, pejorative word-selection, and other techniques to attempt to disparage, undermine, and damage the Plaintiff's case in numerous ways which, if allowed at trial, would violate Virginia evidence law.** Smith has therefore filed a Motion in Limine asking the Court to rule that Thomas's testimony will be limited at trial in accordance with the evidentiary requirements and restrictions imposed by Virginia law.

Argument

Although Thomas is employed at the Medical College of Virginia, he is **not a medical doctor**. Thomas is licensed by the Commonwealth of Virginia only as a psychologist. He is not an "M.D.," but rather is a "Ph.D."

It is equally clear that although defense experts like Thomas are sometimes referred to by defense counsel as performing an "independent" examination, Thomas is not remotely **independent** in this case. He never was involved in any treatment of Smith. No treating healthcare provider ever sought his assistance. He is a well-known defense expert regularly retained in litigation settings and is a witness who earns a great deal of his living testifying for hire for defendants. In this case, the defense hired Thomas, paid him for his work on this case, and will pay him for his testimony at trial. Thomas has never spent a moment on this case that was independent as is the case with the treating doctors. By the time Thomas was hired to assist the defense, this matter was already in litigation and it was clear to him from the moment that he was hired that the defense hoped to prove that Smith did not suffer from impairments caused by a brain injury.

Yet, there is nothing that Thomas can do to change the actual results of his testing, which are adverse to the defense. The tests were given and Smith provided his answers. The results were scored, by comparison to normative data, and fell within various ranges. Smith's performance was impaired in numerous areas. These matters, which are the only scientifically-based topics of Thomas's testimony, are established and unchangeable, and they are adverse to the defense.

Because of his obvious bias, it is perhaps not surprising that Thomas's Report does not properly confine itself to relating the test results and the normative scores. Instead, in manifest efforts to convey his belief that Smith's impairments are not the result of a brain injury, Thomas goes far beyond his field and ranges into comments which are not based on any real science, constitute medical opinions, are subjective in nature, involve marshaling of hearsay medical records entries not properly admitted through Thomas and about which Thomas is unqualified to comment, amount to argument in the guise of expert testimony, are tantamount to comments on credibility, and are otherwise improper.

Before turning to the details of these evidentiary problems as revealed in Thomas's Report, it is useful to revisit the numerous basic principles of Virginia evidence law applicable to expert testimony. If expert testimony violates **any** of these principles, it is inadmissible.

In civil cases, expert testimony is admissible only when the testimony complies with **all** of the following requirements:

(1) **Only a medical doctor can testify regarding diagnosis and causation of brain injuries.**[2] In *John v. Im*, the Virginia Supreme

2. See *Combs v. Norfolk and Western Rwy. Co.*, 256 Va. 490, 495-497, 507 S.E.2d 355 (1998); *John v. Im*, 263 Va. 315, 559 S.E.2d 694 (2002).

Court held that because a psychologist is not a medical doctor he is not qualified to testify regarding issues of diagnosis and causation of brain injuries. The Court held:

> We also hold that the trial court properly excluded Nash's opinion testimony that John [the plaintiff] sustained a mild traumatic brain injury as a result of the automobile accident. **An opinion concerning the causation of a particular physical human injury is a component of a diagnosis, which is part of the practice of medicine.** *Combs v. Norfolk & W. Ry. Co.*, 256 Va. 490, 496, 507 S.E.2d 355, 358 (1998). **Nash was a licensed psychologist, not a medical doctor. Therefore, since Nash was not a medical doctor, he was not qualified to state an expert medical opinion regarding the cause of John's injury.** See id. at 496-97, 507 S.E.2d at 359.

John v. Im, 263 Va. 315, 321-322, 559 S.E.2d 694 (2002) (footnote omitted) (emphasis added).

(2) **Expert testimony must provide expert assistance which is necessary to help the trier of fact in understanding the evidence.**[3]

Expert testimony which is merely argumentative or concerns matters about which the jury should be allowed to reach their own conclusions violates this principle.

(3) **Expert testimony must be based on a fully adequate foundation.**[4]

(4) **Expert must not be speculative in any way or founded on assumptions or beliefs that lack a fully sufficient factual basis.**[5]

(5) **There must not be any "missing variables" that the expert has failed to fully consider (or is not qualified to fully consider).**[6]

---

3. See Code §§ 8.01-401.1 and -401.3; *Keesee v. Donigan*, 259 Va. 157, 161, 524 S.E.2d 645, 647 (2000); *Tittsworth v. Robinson*, 252 Va. 151, 154, 475 S.E.2d 261, 263 (1996); *Chapman v. City of Virginia Beach*, 252 Va. 186, 191, 475 S.E.2d 798 (1996) (reversible error to admit expert testimony which did not assist the jury but rather concerned issues within the range of common experience).

4. See, e.g., *Tarmac Mid-Atlantic, Inc. v. Smiley Block Co.*, 250 Va. 161, 166, 458 S.E.2d 462, 465 (1995).

5. See *Keesee*, 259 Va. at 161, 524 S.E.2d at 648; *Tittsworth*, 252 Va. at 154, 475 S.E.2d at 263; *Tarmac*, 250 Va. at 166, 458 S.E.2d at 466.

6. ITT *Hartford v. Virginia Financial Assoc.*, 258 Va. 193, 201, 520 S.E.2d 355, 359 (1999); *Tittsworth*, 252 Va. at 154, 475 S.E.2d at 263; *Tarmac*, 250 Va. at 166, 458 S.E.2d at 466.

(6) **Hearsay and other inadmissible types of evidence cannot be included in the expert's testimony on direct examination.**[7]

(7) **Only expert opinions formed and held to a reasonable degree of scientific certainty are admissible.**[8] Expert testimony which amounts to subjective thoughts and impressions masquerading as science should not be allowed into evidence. This is particularly true in view of the danger that jurors may place great weight on experts who have impressive academic credentials and are often very experienced and skilled witnesses, and cross-examination may well prove to be inadequate to undo the damage done by such faulty testimony.

(8) **Purportedly "scientific" evidence will not be admitted unless it is actually based upon scientific methodology or testing that produces results that are sufficiently scientifically reliable to be admissible as evidence.**[9]

(9) **The expert must be qualified to give each opinion and each item of testimony he intends to offer.**[10]

---

7. See Virginia Code Section 8.01-401.1 (hearsay data may be brought out on cross-examination). In *Meade v. Belcher*, 212 Va. 796, 188 S.E.2d 211 (1972), the Virginia Supreme Court held that a doctor should not have been permitted to give an opinion which was based upon medical records which were not introduced as evidence in the case. Section 8.01-401.1 was enacted to allow an opinion to be based upon hearsay, such as hearsay medical records, but the statute does not alter the evidentiary prohibition against the introduction of the hearsay itself in direct testimony. An expert must also be precluded from testifying regarding the opinions, conclusions, or observations of others. See *McMunn v. Tatum*, 237 Va. 558 (1989) (expert may not testify to hearsay opinions of others); *CSX Transportation v. Casale*, 247 Va. 180 (1994) (same).

8. *Spruill v. Commonwealth*, 221 Va. 475, 479, 271 S.E.2d 419 (1980); Virginia Code § 8.01-399(C) ("Only diagnosis offered to a reasonable degree of medical probability shall be admissible at trial").

9. See *Satcher v. Commonwealth*, 244 Va. 220, 244, 421 S.E.2d 821, 835 (1992), cert. denied, 507 U.S. 933 (1993); *Spencer v. Commonwealth*, 240 Va. 78, 97-98, 393 S.E.2d 609, 621, cert. denied, 498 U.S. 908 (1990); *John v. Im*, 263 Va. 315, 322, 559 S.E.2d 694, 697 (2002).

10. *Swiney v. Overby*, 237 Va. 231, 233, 377 S.E.2d 372, 374 (1989). See *CSX Transportation, Inc. v. Casale*, 250 Va. 359, 365, 463 S.E.2d 445, 448 (1995).

(10) **Expert testimony must not invade the province of the jury.**[11]

(11) **Issues relating to determining credibility and weighing the evidence are reserved for the jury.**[12]

(12) **Expert testimony should never suggest or imply that there is a scientific way to determine whether a party or witness is telling the truth.**[13] The Court has held that "in reality, in our system of justice, the jury decides what is true and what is not."[14]

(13) **Expert testimony must not be repetitive or cumulative.**[15]

Often, when expert testimony is challenged as inadmissible the proponent of the evidence will argue that any flaws and problems in the evidence can be brought out on cross-examination, and thus there is no need to exclude the evidence. Thus, trial courts may be tempted to allow questionable expert testimony into evidence on the theory that its weaknesses can be exposed on cross-examination and the jury can then determine what weight should be given to it.

---

11. See *Velazquez v. Commonwealth*, 263 Va. 95, 104, 557 S.E.2d 213, 219 (2002); Virginia Power v. Dungee, 258 Va. 235, 259, 520 S.E.2d 164, 178 (1999); *David A. Parker Enterprises v. Templeton*, 251 Va. 235, 467 S.E.2d 488 (1996); *Brown v. Corbin*, 244 Va. 528, 531, 423 S.E.2d 176, 178 (1992); *Grasty v. Tanner*, 206 Va. 723, 146 S.E.2d 252 (1966). The Virginia Supreme Court has continued to apply this rule despite the enactment in 1993 of special statutory provisions relating to expert testimony regarding ultimate issues. See Virginia Code § 8.01-401.3; *David A. Parker Enterprises v. Templeton*, 251 Va. 235, 467 S.E.2d 488 (1996).

12. *Lenz v. Commonwealth*, 261 Va. 451, 469, 544 S.E.2d 299, 301 (2001) ("It was the province of the jury to assess the credibility of the witnesses"); *Kimberlin v. PM Transport, Inc.*, 264 Va. 261, 266, 553 S.E.2d 665, 667 (2002) ("a jury should weigh the evidence, [and] determine the credibility of the witnesses").

13. "The mention of polygraphs in the presence of the jury impermissibly suggests that there is a scientific way to find the truth where in reality, in our system of justice, the jury decides what is true and what is not." *Robinson v. Commonwealth*, 231 Va. 142, 156, 341 S.E.2d 159, 167 (1986).

14. Id.

15. See, e.g., *Harrison v. Commonwealth*, 244 Va. 576, 585, 423 S.E.2d 160 (1992).

This approach is **not** permitted under Virginia law.[16] Rather, the Virginia Supreme Court has made clear that the trial court must always act as the "gatekeeper" charged with the responsibility of limiting expert testimony to its proper bounds.[17] It is "for the trial court, not the jury, to decide whether the proper and sufficient foundation had been laid for the introduction of" the expert testimony.[18] The admissibility of expert testimony presents a "strictly legal question" for decision by the Court.[19] If the proffered expert opinions are not admissible, the jurors should never hear them. Moreover, it unnecessarily lengthens and complicates the trial to allow direct testimony and cross-examination of experts regarding opinions which ought to have been excluded.

Indeed, if cross-examination were sufficient to overcome the effect of inadmissible expert testimony, there would be no need for the numerous decisions of the Virginia Supreme Court carefully limiting the nature and scope of expert testimony that may properly be admitted into evidence. Particularly in the case of testimony from a

---

16. In *CSX Transportation, Inc. v. Casale*, 250 Va. 359, 367, 463 S.E.2d 445, 449 (1995), the Virginia Supreme Court cited a Fourth Circuit Court of Appeals decision **reversing** a trial judge who "held that if an expert does not have an adequate basis for his opinion, it is for counsel to bring out the deficiencies on cross-examination and for the jury to decide what weight, if any, the opinion should be given." 250 Va. 359, 367, 463 S.E.2d 445, 450 (1995). The Virginia Supreme Court quoted with approval the following language from the Fourth Circuit's decision:

> It was an abuse of discretion for the trial court to admit [the expert's] testimony . . . . The court may not abdicate its responsibility to ensure that only properly admitted evidence is considered by the jury. Expert opinion evidence based on assumptions not supported by the record should be excluded.

Id. (quoting *Tyger Constr. Co. v. Pensacola Constr. Co.*, 29 F.3d 137 (4th Cir. 1994), cert. denied, 513 U.S. 1080 (1995)).

17. In cases where numerous aspects of the proposed expert testimony are challenged as inadmissible, the "gatekeeper" role of the trial court becomes particularly active and demanding. For example, if the court has already excluded five other forms of opinion offered by the same expert, the court may begin to feel that at some point fairness dictates that the expert be allowed to state at least some part of his opinions. In these situations, however, the trial court must bear in mind that each and every aspect of the expert's opinions which does not full meet the requirements of Virginia evidence law must be excluded, even if this means that the expert will be allowed to offer few, if any, opinions at trial. It is not the fault of the opponent of the evidence or of the Court that most or all of proffered opinions of the expert are inadmissible. In these situations, the trial court must serve as a "floodwall" against the steady flow of inadmissible expert opinions which would improperly prejudice the jurors. The party offering the expert testimony must show that it fully complies with Virginia law regarding admissibility of such evidence. Any and all such testimony which does not satisfy the admissibility requirements must be excluded as a matter of law.

18. *CSX Transportation, Inc. v. Casale*, 250 Va. at 367, 463 S.E.2d at 449.

19. "In summary, the question before the trial court was one of the admissibility of evidence, not its weight—a strictly legal question." *CSX Transportation, Inc. v. Casale*, 250 Va. at 367, 463 S.E.2d at 450.

highly-educated, articulate, persuasive, experienced, extensively-credentialed expert hired and paid by a party, there is every reason to believe that cross-examination will be insufficient to correct the harm done by allowing the jurors to hear expert testimony which ought to have been excluded. Hence, the Virginia Supreme Court has again and again held that trial courts committed reversible error by allowing into evidence expert testimony which failed to satisfy even just one of the numerous evidentiary requirements which must be met prior to admission of such evidence.[20]

The mere fact that a witness is qualified to testify as an expert does not relieve the trial court of its duty to act as the "gatekeeper." Rather, the court must make the required threshold admissibility determinations as to each and every aspect of an expert's testimony which is challenged. "Qualification of an expert witness does not insure admission of his every statement and opinion."[21]

Application of the evidentiary standards reviewed above to the opinions and statements contained in Thomas's Report demonstrates that Thomas's intended testimony would, if allowed, violate numerous principles of Virginia law, and should be limited in accordance with the foregoing principles.

Some examples will illustrate the numerous evidentiary problems with Thomas's expected testimony. Because these problems are subtle, insidious, and pervade Thomas's Report, identification of them requires a detailed examination of his Report. The evidentiary problems identified

---

20. See, e.g., *Keesee v. Donigan*, supra (trial court committed reversible error in an automobile crash negligence case in allowing an accident reconstruction expert to testify concerning "average" driver perception and reaction times absent evidence that a party fell within the average range; expert testimony cannot be based upon assumptions without evidentiary foundation); *Tittsworth v. Robinson*, supra (trial court erred in admitting expert testimony regarding forces of collision and causation of injuries where experts failed to consider all pertinent variables and relied upon results of dissimilar tests); *CSX Transportation v. Casale*, 247 Va. 180, 441 S.E.2d 212 (1994) (new trial was required because trial court erred in allowing expert testimony which included hearsay introducing a new and different diagnosis into the case); *Chapman v. City of Virginia Beach*, 252 Va. 186, 191, 475 S.E.2d 798 (1996) (case remanded for new trial because trial court erred in admitting testimony by a "human factors psychologist" that the physical properties, configuration, and unsecured condition of a gate section created a hazard and that it was reasonably foreseeable that a child's head could become entrapped in it; this testimony did not assist the jury but rather concerned issues within the range of common experience).

21. *Swiney v. Overby*, 237 Va. 231, 233, 377 S.E.2d 372, 374 (1989). See *CSX Transportation, Inc. v. Casale*, 250 Va. 359, 365, 463 S.E.2d 445, 449 (1995).

below based on statements in Thomas's Report are representative, but not complete or exhaustive. Numerous other instances of the same evidentiary problems appear in Thomas's Report.[22]

A good place to begin a review of Thomas's Report is his ultimate opinion in this case. Thomas's "bottom line" opinion is set forth as follows: **"In summary, comprehensive evaluation did not substantiate a diagnosis of brain injury. Instead, a psychological disorder unrelated to the 2001 incident offers the best explanation for the unusual pattern of symptoms and test results."** Thomas Report at 13 (emphasis added).

Thomas thus makes clear that he intends to opine, both directly and indirectly, on whether Smith suffered a brain injury in the May 15, 2001 incident and whether a brain injury was and is the cause of Smith's symptoms and impairments as indicated by Thomas's testing. Yet, this is exactly what Thomas is **not** permitted to do under Virginia law since he is not a medical doctor. In this regard, it is important to note that the Im case, cited above, did not establish a new rule of evidence in Virginia. Rather, the Im case simply applied long-established principles which had been summarized several years earlier. In 1998, the Virginia Supreme Court held that the diagnosis of injuries and determination of the cause of injuries were matters generally reserved for expert testimony only from medical doctors. The Court held:

> On appeal, Combs argues that the trial court erred in allowing Schneck [a biomechanical engineer] to give an opinion regarding the cause of Combs' ruptured disk. . . . Combs objects, however, to Schneck's testimony concerning the cause of Combs' ruptured disc, arguing that only a licensed, medical doctor is qualified to render such an opinion.
>
> In response, N&W contends that since the study of biomechanics includes the application of scientific and engineering principles to determine forces exerted on the human body, Schneck was qualified to state an expert opinion regarding the cause of Combs' injury. N&W also asserts that Schneck's entire testimony was admissible to rebut Michael Shinnick's testimony concerning the forces placed on Combs' spine at the time of his injury. We disagree with N&W.

22. The defense will presumably argue that Thomas does not necessarily intend to testify to each and every matter set forth in his Report. Perhaps that will prove to be true, but it will nevertheless benefit the parties, the Court, and Thomas to address the numerous evidentiary issues raised by Thomas's Report before Thomas is called to testify.

> The issue whether a witness is qualified to render an expert opinion is a question submitted to the sound discretion of the trial court. *Poliquin v. Daniels,* 254 Va. 51, 57, 486 S.E.2d 530, 534 (1997); *King v. Sowers,* 252 Va. 71, 78, 471 S.E.2d 481, 485 (1996); *Tazewell Oil Co. v. United Va. Bank,* 243 Va. 94, 110, 413 S.E.2d 611, 620 (1992). The record must show that the proffered expert witness has sufficient knowledge, skill, or experience to render him competent to testify as an expert on the subject matter of the inquiry. *King,* 252 Va. at 78, 471 S.E.2d at 485; *Griffett v. Ryan,* 247 Va. 465, 469, 443 S.E.2d 149, 152 (1994); *Noll v. Rahal,* 219 Va. 795, 800, 250 S.E.2d 741, 744 (1979). The fact that a witness is an expert in one field does not make him an expert in another field, even though the two fields are closely related. *Tazewell Oil Co.,* 243 Va. at 110, 413 S.E.2d at 620; *VEPCO v. Lado,* 220 Va. 997, 1005, 266 S.E.2d 431, 436 (1980).
>
> **The practice of medicine includes the diagnosis and treatment of human physical ailments, conditions, diseases, pain, and infirmities. See Code § 54.1-2900. The term "diagnose" is defined as "to determine the type and cause of a health condition on the basis of signs and symptoms of the patient." Mosby's Medical Dictionary 480 (5th ed. 1998). Thus, the question of causation of a human injury is a component part of a diagnosis, which in turn is part of the practice of medicine.**
>
> Schneck was qualified at trial as an expert in the field of biomechanical engineering and he was competent to render an opinion on the compression forces placed on Combs' spine at the time of the incident. However, Schneck was not a medical doctor and, thus, was not qualified to state an expert medical opinion regarding what factors cause a human disc to rupture and whether Combs' twisting movement to catch the toilet could have ruptured his disc.

Combs v. Norfolk and Western Rwy. Co., 256 Va. 490, 495-497, 507 S.E.2d 355 (1998) (emphasis added).

The Virginia Supreme Court has repeatedly reaffirmed the rule of law it applied in *Combs* and *Im.* Thus, for example, in *N&W Railway Company v. Keeling,* 265 Va. 228, 576 S.E.2d 452 (2003), the Virginia Supreme Court held that the trial court properly refused to allow an expert in biomechanical engineering with a specialization in vestibular mechanics to give testimony which would result in him directly or indirectly conveying his opinions regarding the cause of plaintiff's injuries.

In this case, Thomas's "Diagnostic Impression" is that Smith's problems are not caused by real physical injuries, including injuries to the brain, but instead are the result of **Hypochondriasis**. See Thomas's Report at 13. In other words, according to Thomas, the problems are not the result of real physical injuries but rather are all in Smith's head (i.e., are "somatic"). This testimony, if allowed, would transgress almost all the principles of Virginia evidence law reviewed above. Thomas is not a medical doctor and therefore is not qualified to testify that Smith has suffered or has not suffered injuries to his body (including his brain). A diagnosis of Hypochondriasis necessarily depends upon a determination that real physical injuries are not involved. "The essential feature of Hypochondriasis is preoccupation with fears of having, or the idea that one has, a serious disease based on a misinterpretation of one or more bodily signs or symptoms. . . . Repeated physical examinations, diagnostic tests, and reassurance from the physician do little to allay the concern about bodily diseases or affliction." Diagnostic and Statistical Manual of Mental Disorders—IV, 300.7 at page 504 (copy attached as Exhibit C).

Clearly, this "opinion" depends entirely on a medical determination, i.e., whether Smith did in fact sustain injuries to his brain and neck on May 15, 2001. If he did sustain such injuries and his difficulties are caused by those injuries, then he could not properly be diagnosed as a hypochondriac. Thus, for Thomas to say that Smith suffers from Hypochondriasis is the equivalent of Thomas testifying regarding the medical diagnostic and causation issues in this case, which he cannot properly be allowed to do.[23]

Moreover, it is clear that Thomas is not only undertaking to improperly address medical issues, he is also undertaking to comment on the credibility and reliability of Smith's treating health care providers **who are medical doctors**. Smith's treating doctors will testify that he **did** sustain a brain injury and that his continuing difficulties are the result of his brain injury. Thus, Thomas, who is not even a medical doctor, has taken

23. The defense may argue that Thomas should be allowed to testify to a diagnosis of Hypochondriasis based upon the examination and report of Megan Brooke, M.D., a defense expert who is a medical doctor. The fact of the matter, however, is that the diagnosis of Hypochondriasis necessarily involves a medical determination. It should be made, if at all, by a medical doctor. Importantly, Dr. Brooke did not make a diagnosis of Hyponchondriasis in her report. See Report of Megan Brooke, M.D. (attached as Exhibit D). The defense should not be allowed to get this type of diagnosis, which depends upon medical determinations regarding the physical injuries sustained, into evidence through the "back door" of Thomas's testimony. Moreover, it is clear that if Thomas is allowed into the diagnostic territory at all, he will inevitably (and improperly) convey his opinion that Smith did not sustain a traumatic brain injury that caused his continuing impairments. The camel's head should not be allowed into the tent, or the rest will soon follow.

it upon himself to conclude that the diagnosis of Smith's treating medical doctors cannot be believed, and that Smith should have known that his treating doctors' diagnosis was wrong. All of this is very far beyond Thomas's limited role in this case, would violate the principles reviewed above, and should not be allowed.

It is important to note that the defense has already hired an expert who is a medical doctor, specifically Megan Brooke, M.D., and has paid Dr. Brooke to exam Smith and review his medical records. Under Virginia law, Dr. Brooke will be permitted at trial to give her opinions (subject to the constraints of Virginia evidence law) regarding the nature and extent of injuries Smith suffered on May 15, 2001, and the nature and extent of the symptoms and impairments caused by those injuries. Dr. Brooke has issued a report in this case, and it is clear that she will not be bashful about supporting the defense position: For example, Dr. Brooke states in her report:

> While I do believe he had significant musculoskeletal discomfort and associated difficulty in sleeping, concentration and functioning for the first 6–8 weeks following this injury, I do not believe that his current difficulties in functioning are related to a traumatic brain injury.
>
> Even if one wishes to believe that Mr. Smith did suffer a Grade I mild brain injury (concussion), there is no way that his current extreme difficulties in areas ranging from photophobia to emotional stability to cognitive limitations could be related to this.

Report of Megan Brooke, M.D. (attached as Exhibit D), at unnumbered page 4.

Limiting Thomas's opinions to the testing and scoring thereof will therefore not deprive the defense of a "fair fight" at trial. The defense has hired a medical doctor who will give opinions favorable to the defense. The medical doctors in this case disagree about the nature and extent of the brain injuries and impairments caused by the kick on May 15, 2001. These medical experts can testify regarding their opinions and the manner in which they arrived at them, and the jury can then weigh, consider, and evaluate their testimony and credibility. As in *Keeling*, other experts who are medical doctors are expected to testify about the medical issues which Thomas attempts to address in his Report and there is no need to allow Thomas to improperly enter into this area of testimony.

It is critically important, however, that the defense not be allowed to inject Thomas into this battle which is properly reserved only for the medical doctors. Thomas should testify regarding the areas of impaired functioning indicated by his testing of Smith. Thomas should not be allowed, however, to say anything which suggests or implies his beliefs regarding whether a brain injury is or is not the cause of those areas of impaired functioning. The defense also should not be allowed to improperly bolster and corroborate Dr. Brooke's opinions by having Thomas roam far afield of the actual results of his testing (i.e., Smith's performances fell within the impaired, low average, average, and high average ranges). It is clear that Thomas, if given the chance, will convey to the jury that he concurs in Brooke's opinion that Smith did not suffer a brain injury that caused his continuing impairments. Because Thomas is not a medical doctor, however, it is extremely important that Thomas be prevented from conveying his opinions on this issue in any way.

Moreover, what Thomas cannot properly do directly, he also should not be allowed to do indirectly, by innuendo and implication. Thomas's report is replete with instances where he subtly but plainly conveys "in so many words" his opinion that Smith did not sustain a brain injury sufficiently serious to cause the impairments and symptoms he has demonstrated.[24] Thomas relates, for example, that Smith "wore <u>unusual</u> attire" to his testing

24. The decision in *Keeling,* supra, demonstrates that a trial court should not allow testimony which even indirectly violates the prohibition against medical testimony by non-doctors. In *Keeling,* the defense called a biomechanical engineering expert to testify regarding the relationship between blood pressure and cerebral spinal fluid pressure in the area of the inner ear and middle ear. The plaintiff suffered a perilymphatic fistula (an opening between the inner ear and middle ear that allows perilymph fluid to permeate the middle ear from the inner ear) which he contended resulted when he blew into a testing mechanism as part of pulmonary function tests given by his employer. The defense expert's testimony did not directly state opinions regarding the diagnosis and cause of the plaintiff's condition. The plaintiff contended, however, that the defense expert should not be allowed to give testimony which, in effect, intruded into the area of testimony which was reserved for medical doctors. The plaintiff argued that it would violate *Combs* and *Im* for the defense expert to testify that such fistulas are "usually" the result of an infection or something that causes the tissue or the bone to deteriorate. Such testimony obviously would have conveyed the expert's opinion or impression that the fistula in question was probably caused by an infection or bone deterioration, and was probably not caused by the pulmonary function test. The trial court excluded the testimony, and the Virginia Supreme Court affirmed. On appeal, the defense also argued that the trial court also erred in refusing to allow other proffered testimony which purportedly did not address the issue of causation at all. The defense argued that the testimony would have been limited to answering questions about pressure in the inner ear. The Virginia Supreme Court held that, even though the defense's "subsequent proffer did not include questions as to the cause of the fistula," the trial court nevertheless properly excluded this expert testimony too because the trial court concluded that the defense did not intend to limit its questions to pressure in the inner ear and the proffered testimony involved opinions based on both medical and biomechanical matters. 265 Va. at 235. *Thus, the teaching of the* Keeling *decision is that where the substantial import and effect of expert testimony will be likely to address, even partially or indirectly, the issues reserved for medical doctors, the testimony should be excluded.*

sessions. Thomas Report at 2. Clearly, Thomas is not being called as an expert on clothing. Moreover, this comment is highly subjective. What seems "unusual" to Thomas may seem ordinary or at least not "unusual" to someone else. In a similar vein, Thomas charges that Smith wore "Hollywood style sunglasses (though indoors in a darkened room), large earplugs, and a Panama hat throughout the examination." Thomas Report at 2. Once again, Thomas is not being offered as a clothing expert. He is also not a medical expert on light and sound sensitivity caused by brain injury. Moreover, none of Thomas's editorializing about Smith's attire is "scientific." Thomas used no light or sound meter, took no measurements regarding the positioning, direction, and other characteristics of the light and sound sources, and performed no tests regarding the effectiveness of Smith's sunglasses, earplugs, and hat in reducing light and sound.

More importantly, Smith's attire is not "unusual" if, as his treating medical doctor, Dr. Acosta, will testify, he suffers from light and sound sensitivity caused by a mild traumatic brain injury. In that case, the measures which Smith has taken would be quite "ordinary" measures which are widely used to address problems caused by a brain injury. Thomas's statements quite clearly convey his own opinion that Smith did **not** suffer a lasting brain injury and impairments resulting therefrom. Thomas has chosen words which subtly but obviously convey a negative impression—Thomas is clearly signaling that he **disbelieves** the medical opinion of Dr. Acosta that Smith sustained a brain injury causing light and sound sensitivity.

Under Virginia law, however, Thomas is not qualified and not permitted to testify directly as to his opinions on whether Smith sustained a brain injury, or has light and sound sensitivity or other impairments as a result of a brain injury. See *John v. Im*, 263 Va. 315, 559 S.E.2d 694 (2002). Moreover, these matters have not been and could not be addressed by him in any scientific way. He should not be allowed to signal his inadmissible opinions indirectly in subtle but nevertheless effective ways.

In Thomas's "Impressions"[25] at Paragraph 1 he states that the "[m]edical records did not provide evidence that Mr. Smith sustained a neurological injury (e.g., no evidence of altered mental status, normal neurological examination) as a consequence of the May 2001 incident." Thomas Re-

25. Even Thomas's own terminology in his Report occasionally unwittingly reveals that much of what he says is not any type of scientific finding or conclusion, arrived at with any degree of certainty, but rather is merely an "impression" or belief misleadingly presented in the garb of science.

port at 11. Later, Thomas asserts that "[t]he severity, diversity, and intensity of cognitive symptoms reported by Mr. Smith is far in excess of expectations given the nature of his accident." Thomas Report at 12. Thomas is not qualified to review the medical records and testify regarding these medical issues as to the presence, absence, or extent of injuries, including injuries to the brain. See *John v. Im,* supra.

Many of Thomas's "Impressions" consist of marshaling and argumentatively presenting the medical records (e.g. the "[m]edical records did not provide evidence that Mr. Smith sustained a neurological injury"), and reciting secondhand and with approval the report of another defense expert, Megan Brooke, M.D. See, e.g., Thomas Report at Paragraphs 1, 2 [first], 2 [second]. Indeed, Thomas has compiled a six-page Appendix I which consists of a secondhand review and excerpting of Smith's medical records. These matters are not proper subjects of Thomas's testimony. Even where an expert is permitted to offer an opinion which is **based** in part upon hearsay data and information, **he is not permitted to testify to the actual hearsay data and information on direct examination**. See Virginia Code Section 8.01-401.1 (providing that hearsay data may be brought out on cross-examination). Prior to the enactment of Section 8.01-401.1, an expert could not even give his opinion if it was based in part on inadmissible hearsay. See *Meade v. Belcher,* 212 Va. 796, 188 S.E.2d 211 (1972) (doctor should not have been permitted to give an opinion which was based upon medical records which were not introduced as evidence in the case). The statute allows the expert to give his opinion even though it is based in part on inadmissible hearsay, but it does not alter the long-standing prohibition against hearsay.[26]

Thus, Thomas should be precluded from testifying regarding hearsay contents of medical records, and he should also be precluded from testifying regarding the opinions, conclusions, or observations of others, such as the other defense expert, Megan Brooke, M.D. See *McMunn v. Tatum,* 237 Va. 558, 379 S.E.2d 908 (1989) (expert may not testify to hearsay opinions of others); *CSX Transportation v. Casale,* 247 Va. 180, 441 S.E.2d 212 (1994) (same).

---

26. The recent decision in *May v. Caruso,* 264 Va. 358, 568 S.E.2d 690 (2002), establishes additional grounds on which the medical records entries listed by Thomas should be excluded. Such entries often are cumulative, do not assist the jury in weighing and evaluating the testimony of the medical experts, and can potentially overwhelm and confuse the jury.

Thomas also should be barred from testifying regarding the medical records or the medical opinions of Dr. Brooke, Dr. Acosta, or Dr. Jacobson, on the additional independent ground that Thomas is not a medical doctor, and he therefore has no proper role to serve in commenting upon or testifying regarding these matters. Thomas also should not be allowed to testify regarding any alleged previous loss of consciousness or brain injury in a sleigh-riding accident when Smith was a child. Because Thomas cannot diagnose the presence or absence of a brain injury, testimony regarding previous alleged brain injuries is also irrelevant to Thomas's testimony in this case and beyond his expertise.

In order to introduce any portion of the medical records, the defense would have to authenticate the records properly, and then bring the entries involved within an exception to the hearsay rule. Often, medical records involve multiple layers of hearsay, and thus cannot be admitted into evidence unless the proponent of the evidence establishes that each level of hearsay falls within an exception to the hearsay rule. The contents of medical records and the opinions of other defense experts, if admissible, should be introduced in a proper manner through other witnesses, and not in a back-door, cumulative, repetitive, argumentative, hearsay fashion through Thomas.

In Paragraph 3 of his "Impressions," Thomas asserts that "[c]omprehensive neuropsychological evaluation of this 52-year-old man revealed an abnormal profile of results with impaired-range performances within several areas assessed: auditory attention and concentration; visual and verbal learning; hypothesis testing, visuoperception." Thomas Report at 12. Thomas's actual test results, therefore, demonstrated impaired functioning by Smith.

Rather than confine himself to the actual results of his testing, however, Thomas then attempts, in effect, to undermine his own test results, and thereby cast doubt and suspicion on Smith. Thomas states:

> For example, on a test of verbal learning, Mr. Smith did not benefit from additional exposure to word list items over a number of trials as most other people; he recalled as many words after Trial 3 as he did after Trial 5. Additionally, he also recalled more numbers in reverse sequence (6) than he did during the forward sequence (5) on test of auditory attention. This result is unusual, given the fact that adequate attention to the forward

> trial is necessary for satisfactory performance on the backward trial. **The severity of observed cognitive deficits indicated by quantitative testing is greater than expected for most persons with a severe brain injury.**

Thomas Report at 12 (emphasis in original).[27]

Thomas wants to say, in so many words, that Smith did not do as well on the testing as Thomas thought he should do, that he should have done better, etc. Yet the very purpose of the testing was to test and measure Smith's performance in various areas of functioning. If the tests are a scientifically reliable measure of mental functioning, then Thomas should testify to the ranges into which Smith's performances fell, and should say no more. If the tests are not a scientifically reliable measure of functioning, then Thomas has no scientifically reliable testimony at all to offer. Either way, his editorializing about what he expected and about his impressions and beliefs about Smith's performance is unscientific, unreliable, and inadmissible.

Clearly, what Thomas intends to do is not only to testify that the results of his testing indicating areas of impaired performance, but to then suggest and imply that these results are not to be believed, that these measured impairments are **not caused by a brain injury**, but are rather are exaggerated and **made up** by Smith.

Thomas persists in this vein:

> Our experience has been that persons presenting with similar patterns of very severe impairment require close supervision and assistance with daily living activities within a structured living environment (e.g., skilled nursing facility). Nevertheless, the patient is functioning independently in most activities of daily living and drives.

Thomas Report at 12. Once again, Thomas is essentially saying that the performance impairments of Smith cannot be believed. He is also

27. Thomas's quoted opinions are very similar to the opinions that were excluded in *Keeling*. In that case, the biomechanical engineer testified that a fistula is "usually" caused by an infection or bone or tissue deterioration. The Supreme Court held that this testimony was improper. Thomas's quoted opinion asserts, in effect, that severe symptoms and impairments like those suffered by Smith are not usually caused by brain injuries. In both cases, the opinions are equally improper since their practical effect is to indicate the nonmedical expert's beliefs regarding what caused the plaintiff's condition and impairments.

testifying about matters as to which he lacks personal knowledge, lacks a sufficient foundation, and has not performed any scientific inquiry. Thomas did actually not perform any detailed or scientific study of the extent to which Smith "is functioning independently in most activities of daily living and drives," or of the degree to which Smith is actually successful in these activities.

Thomas also asserts in a subjective manner that Smith "did not evidence difficulties with carrying out instructions[.]" Thomas Report at 5. Yet, the actual results of Thomas's own testing showed that Smith's "recall of a set of instructions was within the Impaired range immediately following presentation" and that "[f]ollowing a second presentation and a 10-minute delay" his performance was "in the Low Average range." Thomas Report at 6. Thomas should be confined to testimony which is scientifically based and is relating the actual results of his testing.

Another example of improper comment and innuendo by Thomas lies in his commentary regarding a test of recall of 15 items. Thomas indicates that Smith recalled 11 of 15 items and four of five sets. He then editorializes: "Patients with a severe brain injury often obtain perfect or near perfect scores on this measure." Thomas Report at 6. The clear implication is that Smith's results are so poor that Smith must not have been doing his best, that the impairments must be exaggerated, and perhaps even are the result of malingering. Yet, neuropsychological experts agree that their field of expertise does not include any scientifically reliable method of determining whether someone is malingering or faking a brain injury. See infra. Moreover, under Virginia law only a medical doctor is qualified to testify to opinions regarding whether impairments are caused by a brain injury. See *John v. Im*, supra.

Thomas concedes that Smith's overall performance on a test of verbal learning "was in the Impaired range[.]" Thomas Report at 6. Not content to leave it at that, however, Thomas wants to testify not only regarding the scoring of the scientific test results, he wants to editorialize that "[a]n abnormal learning curve was observed. Most people recall an increasing number of words after each consecutive trial. Mr. Smith, however, recalled as many words after Trial 3 as Trial 5 (8 words)." Thomas Report at 6. It is apparent, however, that Smith **did** recall an increasing number of words after Trial 1, Trial 2, and Trial 3. Figure 1 to Thomas's Report shows that Smith scored as follows: Trial 1—4 correct, Trial 2—5 correct, Trial 3—8 correct, Trial 4—9 correct, Trial 5—8 correct. In other words, **just like the normative group**, Smith's results improved after each trial on the first four trials. The only place where Smith's pattern of results deviated from the normative pattern was that after Trial 4 his score fell by one.

Thomas has thus "cherry-picked" the test data in a manner that seems to support his own subjective, unscientific belief that Smith's impairments are not the legitimate result of a brain injury, and to imply that Smith's pattern of performance is somehow suspicious-looking. Yet, this is not the proper or scientifically reliable function of neuropsychological testing. This type of minute variation in a few isolated test responses (out of the hundreds and hundreds of responses given) is simply not a sufficient basis for any scientifically reliable opinions regarding Smith and his impairments. That this is true is obvious from the fact that Thomas has given such extensive tests over a two-day period, and then scored the results by major categories against a vast body of normative data. Thomas should be confined to testifying to overall results of his testing and the scoring of his test results since this is the only area which neuropsychological testing has achieved any scientific reliability. Yet another reason Thomas should not be allowed to testify to the minute details of individual test results is that these individual results constitute hearsay test data which may be explored on cross-examination, but cannot be brought out on direct examination. See Virginia Code § 8.01-401.1.

Moreover Thomas's own data shows that not all test subjects improve their performance from Trial 4 to Trial 5. This is evident from the fact that the normative group results go from an average of about 11.3 to an average of about 12.0 on Trial 5. This is indicated by Figure 1 attached to Thomas's Report, which plots the normative group results at approximately 11.3 on Trial 4 and 12.0 on Trial 5. The normative group test results thus do not increase by an entire point (1.0) from Trial 4 to Trial 5. The only way that the normative score could have increased by less than a full point is if at least some members of the normative group did not increase their performance at all from Trial 4 to Trial 5, or perhaps even declined in their performance. If everyone had improved their score by one or more, the average score of the normative group would have gone up by at least one point. **Thus, even within the normative group there were some people who did not improve their score after Trial 4.**[28]

It is unsound and improper for Thomas to create the impression that Smith's results are "suspect" or "fishy" when he does not have a scientific basis for arriving at that opinion. Moreover, if Thomas believes his test

28. This attack on Thomas's opinions using a careful review of his own data may very possibly invite the observation, "Well, that can be brought out on cross-examination." As noted earlier, however, where expert testimony is not based on a scientific foundation, is not reliable to a reasonable degree of certainty, and violates other evidentiary requirements, it must be excluded and cannot be allowed into evidence subject to cross-examination. Cross-examination is simply not an adequate remedy for the introduction of inadmissible testimony.

results are not trustworthy or scientifically accurate, then he should say so, in which case his results would very likely have to be excluded completely. He should not be allowed, however, to have it both ways, i.e., to testify to results of neuropsychological testing, and yet at the same time suggest and imply that the test results are "suspect" (not a reliable indication of the functioning they are designed to measure and purport to measure) and instead mean something entirely different (that the measured impairments are not the result of a brain injury but rather are all in Smith's head).[29]

Thomas also comments on the Minnesota Multiphasic Personality Inventory-2 test results that "[p]sychological distress was suggested by the patient's response style. Such individuals often 'cry for help' and report a number of physical problems. Somatic complaints such as headache, body pain, dizziness, nausea, and fatigue are common." Thomas Report at 10. Once again, Thomas has gone far beyond the proper bounds of his testimony. Because Thomas is not a medical doctor, he is not qualified to offer any opinions which directly or indirectly convey his views regarding whether Smith's headache, body pain, dizziness, nausea, and fatigue are the results of real physical injuries to his brain and neck or are **somatic**, i.e., not the result of **real** physical injuries. An individual who has **real** physical injuries and reports a number of physical problems is not manifesting **somatic** symptoms or manifesting some type of psychological tendency toward "cry for help" behavior, but rather is simply telling the truth about his injuries. Because Thomas is not qualified to offer diagnostic opinions regarding the nature and extent of the actual physical

29. Once again, the requirements of scientific reliability and a reasonable degree of scientific certainty must be rigorously applied to each link in the opinion-making process. Thus, for example, in *Santen v. Tuthill*, 265 Va. 492, 578 S.E.2d 788 (2003), the Virginia Supreme Court held that even though a preliminary breath test may be a generally reliable method of testing blood alcohol level, testimony regarding such test results was inadmissible since there was no evidence to show specifically that the particular machine used had been regularly calibrated to make certain that it was accurate. Similarly, Thomas should not be allowed to testify regarding any purported "unusual learning curve" purportedly indicated by one or two responses since there is no evidence to show that any scientifically-reliable and verifiable process or methodology enables a neuropsychologist to arrive at any opinion based on such extremely limited data with any degree of scientific certainty. Figure 1 should be excluded because it purports to depict this "unusual learning curve," because it does not support any scientifically-based opinion, because it will distract and confuse the jury, because it violates the prohibition against the introduction of hearsay test data on direct examination, and because its improper prejudicial effect outweighs any probative value it may have.

injuries to Smith, he should not be allowed to give any testimony which suggests that Smith's reports of symptoms are **somatic** rather than the result of real injuries.[30]

Similarly, Thomas should not be permitted to testify that Smith's report that his speech is not "the same as always" is an example of "Mental Confusion and Deviant Thinking" (Thomas Report at 10). If Smith has sustained a traumatic brain injury, then his speech is almost certainly **not** the same as always. This item is therefore indicative of "mental confusion and deviant thinking" only if one assumes, as Thomas has, that Smith did not in fact sustain a brain injury. Yet, Thomas is not qualified to make that determination. The same is true of virtually all of the items highlighted by Thomas under the headings at the bottom of page 10 and the top of page 11 ("Somatic Symptoms, Mental Confusion and Deviant Thinking/Belief, Anxiety and Worry, Depression, Sexual Concern, Beck Depression Inventory"). These items are common symptoms of brain injury, and are noteworthy as examples of somatic symptoms, mental confusion, deviant thinking, etc., only if one assumes that Smith did not in fact sustain a brain injury, a determination which Thomas is not qualified to make.

Thomas should also be precluded from giving any testimony which suggests or implies that Smith has not done his best on the testing or has somehow exaggerated his problems. This is the obvious implication of many of Thomas's statements and the innuendo and "spin" he places on certain isolated details of the test results which he clearly views with suspicion and disbelief. Yet, the truth, which is widely recognized even in the field of neuropsychology, is that there is no scientific way by which a neuropsychologist can determine that a test subject is not doing his best, is not performing up to his true capabilities, is exaggerating his symptoms, or is faking or malingering. This type of testimony should not be allowed because it is not scientifically reliable, is unduly subjective, involves numerous assumptions and "missing variables," invades the province of the jury, and violates numerous other principles of Virginia evidence law. See "Role of Defense Neuropsychologists Should Be Limited Under Virginia Evidence Law," Vol. 14, Number 4, *The Journal of the Virginia Trial Lawyers Association* (Fall 2002). [A copy of the cited article is attached hereto as Exhibit E, and the arguments made and authorities cited therein are hereby incorporated herein by reference.]

30. Figure 4 should be excluded on the same grounds asserted in the preceding footnote with respect to Figure 1, and for the additional reasons discussed in the text.

Neuropsychological testing and opinions regarding test-taking motivation, use of "best efforts," exaggeration, malingering and similar matters have not achieved scientific reliability, but rather are riddled with problems, uncertainties, and inaccuracies. Research that has directly examined the capacity of neuropsychologists to detect exaggeration of impairments and malingering "has provided little basis for confidence in their success."[31] There is little or no evidence that the subjective opinions of neuropsychologists regarding exaggeration of impairments and malingering are reliable.[32] A 1994 study indicated that even neuropsychologists who performed comprehensive assessments including face-to-face contact with examinees still had problems accurately detecting malingering.[33] Clinicians with extensive experience did no better than those with limited experience.[34] Additionally, "there is no credentialing or related process that provides a direct and representative assessment of a neuropsychologist's capacity to detect malingering."[35]

These studies indicate that neuropsychological methods and tests for detecting malingering have not achieved anything that even approaches scientific reliability. Indeed, in the clinical and forensic context, assertions that malingering opinions are reliable are almost entirely speculative since, "[i]n many, if not most, instances, the clinician does not receive feedback on the accuracy of positive or negative identifications of malingering."[36]

Just last year, a Virginia Circuit Court applied the evidentiary principles reviewed above to testimony of two defense neuropsychologists (one of whom was Thomas himself) and carefully limited their testimony in accordance with the evidentiary requirements set forth herein. In ruling on a Motion in Limine prior to a jury trial in mid-2002, Fairfax Circuit Court Jane Marum Roush held that the neuropsychological experts "will not, in direct testimony, opine that the plaintiff is lying, faking, malinger-

31. David Faust & Margaret A. Ackley, "Did You Think It Was Going To Be Easy? Some Methodological Suggestions for the Investigation and Development of Malingering Detection Techniques," in Cecil R. Reynolds (ed.), *Detection of Malingering During Head Injury Litigation* at 1 (1998).

32. David Faust & Margaret A. Ackley, supra, at 3. Neuropsychologists Faust and Ackley survey the limited neuropsychological literature and studies regarding "malingering," and additional citations to the materials that support the problems and concerns discussed in the text of this article can be found in their article.

33. Id. at 2.

34. Id. at 3.

35. Id. at 21.

36. Id. at 5.

ing, or not credible."[37] Judge Routher further stated from the bench that no expert would be permitted to state opinions that amounted to "any variation" of these opinions.[38] Additionally, Judge Roush stated from the bench that any reference to "secondary gain" would "invad[e] a province of the jury."[39] At trial, Fairfax Circuit Court Judge Gaylord L. Finch amplified the Court's earlier Order to preclude the defense neuropsychologists from giving any opinions or testimony that the plaintiff did not use his "best efforts" on their testing, was "not trying," "exaggerated his symptoms," or produced results that were "worse than you might have expected." The Court ruled that all of these variations were also inadmissible under Virginia law, and limited the testimony of the defense neuropsychologists accordingly.[40]

It is of no consequence that Thomas's Report does not explicitly use the words "faking," "exaggerating," "not doing his best," "malingering," or similar words. Thomas has nevertheless signaled his beliefs, impressions, and suspicions along these same or similar lines. Any version of this type of testimony should not be allowed at trial because this testimony, in effect, amounts to offering opinions which are subjective, unscientific, unreliable, and violates numerous principles of Virginia evidence law. See article attached as Exhibit E and authorities cited therein.

---

37. *Batzel v. Gault,* Law No. 195596, Order entered April 12, 2002 (Fairfax Circuit Court 2002) (copy attached hereto as Exhibit F).

38. *Batzel v. Gault,* Law No. 195596 (Fairfax Circuit Court 2002), Transcript of April 12, 2002 Hearing at 32 (copy attached hereto as Exhibit G).

39. *Batzel v. Gault,* Law No. 195596 (Fairfax Circuit Court 2002), Transcript of April 12, 2002 Hearing at 21 (copy attached as Exhibit G).

40. *Batzel v. Gault,* Law No. 195596 (Fairfax Circuit Court 2002), Transcript of May 2, 2002 Trial Proceedings at 3-4 (copy attached as Exhibit H).

Conclusion

Therefore, the Plaintiff requests that the Court enter its Order ruling that Thomas's testimony at trial shall be limited in accordance with the principles of Virginia evidence law set forth herein. A sketch Order is submitted herewith.

PAUL R. SMITH

By:____________________
Of Counsel—Roger T. Creager

John C. Shea

Roger T. Creager

Marks & Harrison, P.C.

1512 Willow Lawn Drive

Post Office Box 6569

Richmond, Virginia 23230-0569

(804) 282-0999 phone

(804) 288-1853 fax

CERTIFICATE

I hereby certify that a true copy of the foregoing Memorandum In Support of Motion to Limit Testimony of Paul R. Thomas, Ph.D. was mailed (together with all Exhibits thereto and the sketch Order referred to therein) to all counsel of record on this _______ day of December, 2003.

Roger T. Creager

INDEX